AFRICAN LITERATURE TODAY

10 Retrospect & Prospect

AFRICAN LITERATURE TODAY
10 Retrospect & Prospect

A review
Edited by ELDRED DUROSIMI JONES

HEINEMANN
LONDON · IBADAN · NAIROBI

AFRICANA PUBLISHING COMPANY
NEW YORK

896 J714a
no. 10, C. 1

Heinemann Educational Books Ltd
22 Bedford Square, London WC1B 3HH
PMB 5205 Ibadan · PO Box 45314 Nairobi
PO Box 3966 Lusaka
EDINBURGH MELBOURNE AUCKLAND TORONTO SINGAPORE
HONG KONG KUALA LUMPUR NEW DELHI
JOHANNESBURG KINGSTON TRINIDAD

ISBN 0 435 91653 X (cased)
ISBN 0 435 91654 8 (paper)

© Heinemann Educational Books 1979
First published 1979

Published
in the United States of America 1979
by Africana Publishing Company
a Division of Holmes & Meier Publishers Inc
101 Fifth Avenue
New York NY 10003
All rights reserved
Library of Congress Card No 72–75254
ISBN 0–8419–0397–2

BRITISH LIBRARY CATALOGUING IN PUBLICATION DATA

African literature today.
No. 10: Retrospect and prospect
1. African literature (English) – History and criticism
2. African literature (French) – History and criticism
I. Jones, Eldred Durosimi
820'.9'96   PR9340

ISBN 0–435–91653–X (cased)

ISBN 0–435–91654–8 (Pbk)

Set in VIP Melior
Printed in Great Britain by
Cox & Wyman Ltd, London, Fakenham and Reading

Contents

Ten Years
of *African Literature Today*

T his is the tenth year and the tenth number of *African Literature Today*, a journal which grew indirectly out of a conference held at Fourah Bay College, Freetown in 1963 to
discuss the place of African literature in the academic programmes
of universities principally, but by no means exclusively, in Africa.
The enthusiasm generated by this conference (another on francophone African literature had been held in Dakar slightly earlier)
led to the formation of a very short-lived Association for the Study
of African Literature, and the publication of a slightly longer-lived
Bulletin of the Association for African Literature in English which
was primarily intended as a newsletter linking various African
universities and individuals who had taken out membership of the
association. The first number was edited by Professor Tom
Creighton, then head of the Department of English at Fourah Bay
College, and the subsequent numbers were edited by the present
writer.

The *Bulletin*, typewritten and cyclostyled in the English
Department of Fourah Bay College, ran into four numbers, each
threatening to be the last because of the precariousness of the
funding of even such a cheaply produced medium. The four numbers demonstrated very clearly the need for a forum in a different
format and with a wider circulation, specificàlly devoted to the
discussion and criticisms of African literature, a need which
African Literature Today, with more secure financial backing,
stepped in to meet.

The last ten years in Africa have seen the settling of the various
newly independent countries into the realities of their autonomy.
The period of colonial protest and struggle gave way to the establishment of independent regimes, to a stock-taking and a pre-
liminary assessment of the fruits of the new state of life. The writers
of Africa looked about them, and applied to life under their own

kind the same critical examination, through their art and conduct, which had been given to the earlier colonial regimes. The resulting examination produced less and less enthusiastic responses. Thus the trend over the last ten years or so has been a greater degree of alienation or dissidence of the principal writers from established regimes and a movement towards a closer identification with what they see as the needs of the ordinary people. Writers increasingly found themselves in difficulties with their respective governments, with ensuing consequences of loss of favour, of exile – enforced or voluntary – or worse still of detention or imprisonment in their own countries.

Before 1968, Wole Soyinka had become established as one of Africa's major dramatic writers; his *Dance of the Forests* (after a number of short plays) had indicated a perceptive visionary gloom; and he had produced his first volume of poetry *Idanre and Other Poems*, and his novel *The Interpreters*. He was imprisoned in 1969 for activities connected with the Nigerian Civil War. In retrospect it seems inevitable that the writer who had pictured so compellingly the possible fate of newly independent African countries unless they squared themselves to face both the positive and negative potential of their own humanity should have been galvanized into some sort of action, however futile, to try to prevent the enactment of a scenario that to him would have appeared so clearly as a disastrous as well as an unnecessary civil war. That war also caught up in its wake, but in different ways, Chinua Achebe, Christopher Okigbo, Cyprian Ekwensi, Elechi Amadi, to name a few, in the sense that it completely changed their manner of life, at least for its duration. Christopher Okigbo did not survive. The war has since been a dominant thematic influence in the postwar work of these and other Nigerian writers.

On the other side of the continent, Ngugi's work has also been dominated by a war. His vision of the real meaning and consequences of the Mau Mau struggle and the subsequent political independence for the ordinary Kenyan has deepened and saddened over the last two novels, *A Grain of Wheat* and *Petals of Blood*, and the deadlier relevance of this vision has brought him the unwelcome attentions of authority in his own country. Curiously, Ngugi's *Petals of Blood* was launched in Nairobi by a government minister, and his play *The Trial of Dedan Kimathi* – written jointly with Micere Githae Mugo – was the official Kenyan entry at FESTAC.

His play (co-authored with Ngugi wa Mirii) *Ngahiika Ndenda* was by contrast banned after a short run. Ngugi himself was arrested soon afterwards and, at the time of writing, is still detained without trial or charge; but reports which have come out of the country suggest that his political and social sympathies – which could be urbanely ignored while canvassed in sophisticated novels and plays written in English – are regarded as potential catalysts of action, now that they are appearing in plays in Kikuyu and played with total communication to village audiences, as *Ngahiika Ndenda* was until its licence was withdrawn.

That Ngugi should be released or brought to a fair trial must be the wish of all civilized men, and an outcry to this effect has gone out from many parts of the world, to which Kenya must listen if it is not to earn comparison with regimes whose ideologies it openly (and rightly) opposes. The plight of Ngugi is, however, only a symptom of the larger problem of how societies which themselves have emerged through vocal protest, and even war, to self-rule, can themselves be governed and progressively reformed by the thought and action of their own people.

In seminars, conference discussions, and passionate essays during the 1960s the role of the writer in developing countries and the writer's commitment as a citizen were constantly recurring themes; but nothing signals so clearly the relevance of the African writer to his social environment than the actual fates of several, of whom Soyinka and Ngugi are only examples. The majority of writers still remain true to their vision.

In this connection, the case of Senghor is remarkable. He was an established literary as well as a political figure decades before *African Literature Today* was born, and is now an elder statesman in both fields. To have survived, as he has, the raw practicalities of politics and government (which Machiavelli saw so clearly), with his reputation as an artist and humane philosopher still as high as it is, is one of the more extraordinary feats of contemporary political life in Africa. The more dismal influence of so many other regimes makes Senghor still a shining example. The influence of Negritude as an active critical and philosophical force has certainly waned, but its residual influence is still apparently benign.

Critical industry has grown with the stature of the writers themselves and has helped to place the literature in the context of other literatures. There is very little left of the tentativeness of a decade ago, and although the hardy perennials – what is African literature? who should criticize it? – are still heard (even in this journal), the actual business of criticism has proceeded apace.

African Literature Today has been joined by *Research in African Literatures* edited by Bernth Lindfors of the University of Texas as an international journal devoted exclusively to the study of African literature, while many others now publish criticism as part of either Commonwealth literature or world literature. The numerous critical articles on the major figures are now beginning to yield book-length studies of individual authors, as well as anthologies of criticism on different aspects of the corpus. Most of the principal names have been seriously examined in critical books – Soyinka, Achebe, Senghor (several times each), as well as Ekwensi, Peter Abrahams, Okigbo, p'Bitek, and others.

Since the mid-1960s several bibliographical guides to the literature have been compiled – Margaret Amosu, John Ramsaran and (massively) Janheinz Jahn were the pioneers. *The Journal of Commonwealth Literature* included a running bibliographical section on Africa. These general bibliographies are still useful, but they are being joined by specialized compilations on individual authors, first as an inevitable part of the book-length studies, then for their own value. James Gibbs has a book-length bibliography on Wole Soyinka, still in manuscript, but already indicating the seriousness and the industry with which that author, like others, is studied. Others will not be far behind.

African literature is now established in schools and universities all over the world as an academic discipline, and most people have a good idea what is meant when the term is used. There is little doubt that while the work of critics probably has a minimal influence on what is produced as literature (this is certainly disputable), criticism has helped to create a receptive climate for the literature at home, has helped to establish the study of it on a serious level, has introduced the writers to the wider world, and has thus helped to establish their reputations. Given the impertinence of the very act of criticism, this activity has generally served the literature well.

In the first number in 1968 we staked out our modest patch of ground:

> *African Literature Today* is intended to be a forum for the examination of the literature of Africa. Its language is English but it will publish criticism of literature no matter what its original language. The Editor wishes to encourage close analysis of individual works or the output of particular writers or groups of writers. Publishers publish what they decide to publish for a variety of reasons, not least among them the reason that they are in business to make money. Readers also read books with a variety of expectations, not the least being their wish to be

entertained. It is the critic's business to read discerningly and demonstrate the qualities of a work and thus (a) to make it accessible to a larger readership than the absence of criticism might have opened to it, and (b) by an accumulation of such examinations to help establish literary standards. The more permissive the publisher's policy is, the more necessary becomes the function of the critic.

We hope we have remained faithful to our original vision and have in that way done some service to African literature.

The Next Two Numbers

Number 11 will explore the influence of the traditional African heritage on contemporary writing under the general title of 'Myth, History, and Contemporary Literature'.

Number 12 will concentrate on new writers or writers whose works have not received sufficient critical notice. The established writers will be given a well-deserved rest. Articles should reach the Editor by 15 September 1979 but contributors are advised to write beforehand proposing topics on which they wish to write.

STOP PRESS

Readers of this journal will probably know that the new President of Kenya, Arap Moi, announced on 12 December 1978 that Ngugi and all other political prisoners in Kenya were to be released.

Professor Eldred Jones passed the proofs of this journal before the welcome amnesty was announced.

All articles and editorial correspondence to
Professor Eldred Durosimi Jones
Department of English
Fourah Bay College
University of Sierra Leone
Freetown
Sierra Leone
It is regretted that unsolicited manuscripts
cannot be returned unless the authors provide
return postage

Issues in the Reassessment of the African Novel

Dan Izevbaye

On the Need for Reassessment

A periodic revaluation of the African novel is necessary in order to develop a lively critical heritage as support for its growth. One function of such a revaluation would be to sift the recent past for significant contributions to fiction in order to affirm our continuity with it, and encourage a redefinition of existing literature in the light of new knowledge about literature and society. Since our attitudes to existing novels are constantly being affected by the publication of new ones, it is important for us constantly to re-examine our critical attitudes and perhaps find a new critical language to reflect our modified consciousness of what the literature means to us. An important example of such a redefinition of concept occurs in two examples of how the meaning of 'culture' has been modified. In the light of the South African experience, Ezekiel Mphahlele, rejecting the West African view of culture as something handed down from the past, points out that for Southern Africans the 'very bloody struggle helps to determine the shape of their culture'.[1] There is also the question of whether the novels of Achebe should be read as novels about culture *conflict* or about *adaptation* when they seem actually to affirm the resilience which ensures the survival of the group. Early twentieth-century missionaries and anthropologists used the more cautious euphemism 'culture contact'. The concept of conflict itself seems to encourage a rather inflexible way of reading novels which subtly depict the ironic resourcefulness of the ordinary man caught in the most trying situations. This applies even to fictional accounts of contemporary human behaviour. Achebe's Rufus in 'The Voter'[2] quietens his conscience by resourcefully voting for both election candidates to whom he has made promises, reminding us somewhat of a similar compromise in *King Lazarus* where the chief of the Essazam finds himself adapting the traditional custom of polygamy to the changing circumstances caused by Christianity. What is urgently needed now is not so much a study of new directions and literary departures from existing practice as an emphasis on continuities in order to renew and consolidate the literary gains made so far, in African novelists' gradual contribution to the making of a tradition of African fiction.

Among the most important problems in any reassessment of the African novel are the need to avoid an exclusively formal approach, and, in view of the great diversity of African cultures, a critical point of view for controlling and bringing unity to an account of the African literary experience. Since colonialism has imposed a similar pattern of linguistic relationships and a common political experience on African societies, the theme of colonialism has provided a compulsive point of view for many critics. But the political point of view is not wholly sufficient, and there is need to take into account other bases for the discussion of the African novel. It is necessary, for example, for criticism to recover and re-emphasize the central concern of the novel in particular, and of literature in general.

One general concern is stated in Achebe's insistence that 'art is, and was always, in the service of man'.[3] This is a fundamental view of the function of art. For example it embraces the religious function of art, since man makes art, and since the gods themselves exist to serve man, to re-state an attitude expressed in *Arrow of God*. Margaret Trowell's classification of African art into 'Spirit-regarding Art', 'Man-regarding Art', and the transfunctional 'Art of Ritual Display'[4] will, however, be found a useful means of making formal or generic distinctions in the study of art.

We can relate this general function of art to the central concern of the novel by distinguishing the essential humanism of the novel from other verbal forms which are not exclusively centred on man. Then, even a work as crowded with spirits and deads as *The Palm-wine Drinkard* will be seen as a celebration of the triumph of man over the non-human world.

Human interest is a useful point of departure in considering the African novel. The question of the place of man in the world of fiction may be posed in different ways. The three areas of major preoccupation in the African novel indicated in the subsections which follow are related to the question of the treatment of man. If we seek to classify the African novel by asking the question 'what is the real subject of the novel?' or 'who is the real hero?', we are likely to get fictional categories in which the author is hero, society is central, or debased materialism is triumphant. If we pose the same question differently by relating it to the sources of the author's approach to narrative, our categories become dependent on the different disciplines which influence the novelist's conception of story, and we then see novels in terms of their relation to autobiography and psychology, to social anthropology, and to history and politics. It would, however, be necessary in this case for us to remind ourselves that the disciplines from which these categories derive are not identical with the literary products which 'imitate' them, and to stress the importance of form and *fiction* for drawing the lines of distinction.

The Story of the African by Himself

African autobiography enjoys a dual status as personal history and as a literary genre. This sometimes leads to some difficulty in determining the actual value of individual autobiographies. As one of the earliest and most popular prose forms in Africa, the autobiography was especially valued early this century as an important source of enlightenment and insight into a little-understood continent. The author was considered a representative of Africans in general, and his story, the story of the African. More recent autobiographies have enjoyed a similar prestige. Studies of African autobiographies which show that 'the natural mother' and 'the earth of Africa ... cross-fertilize and link together to form a single symbol'[5] do so partly because the hero is a typical member of a Westernized élite whose career is expected to reflect the destiny of a continent that is being guided into the modern world through Western literacy.

Much of this is true of the political autobiography, the personal story of the African nationalist who has helped in shaping the history of his country and whose career is therefore almost synonymous with the development of his nation. There is a comparable political significance in the eighteenth-century attempt by Equiano to draw attention to the black man's need for humane attention by writing an autobiography. The use of writing – itself clear evidence, in the eighteenth century, of the black author's capacity for reason and cultivation[6] – is important for describing the black man's reaction on his first introduction to literacy, and thus to writing as a literary medium.[7]

In recent times the literary autobiography also has political significance, mainly in South Africa where political issues so pervade the everyday life of the individual that his story is in large part that of his society. Elsewhere in Africa there are so many other concerns which are not likely to receive attention because they are not a part of the experience of the educated man that it is not often clear what the status of the autobiographer is, and with what authority he speaks on behalf of his people. The theme of education and Westernization has been so central to African literary auto-biography that it is mainly in other forms of writing – like the dramatized lyrics of Okot p'Bitek – that it has been possible for other Africans to speak through the writer.

The African autobiography often turns out to be addressed to a mainly Western audience. Both *The Dark Child* and its 'sequel', *The Radiance of the King*, are manifestly written for a white audi-ence. In handling the theme of the loss of innocence Camara Laye aims to achieve poetic justice by reversing the process by which the hero of *The Dark Child* sets out to acquire the white man's edu-cation and technical skills, at the expense of his own heritage of education and skills. In contrast, the English-speaking African autobiographer sometimes treats the theme of Western education as a success story rather than as a force making for cultural alienation, and a powerful and near-inevitable alternative to tradi-tional forms of education. The satire on the literate African élite in many novels indirectly gives voice to the inarticulate, because non-literate, majority of Africans, including the commercial élite and traditional rulers. The process of individuation and con-sequent alienation which the satirical novel frequently takes as its target is not often stressed by the autobiographer, whose élite status makes him at best only the representative of a class. Thus many autobiographers do not concern themselves with the psychic and cultural tension inherent in the African quest for Western edu-cation. This tension is represented by the contrast between the attitude of the two parents in *The Dark Child*, and in the hero's fatalistic acceptance, even while he reflects nostalgically on the cultural inheritance he is leaving behind.

A latter-day consciousness of the alienation inherent in the pro-cess of learning the skills of the West has produced an indictment as violently and unambiguously phrased as the diary entry in *Why Are We So Blest?* which denounces Westernized Africans as 'privileged servants of white empire' selected by an educational process which has been 'turned into an élitist ritual for selecting slave traders' (p. 222). This denunciation goes beyond earlier accounts of the educational process, beyond the absurdity of Mongo Beti's Medza, the agony of Samba Diallo's spiritual questioning, and Achebe's sympathetic handling of Obi Okonkwo's pathetic fate.

To see the hero of the autobiography as a cultural type or model the reader needs to be fully aware of the extremely complex cultural condition from which the hero emerges. There will then be no doubt about the true cultural status of the hero. But this need not be the only measure of the value of an autobiographical work; we can still judge the author by the use he makes of the literary characteristics of the form. There is much food for thought in Mphahlele's doubt if there is any 'such thing as autobiography: maybe there is only autobiographical fiction or fictional autobiography in the final analysis'.[8] Perhaps, then, the best of autobiographies is no more than the true history of a man's consciousness of particular places at particular times. In spite of what South African critics describe as the cliché of the South African experience as material for art, it has been pointed out that the essay and the autobiography thrive better than other forms in that social environment because they satisfy both the creative urge and a concern with social relevance. Because of the simpler issues involved in the South African reality – that is, the relatively unvarying and clear-cut nature of its policies and their application – there is a more immediate formal response to the requirements of theme in *Down Second Avenue* than we find in most autobiographies from elsewhere in Africa, and the form comes close to realizing its function as social document and psychological mirror.

The point has been made earlier that many other African autobiographers tend to treat education and literacy as a means of improving the hero's social status and material well-being, usually without a full consciousness of the cultural implications of the hero's alienation. An early South African autobiography, *Tell Freedom*, shows how a formal education leads only to the frustration, rather than the fulfilment, of the non-white's social expectations, as we find also in a much later personal narrative, *Down Second Avenue*. 'Alienation' in this case wears a fundamentally different aspect from the West African one. It takes the form of a deliberate choice of exile. And a child's natural predilection for daydreaming now seems an unconscious preparation for exile and a kind of prophecy. The childhood dreamer is led on to his illusory world by celluloid images: 'It was grand to dream of unknown tulips, roses, lazy lagoons, mandolins in Santa Lucia, beautiful ladies in blue, old Father Thames, the unknown sunny side of the street.'[9]

This escapist mood was apparently shared by Peter Abrahams, whom Mphahlele met at St Peter's School and described as 'someone who was always yearning for far-away places' (p. 129). The contrast with the writing from the rest of Africa is obvious. In spite of intervening time and the emotional return to a childhood experience, the longing is not so much for a lost childhood as for a lost homeland. The writing is nostalgic rather than elegiac, because it is still possible for the hero to return. It is this treatment of the childhood theme in Down Second Avenue which gives the South African autobiography an adult relevance and interest in spite of its nostalgic use of childhood material, and raises it above the level of 'what is after all a story about a boy' in Kossoh Town Boy, an autobiography which subordinates the bitterness of adult consciousness to the sweetness of childhood.

The persistence of nostalgia in personal narratives suggests that it is an essential ingredient in the raw material of autobiography, although it is not usually associated with the novel. It may be true that the example of Joyce is there to show a fictional autobiographer how to protect himself from sentimentality by keeping at a safe distance from the emotions of infancy;[10] but we are still aware that it was not that the emotion was originally absent but that it had been controlled. The absence of this control is generally accepted as a serious flaw in a novel.[11] The basic difference between a novel and an autobiography, apart from the relationship of the author to his material, is the relation of the present to the past, of adult narrator to child subject, both subject and narrator being one and the same person divided by time.

The autobiography, then, is not a form transitional to the novel, but a genre in its own right. It has its own peculiar limitations and advantages. In South Africa it is the genre for the formal control of sustained anger and personal frustration for which the cathartic essay and the short story are clearly inadequate. Nostalgia has its place within this form; 'memories knot into a lump of grief' for Mphahlele, in his introduction to an edition of Down Second Avenue: 'nostalgia tugs at your heartstrings, but you learn to live with it'.[12]

One of the literary uses of nostalgia is for evoking a community that is distant and therefore inaccessible in order to seize upon it and make it one's own again. In certain social circumstances, and especially for the condition of the alien, whether as black slave in eighteenth-century England, or as black student and apprentice in twentieth-century France, nostalgia is the literary means of affirming a sense of belonging and forestalling the despair that is attendant upon alienation. But this calls for the art of the novelist rather than that of the historian or reporter, since it is not the bare recall of the material world or of social customs that is required, but the psychological or emotional acceptance of that world or of those customs. Mphahlele relies on the techniques of the novelist in *Down Second Avenue*, especially for the imaginative reconstruction of dialogue and the evocation of dramatic situations, as we find in the fiction-like characterization of remembered personages like Aunt Dora and Ma Lebona. But there is a contrast between, on the one hand, the way that a novelist consciously organizes his work, even simulating the flow of experience through memory by means of the techniques that we know as interior monologue and stream of consciousness, and on the other, Mphahlele's hesitation in relating form to memory. Though the political meaning of his material appears to provide him with a means of selecting and presenting his remembered experience, it does not provide him with a satisfactory solution to the problem of form:

> At first it was all a jumble of words to me when political debates went on. Gradually, as I listened, I was beginning to put into their proper places the scattered experiences of my life in Pretoria ... But I only succeeded in reconstructing the nightmare which in turn harassed my powers of understanding. (pp. 127, 128)

The formal problem is also complicated by the limitations imposed by the point of view and the subject. The Second Interlude of *Down Second Avenue* suggests Mphahlele's awareness of the formal inadequacy of the linear, episodic narrative which seems the natural form for an autobiography. He recognizes in this Interlude the difficulty of 'trying to put pieces together. Pieces of my life' (p. 74). In fact it is to be asked whether an addition of form to autobiographical material will not interfere with the truth of its matter and turn it into fiction. In contrast to *Down Second Avenue*, we find a consciously formal pattern in *The Dark Child*. Here a symbolic tension between the father's encouragement and the mother's disapproval is later reflected in the narrator's nostalgia for the world left behind, even though the choice of 'exile' and education abroad has been freely made by the hero. Mphahlele implies in his own book that the problems of portraying a balanced and accurate account of human relationships are inherent in the restrictions imposed by the narrator's point of view. The unpleasant memories of the father raise in the narrator's mind questions about the editorial character of reminiscence and a subjective point of view: 'My father's image keeps coming back only to fade. I can't think of him but as a harsh, brutal, cold person. Like his mother. And that brutal limp of his' (p. 75).

The critical view of reminiscence occurs less ambiguously in Ngugi's *Petals of Blood* where one of the main characters, Munira, asks, 'what are recollections but fiction?... how can one truly vouch for the truth of a past sequence of events?' (p. 191). This questioning contrasts with the usual confidence of the African autobiographer who tends to view the child's mind as a blank screen on which to project the images of his adult desires.

We expect a limit in the range of interesting situations which an autobiographer can re-create since, because he depends on reminiscence, his evocative power will also depend mainly on the vividness of events which he has directly experienced. But while the personal reminiscence depends wholly on an actual experience as a fictional event does not, the literary autobiographer can also recognize the difference between the actual event and an artistic imitation of that event. If he is emotionally involved with his material in a way that the novelist is not, he is aware of the importance of temporal distance, as Mphahlele makes clear in his epilogue: 'It is the lingering melody of a song that moves me more than the initial experience itself ... Too dumb to tell you how immensely this music or that play or this film moves me, I wait for the memory of the event' (p. 219).

In spite of the distance made possible by the passage of time, the autobiography is still more subjective than the novel. It nevertheless has a special contribution to make by showing that the exploration of inner motives is a valid alternative to the type characterization common in the African novel. The first-person point of view gives an authoritative, because privileged, insight into the thoughts and feelings of the hero. It is therefore the least troublesome form of characterization, though limited in respect of the inner lives of other characters.

The novelist sometimes uses the autobiographer's mode by wearing his hero's mask like an actor and speaking with his voice, though not many African novelists have sought to do this. One exception is Achebe who speaks in the mask of Odili and thus gives himself abundant opportunity to put his skill of irony to profitable use. Others have been less directly 'autobiographical'. Armah, less successfully in *Why Are We So Blest?*, uses the diary, a modified form of epistolary narrative, for telling the story of three characters who meet in Congheria. *Why Are We So Blest?* seems to present autobiographical matter in a raw and untransformed state. We are constantly aware that the story is not wholly feigned, for the characters do not seem to exist independently of the views held by their author. Armah achieves an appropriate distance in his earlier and much better second novel, *Fragments*. This fictionalized life story is told mainly in the third person, especially in those parts of the book where events are seen from the hero's point of view. We recognize in *Fragments* the autobiographical limits of fiction. When we read Soyinka's *Season of Anomy*, fiction has taken over from fact, and we no longer identify it *directly* with the autobiographical record of experiences in *The Man Died*.

Portraits of Man and Society

The place of characterization and the social background have always been important questions in the discussion of African novels. Some early reviewers of Achebe's books used to wonder whether to judge them as fiction or as the reporting of 'native customs and idiom'[13] or, as another reviewer asked of *Arrow of God*, a work now generally considered Achebe's best novel so far, is Achebe a 'novelist or sociologist?'[14] More than ten years after these reviews it is now possible to give a clear picture of the literary politics and the problem of literary genre which were not clear at that time; that is, to attempt to show the relationship of subject matter to the literary form in which it is expressed.

The first issue is that of narrative strategy: in what literary manner was the young novelist to react to the prevailing conceptions of culture and civilization which, because they were based on the existing state of European knowledge and scholarship about Africa, were considered by the African intellectual as contributing to an inadequate and unpleasantly romantic view of Africa? This theme occurs regularly in Achebe's explanations of his work, and is encapsulated in his statement that Africans did not hear of culture for the first time from Europeans.[15]

The narrative strategy adopted for correcting this romantic view of Africa – a fictional documentation of cultural and sociological details – is reminiscent of the literary reaction of Western realists to romantic literature. But since in this case the literary 'revolution' occurred not within the same culture but as a confrontation of two cultures, some critical problems are inevitable. The most important of these is the question of when sociological description becomes a literary portrait of society. While conceding the difference between the fictionalized sociology of *Wand of Noble Wood* and the sociological fiction of *Arrow of God*, it is enough to point out that as Westernized readers we tend not to notice the abundant sociological details in European novels because of our familiarity with their cultural meaning. For any one of Sir Walter Scott's historical novels of Scotland or the fairly contemporary account of London life which we find in Virginia Woolf's *Mrs Dalloway*, a 'truly African' reader – if it were possible for him to read English without a good knowledge of its cultural background – would require as full a glossary as the average English reader would need to enter the literary world of *The Interpreters* and *Petals of Blood*.

The second and more important issue raised in the early reviews is the novelist's departure from the standard conventions of the novel. The problem here is different from that posed by the works of Tutuola which, because of their extreme deviation from standard novelistic practice, are recognized as belonging to a different fictive mode from conventional novels. The so-called anthropological and sociological novels are not different in kind from the conventional type of novel. Their formal innovations relate not so much to existing conventions of literary form as to the methods of the disciplines of anthropology and sociology. Such novels are not necessarily in competition with the discipline whose method they adopt; we do not expect that the writer of science fiction has conceived his work as a substitute for science, since he merely puts to narrative use the assumptions and knowledge made available to him by science.

Sociology and anthropology may be said to make a similar contribution to the novel form. The sociological novel came into its own in France and the United States when the realists and the naturalists attempted to develop a narrative method which would expose, by concentrating on sociological details, the causes of contemporary social decadence. But long before this the novel had often explored the problem of nurture and human nature, especially through satire and the travel tale, in what we may describe as non-sociological writing. The question of man and society has been so frequently explored in the English novel that, by building on an existing intellectual debate about the ability of their inherited civilization to triumph over the savage inclinations of the human heart, novels about Europeans beginning in a naked, unadorned state have taken on the character of a significant tradition of fiction and produced a distinct fictional convention, the novel without the background support of the hero's society. By using the setting of Africa and the new world, this convention has brought into being a set of literary characters – the desert island family. These build their often exploitive estate from a state of savagery, though going by the civilized names of Crusoe and Kurtz, or maybe bearing no Christian names although they are of authentic Christian stock, like the tribal group of savage children in *Lord of the Flies*.

We may describe as primarily anthropological, then, a European work like 'Heart of Darkness' which not only makes literary use of the anthropological assumptions of its time, but is basically intended as a study of human nature stripped of its European vestments. Conrad's quest for an understanding of human nature is fulfilled by subordinating the sociological material to Marlow's analysis of the personality of Kurtz. The subject, Kurtz, is removed from his sociological setting, the accustomed social restraints of butcher and postmaster, and put among people who, according to Marlow giving voice to the assumptions of Victorian anthropologists, 'still belong to the beginnings of time – had no inherited experience to teach them' and are therefore closer to man in a supposedly original state.

The African novel cannot be said to be anthropological in this sense. Although there is a difficulty in accepting anthropology as the defining feature of the conventional novel because of the over-tones it has acquired from association with the study of the so-called primitive peoples, there is a sense in which, because of the essential humanism of the novelist, the moral pressure of the novel tends towards the 'anthropological' when the novelist develops the art of irony as a means of exposing the savage instincts beneath the veneer of material civilization and sophisticated behaviour, as in some of the novels of Jane Austen, Henry James, Edith Wharton and F. Scott Fitzgerald. The novelist then is not a mere observer and recorder of social institutions and material culture. His art re-creates for us the problems and effort of a people creating a viable culture in response to the demands of their environment, and it gives us frequent insights into the effect on men of the culture they have created. Readers of *Batouala* will be struck by a different conception of culture implied in its French reviewers' objections to the 'crude' or 'obscene' sections in the expurgated first edition.[16] René Maran's 'objective' portrayal of Ubangi-Shari, the present-day Central African Empire, was an ironic means of commenting on its relationship to imperial France, and an attempt to vindicate its culture.

The civilizing function which literature performs by tearing down the veil of sophisticated drawing-room manners and fashionable clothes behind which the character can allow free play to the savage in him becomes of central interest to the African novelist, whether he is dealing with the African image in the past or the politics of the present. As a humanist, the novelist can hardly deal with politics, society, or civilization without relating it to its effects on the human personality. The issue is of importance to the African novelist. If European man in fiction disintegrates when stripped of his cultural supports, like Kurtz or Clarence, or builds a home from home, like Crusoe, or, like a Jane Austen character, convinces us of the need for the gentle art of ridicule to bring the human heart to order, what artistic mode should suit the novelist whose characters are modelled on men who are not only excluded from the material comforts of civilization but are denied the basic freedom on which humanity is nourished?

We will find the nearest answer to this question in the South African novels of Alex La Guma whose fictive reality, to the rest of us comfortably placed Africans, consists of an unreal world inhabited by the dehumanized beings of *A Walk in the Night* and the creatures fighting for animal survival and for blankets and food in *The Stone Country*. The restricted arena of action in this novel at first seems an ideal symbol for the geographical and mental constraints on the non-white South African. But our conception of the tiresome routine of prison life soon makes us aware of an obsessive reliance on violence for the progress of the plot, so that we are forced to recognize in the story an allegory of the violence of ghetto life in South Africa, and not just a concretely realized story of life in a particular South African prison. The reader's appreciation of La Guma's skill is partially affected by the melodramatic effects inherent in his material. But there is a difference between the use of violence for political comment in this work, and the glorification of violence for the sadistic pleasure of the reader which can only result in the cheapening and simplification of human emotions such as we find in the imported thrillers which fill our bookshop shelves and cinema houses.

Apart from its usefulness for determining literary worth, human interest is also useful for distinguishing the novel from other extended forms of prose narrative, since the novel form is perhaps the most expressive of a writer's humanism. Generally it is the traditional epic which glorifies the collective achievement of a human group by embodying this in the actions of a group of heroes, ignoring ordinary individuals who do not attain the elevated stature of men who best embody the group's most valued ideals. The entry into the epic world of non-heroic human values produces forms that are closer to the novel than to the epic.

To produce the novel the West has had to turn from the heroic and poetic to the comical and prosaic, from larger-than-life heroes and warriors to rogues and coney-catchers. We have witnessed a comparable occurrence in the African novel, with the difference that the continuity of epic and 'comic epic in prose' has not had to develop over a long period as in the English novel, but is formally represented in a single work, *Things Fall Apart*. In view of the overwhelming critical attention now given to *Arrow of God* for its superior place among Achebe's novels, it is necessary, at this point, to affirm the importance of *Things Fall Apart* not only for its simple dramatization of a theme that has significance for a whole race, or for its frequently discussed adaptation of Ibo ideas and modes of verbal communication, but for its equally important place in the development of the African novel as a literary genre. *Things Fall Apart* is a formal representation of the impossibility, at that moment in history, of upholding those social values which gave rise to and, for a long time, continued to sustain the traditional epic. The point is implicitly made in the characterization of Okonkwo whose only human weakness is his fear of weakness. This repressed fear, which much of the time finds sublimation in his masculine drive for leadership, periodically erupts in the unusual form of physical brutality. So, although Okonkwo commits no wilful crimes of inhumanity, his characterization does not include the alleviating emotions of human remorse or anguish which we find even in Mofolo's Chaka, a historical leader who remains a monster in the portrait mainly because of Mofolo's Christian hostility to him. Obierika's answer to the white man's inquiry about Okonkwo's suicide denies Okonkwo a human status in his community and, ironically, of the manhood he has spent all his life achieving:

> 'Will you bury him like a man?' asked the Commissioner.
> 'We cannot bury him. Only strangers can ... You drove him to kill himself; and now he will be buried like a dog.' (pp. 184–5)

The defeat of epic values in the two traditional novels of Achebe makes place for the world in which the form of the novel can be developed in more conventional terms. The epic hero – that man of uncommon abilities who combines in himself the most highly rated values of his race – seems to have disappeared from recent African fiction. Instead we have a democratization of the heroic ideal, with many more ordinary men and women personifying the various qualities required to transform their communities. Ousmane's Bakayoko, like Soyinka's Bandele, come closer in conception to the ideal of the hero which we find in Okonkwo than most other heroes of contemporary fiction. But, like Ezeulu, they are men who think, not men who fight like Okonkwo whose 'fame rested on solid personal achievements'.

Nkem Nwankwo's *Danda* mocks those values by celebrating the *akalogholi*, a kind of African *picaro* who, like Okonkwo, would not heroically endure hunger and failure, but would spring away in human terror from the endurance test of manhood and responsibility about to be administered on his face with a scarring knife. Danda has literary relations who, though contemporary in the literature, historically belong to a much later age group. These include Barrabas, the chief in Soyinka's *The Interpreters*, who flees in fear from the exalted role of community patriarch which Lazarus has designed for him, and a whole new generation of housegirls exploited and driven to the streets like Araba in Armah's 'Offal Kind',[17] Vero in Achebe's 'Vengeful Creditor',[18] Moni in Kole Omotosho's *The Combat*, and the prostitute in Okello Oculi's novel of that name.

This change from the portrayal of heroes to the depiction of the lot of rogues and other underprivileged characters contains two elements. First is the ancient moral rage of the poet against social injustice, which gives him the courage to remind us that 'Thieves for their robbery have authority / When judges steal themselves'[19] or, in the more contemporary language of Soyinka commenting on the pursuit of Barabbas the thief, 'Run, you little thief, or the bigger thieves will pass a law against your existence as a menace to society'.[20] The second element, closely related, is ideological; it follows on a shift from the theme of colonialism to that of local politics. The authors of these narratives often try to explore the sociological sources of human privilege, in order to assert the humanity of those characters who are denied full status by their society, as novelists have earlier done in depicting African characters under colonialism. And as the very scope and elasticity of the novel ensures that the epic survivals in the form are never completely lost but can be retrieved and put to new use as new ideological needs arise, one expects a compensating idealization of the common man to follow. The two most important novels of the common man, *God's Bits of Wood* and *Petals of Blood*, make use of some features of the epic. *Petals of Blood* is sociological in the specialized sense of the term, being a radical exploration of the material sources and economic condition of contemporary Kenyan peasants against a background of land tenancy and the political and educational privilege of the post-independence class of Westernised élite. Its characters, like the characters in *God's Bits of Wood*, are not rogues and outcasts, but mainly peasants and workers aspiring to normal human rights through collective action. In these two 'socialist' novels there is a deliberate rejection of the heroic view of individuals and an attempt to demonstrate the limitations of individualism through actions which show the failure of characters who act alone.

In *Things Fall Apart*, where the setting of a traditional society and the theme of one man's futile resistance of colonialism provides the basis of epic action, the humanism of the novel occurs ironically in the tragic defeat of the hero. Taken together, both *Things Fall Apart* and *Danda* show that either tragedy or comedy is necessary as the instrument through which the heroic world of the epic and the realistic world of the novel may interact. *The Interpreters* is epic in scale and attitude, but it remains in the realistic world of fiction not only because of the non-heroic presence of Mathias and Barrabas, but also because of the pitiable but very human failure of the interpreters themselves, as they fall below the epic demands of the author because of their very human weakness for wine and women.

The power of an unusual woman over a number of men has a different effect on the mode of Amadi's *The Concubine*. This novel takes us, not into the physical world of the epic, as does Amadi's second novel, *The Great Ponds*, but into a society where actions are strongly influenced by the supernatural. The sociological nature of *The Concubine* does not lie in its use of everyday details. It is rather in the fact that the diviner's solution to the heroine's problem is seen not in terms of her personal cure but in relation to his general conception of the need for social order which the personality of the heroine threatens to disrupt. Seen in these terms, the function of the divination in *The Concubine* is indirectly related to the larger question of social order and the government of men, even if, in this case, it is the control of human behaviour through the agency of the supernatural that is invoked.

On the Governance of Men

The third area of major concern in African fiction is politics as it applies to both colonialism and post-independence rule. If we accept the Aristotelian position that society itself is political since it involves the organization and the government of men, then all African novels are political, even when they are not explications of the colonial theme or of party politics. It is however in the narrower sense of works dealing with an explicitly political subject that the meaning and nature of the political novel is most easily defined and understood. Politics in this sense is closely allied to the African novel in as much as decolonization has always been a central concern of the novelist. Apart from novels about colonization, the bulk of African novels are political in the narrow sense. The themes of the African novelist have so far been related mainly to national politics. In some countries there is a close relationship between the colonial past and the present, as in the shelf-full of Kenyan novels about the Mau Mau forest fighters on whom Ngugi also bases his theme of the forgotten peasants who fought for freedom. In other countries the literary fascination is with post-independence politics – Nkrumah's Ghana in *The Gab Boys* and *The Beautyful Ones*, Nigerian electioneering campaigns in novels by Ekwensi, Aluko, Nkem Nwankwo and others, university politics in *The Naked Gods* and *The Interpreters*, and the ubiquitous prison and policeman in South African fiction.

The African novelist has often considered political awareness an important part of his role as writer, in addition to his earlier attempt to bring about a change of consciousness in the African as regards his cultural and political relationship to the colonial condition of the African. But the literary problems implied in this commitment are obvious to everyone. Although the importance of a writer's political conscience is recognized, it is also recognized that a distinction should be made between a novelist's gift for creating a plausible fictional world and the maturity of his political ideas. This is important because the authority of the novelist resides less in his political influence than in his artistic ability. The novel as a political force has a less decisive influence on political policies than the economic and scientific realities of today's world. The value of protest literature for effective political action is felt, not as a practical contribution independent of other, practical forms of political action, but as an advance suggestion of a course of action, an expression of political faith, or an artistic support for more direct and effective struggle. Art is in fact subordinate to revolutionary action, to summarize Fanon's position in his definition of national culture.[21]

Many novelists have sought to overcome the problem of political relevance by adapting to the novel form the use of overt explications or the direct statement of important political issues. This contrasts with another literary method which we recognize as political allegory and in which there is a subtle relationship between literary form and political implication, so that we expect a complete interfusion of story and meaning. If the subtle relationship of art and propaganda breaks down, the basic fable shows narrative absurdities and betrays the author's political designs on us.

We find an attempt at political allegory in a novel like Omotosho's *The Combat* which adopts a recognizably orthodox allegorical mode and thus casts the weight of evaluation on the consistency and intrinsic interest of the narrative, so that it invites us to seek the primary value of the novel in the quality of the fable, not in the meaning which should be felt as implicit. The combat of the title, a much publicized fight between two claimants to the child of their common lover, is sufficiently improbable and farcical for the satirical purpose, but the main cause of the farce, as the direction of some of Omotosho's more recent writing suggests, is a formal concession to an audience who require clarity and explicitness. So far in African fiction the full potential of the political allegory is still to be exploited. But the union of vehicle and political idea which we expect of the political allegory is at its best in *Season of Anomy*.

In contrast to the art of implication which requires that the reader be capable of understanding and interpreting the secondary meaning of the allegorical narrative, political novels make use of reflection and discourse, as in Armah's *Why Are We So Blest?*, or they rely on even more explicit forms of political analysis and statement, as in Ngugi's *Petals of Blood*. This method is no less difficult than that of indirection, for the novelist still needs to reconcile doctrine and creation, politics and art. In *Why Are We So Blest?*, where Armah bends his gifts to non-literary ends, this is attempted through the combined use of diary and dramatic monologue reconciled in the final account of the last character into whose hands the complete record of events falls and who, by implication, is now the real 'author' or compiler of the events narrated. *Petals of Blood*, on the other hand, tries to take advantage of the scope and variety of the epic form which makes it possible to combine a variety of narrative forms, from political essay to factual and speculative prehistory and myth. Even the use of myth and folklore, which would normally require explication and exegesis in a work as dense with symbolism as *The Interpreters*, becomes in *Petals of Blood* mainly reinforcement and amplification of its political argument. Apart from the Kikuyu words which are left unexplained, the novel provides its own explication of the basic folklore used in the narrative.

The relationship of politics and the novel in Africa has been explored in these two ways, by implication and through explication. In contrast to *Season of Anomy* where the narrative is consistently fiction and where the relationship of art and politics is mediated by myth, *Petals of Blood* frankly announces its own political intent as part of its story, in spite of its own heavy reliance on folktale and myth for its structure and imagery. From the point of view of this novel, myth-as-literature is all very well, but it is only a vehicle for ideas and it will pass away in that form, like the mythical song which Karega, one of its main characters, heard, feeling very sad at its end because it was 'like listening to a solitary beautiful tune straying, for a time, from a dying world' (p. 210). The aesthetics here, in some ways almost like that of Armah's *Two Thousand Seasons*, seeks a close identification of politics and the novel through a mode where both are as one. But the human affirmation necessary for all important novels is made possible by its focus on the lives and relationships of individuals desiring, loving, and suffering, not on the actual machinery and strategy of government and politics. For though these are important when properly manipulated for the attainment of human goals, they belong centrally to the realm of politics rather than of art.

Our view of the African novel has been directly influenced by politics, especially in the descriptions of the change of mood from cultural nationalism in the 1960s to the satire of the years after independence. The literary experience of the five years between the publication of *The Voice* and *The Beautyful Ones Are Not Yet Born* reflects a change of political attitude, not the emergence of new narrative modes. In spite of important formal innovations in *The Voice* and *The Interpreters*, satire, the basic mode for social criticism in the 1960s, was not new in the African novel. It had been the means by which the French novelist criticized the French inheritance in Africa. Just as we speak of the mid-sixties as a new direction in African writing, so at least one study of the African novel in French saw the colonial novels of Oyono and Mongo Beti as 'the watershed in contemporary African literature in French'.[22] What seems important, from the point of view of the development of form, is the revised application of an existing literary method to new political situations. The first method is to criticize an unacceptable political administration by contrasting it with the social organization of another time or place.This other society belongs to a more or less idyllic past, or is envisaged as an African utopia. Whatever criticism is made of the past, a fair amount of idealization is implied in the defence of indigenous cultures in *Batouala, Things Fall Apart* and *The Dark Child*. This idealization is as much a criticism of colonial administration as the use of contrast between pastoral and contemporary African societies is one mode of criticizing contemporary African governments. The commune of Aiyero in *Season of Anomy* and the village of Ilmorog in *Petals of Blood* are local Arcadias threatened by, or threatening by, their model socialist nature, the evil character of the larger world outside their boundaries. They are seen as crude archetypes for a future Afrotopia.

The other method of social criticism, the direct satire of the acquisition and use of political power, is common to both *King Lazarus* and post-independence novels like *A Man of the People* and *The Beautyful Ones*. The more hopeful outlook in the earlier novel comes from the fact that the subject dealt with here is not local politics but foreign rule. The later despair comes from the shocking discovery that there is in effect not much difference between the former white rule and the new black rule. The change of rulers has not meant a change in the circumstances of the governed, but a continuity of oppression.

The problem with satire is its simplification of the characters and the situations portrayed. A European critic will object to the DOs, the Winterbottoms, and the Thompsons in African fiction as mere types, just as the political scientist and the African nationalist will argue against the portrait of Nkrumah in some Ghanaian novels. In answer to the narrator's statement in *Petals of Blood* that 'a politician was [always] a politician' (p. 181), the politician will tell you that politics is the art of the possible, and that stereotypes ignore the stress of practical situations on human conduct. Thus, although a novelist is essentially a humanist because his ruling passion is the preoccupation with the human condition, satire and character types can become, in the hands of a skilful novelist, a verbal weapon against political injustice and misrule. The novelist's interest therefore is in human beings rather than in forms of government. In a consciously socialist novel like *Petals of Blood*, the economic dispossession of the peasants finds its most effective symbol in the degradation of Wanja the barmaid, who rises from prostitution to economic independence and womanhood, but is forced back to the humiliating status of a prostitute who sells her love because she sees that nothing is obtained free of charge in her country.

A brief thematic account of one of the primary symbols used in African political fiction will show how the novelist's humanism expresses itself in interests which are human rather than institutional, and that party politics are of secondary interest to the exploration of human fate. The use of the car as an indicator that material possession is at the heart of human transactions has become familiar to us from the excitement caused by cars among the characters in *A Man of the People* and the first two novels of Armah. But the more telling use of the car symbol occurs in the short stories of Acheme and Ngugi. The real issue that is fought in the elections in Achebe's 'The Voter' is the choice to be made between humanism and materialism. The choice is indicated on the ballot box symbols:

'Do not forget, ... our sign is the motor-car ... Don't look at the other [box] with the man's head: it is for those whose heads are not correct... Vote for the car and you will ride in it! ...
'Or if we don't, our children will.' (p.18)

Alienation is the social and spiritual consequence of this making of the motor-car into a fetish. It is only a step from here to the confusion of values in Ngugi's 'A Mercedes Funeral' where the hero's dream of dying in a Benz gets an ironic response in the offering of the strangest of funeral gifts by a friend. This friend 'did not want to bring politics into what was a human loss', though he makes a most political offering to enable the hero to fulfil his 'drunken dreams and impossible schemes.'[23] As Armah's Koomson tells the Man, politics is the art which makes all things possible. Estella's sister

'... has fallen in love with a Jaguar, and she's going to kill herself if she can't have it. She wants us to get the foreign exchange for it.'
'I thought that was no longer possible,' said the man, looking at Koomson.
'Everything is possible,' Koomson said. 'It depends on the person.' (p. 175)

An identical displacement of moral integrity by materialism occurs in Odili's description of the power of a long, chauffeur-driven

American car to pass through the eye of a needle. Always, the African novelist associates a big car with power and sex – in *Fragments*, in Ngugi's brief sketch of the life-style of an educated, car-owning class in 'The Mubenzi Tribesmen',[24] in Oculi's *The Prostitute*, and with a different emphasis in *Jagua Nana* where the prostitute gets her nickname from a prestige car, and also in the melodramatic *My Mercedes Is Bigger Than Yours* where the hero virtually has an orgasm driving his new Jaguar to his home village.

The use to which the car symbol is put in African fiction suggests that the political novel is ultimately humanist in purpose. The end of government is not just to rule over people, but to choose between – or reconcile – the apparent material prosperity of the nation and the welfare and dignity of her nationals as human beings. The moral dilemma of how to behave with decorum in the face of money is resolved in 'The Voter' only because the elders 'knew how far to go' with their bargaining in order to still be able to stoop and pick up money from the floor 'without great loss of dignity' (p. 15). The story shows that political fiction is often also moral.

There seems to have been a thematic shift in political writing outside South Africa from the political face of imperialism to its economic aspect. From the treatment of politics in *Xala* and *Petals of Blood*, and even in what is primarily a civil war story, *Season of Anomy*, the main direction of political writing seems to seek a choice between capitalism and socialism. In the long run what seems to be a literary debate about forms of government is essentially a concern that rulers should make possible a restoration of human dignity and worth, and seek a devaluation of material wealth which is the main obstacle to this goal.

Form and Ideas in the Novel

It is only about twenty or twenty-five years since the African novel attracted sustained critical attention, and it is too early to forget that, in addition to working in a second language, African novelists have no modern tradition of fiction to sustain them. It is necessary to identify those issues which help or hinder the direction of our literary tradition. The most important of these is the inevitable but difficult decision a novelist has to make about the relationship of his political commitment to his art. The novelist who is set on a didactic path still needs to perfect his art if he hopes to teach effectively; an oracular pronouncement is remembered because its verbal form is memorable. But since the history of the African novel has been essentially a history of an evolving racial consciousness, it cannot be denied that political relevance is a key factor in the revival of certain novels, as is the case with Ethiopia Unbound.[25] But the literary value of this work is hardly higher than that of Obeng's Eighteen Pence.[26] Their common interest for the literary scholar is mainly historical. Of greater merit are both Batouala and Sol Plaatje's Mhudi. The most recent revival of Mhudi is partly due to the faith of Tim Couzens.[27] Mhudi's chief interest today includes Plaatje's dramatization of his insight into the implications of the Mfecane. But it has dated somewhat. In contrast, Mofolo's Chaka – a translation – is of greater literary interest, and still attracts literary respect after half a century, in spite of its outdated view of Chaka's career.

We may learn much about what helps art to endure beyond its time by looking at the example of Mbari, an artistic form which exhausts itself in the performance of its function, although this feature is present in fiction only in the cathartic or religious expression not intended for an audience. Apparently what the Mbari artists transmit through time are artistic forms, and the art renews itself when 'other people who want to make their own [Mbari house] come to copy artistic designs'.[28] A novel ensures that its original function will not be forgotten because it is an art form which depends on the printed word for its transmission and preservation. The library and the bookshop help us to keep alive our contact with its past and ensure an understanding of the original functions of each novel. Although the novel implicitly preserves the nature of its function in its text, what it in fact transmits is not its ideas – which remain mainly of historical interest to us after the novelist's goal has been fulfilled or frustrated – but its literary conventions for the use of other novelists. A useful hint of this historical process is present in Andre Malraux's argument that important works of art are 'victories over forms achieved by forms [and]... not the allegorical expression of some ideology'.[29] While this is not adequate for showing how a novelist's ideology may significantly affect his choice of a particular medium for his ideas, it is nevertheless useful for helping to point out that the one significant thing that an African novelist hands down to his successors is not his ideas but the literary conventions of style and form. Malraux's definition of an art museum as 'a place where the work of art has no longer any function other than being a work of art',[30] because it deals with specialized art collections, does not take into account the power of artistic form to stimulate new ways in which the art work may function in new contexts so that its form acts as an imaginative bridge between past and present, as did those Ife stone sculptures buried generations ago and later dug up to be put to completely new use by a people who had no recollection of the original functions of the objects.[31]

A writer's imitation of style and form often provokes a charge of plagiarism against him. This mark of the change from an oral to a written transmission of literary texts is brought about because print has made possible the idea of property ownership, and not because of the use of print *per se*. Plagiarism posed no problem in oral societies mainly because there were no tangible records for ascertaining that language and manner had been reproduced as well as form and content, as will be seen in the fact that there is copyright for modern pop singers though they do not operate in a printed medium. It will be remembered that Ouloguem, whose *Bound to Violence* has been at the centre of the plagiarism controversy, borrowed from both the oral as well as the printed traditions, but it is only for copying from print that he has been taken to task. The issue of copying another writer's actual words and manner noted by Nwoga[32] has been taken care of by the distinction, in copyright laws, between the reproduction of ideas and the reproduction of words: 'One is safe if one reproduced in one's words, the original ideas of an author provided one does not actually copy his words.'[33] The law, being no ass, accepts, like the best of critics, that literature is essentially an act of language.

The existence of copyright laws indicates the changed status of the verbal artist in our newly literate cultures, with critics exerting pressure to ensure the originality of the artist, in a manner unprecedented in the oral tradition. There is a similar official pressure on the artist for a dissociation of his literary medium from his political ideas. The various symptoms of the resulting tension are seen in the image of the felon sometimes attached to the profession of the artist, and the fact that now and then a major writer is forced to try his hand at the new genre of the authentic prison diary.

NOTES

1. *The African Image*, London, Faber, 2nd rev. edn, 1974, p. 23. New York, Praeger, 1974.

2. *Girls at War*, London, Heinemann (AWS 100), 1972, p. 19. New York, Fawcett World, 1974.

3. *Morning Yet On Creation Day*, London, Heinemann, 1975, p. 19. New York, Doubleday, 1975.

4. *Classical African Art*, London, Faber, 3rd rev. edn, 1970, p. 23.

5. Wilfred Cartey, *Whispers from a Continent*, London, Heinemann, 1971, p. 3.

6. *Equiano's Travels*, ed. Paul Edwards, London, Heinemann (AWS 10), 1967, p. 73: 'you assert that they [i.e. black slaves] are incapable of learning, that their minds are such a barren soil or moor that culture would be lost on them.'

7. ibid., p. 40, and Paul Edwards's footnote on p. 188.

8. Mphahlele interviewed by Pieterse in *African Writers Talking*, ed. Dennis Duerden and Cosmo Pieterse, London, Heinemann, 1972, p. 111. New York, Africana Publishing Company, 1972.

9. *Down Second Avenue*, London, Faber, 1959, p. 97. All quotations are from the 1971 edn. New York, Anchor Books, 1971.

10. Gerald Moore, *The Chosen Tongue*, London, Longman, 1968, p. 206.

11. E.g. by Paul Edwards and Kenneth Ramchand, 'An African Sentimentalist: Camara Laye's *The African Child*', *African Literature Today*, 4, London, Heinemann, 1970, pp. 37–53. New York, Africana Publishing Company, 1972.

12. *Down Second Avenue*, New York, Anchor Books, 1971, p. xix.

13. Ronald Christ, *New York Times Book Review*, 17 December 1967, 22.

14. I. N. C. Aniebo, *Nigeria Magazine*, 81, 1964, 149.

15. 'The Role of the Writer in a New Nation' (1964), in *African Writers on African Writing*, ed. G. D. Killam, London, Heinemann, 1972, p. 8. Evanston, Illinois, Northwestern University Press, 1973.

16. René Maran, *Batouala* (first published 1921), introduction by Donald E. Herdeck, London, Heinemann (AWS 135), 1973. Washington, D.C., Inscape Corp., 1973.

17. *Harper's*, ccxxxviii, 1424, January 1969, 79–84.

18. In *Girls at War*.

19. Shakespeare, *Measure for Measure*, ii, ii.

20. *The Interpreters*, London, Heinemann (AWS 76), 1970, p. 114. New York, Africana Publishing Company, 1972; New York, Macmillan, 1970 (paperback).

21. *The Wretched of the Earth*, Harmondsworth, Penguin, p. 189. New York, Grove, 1965.

22. A. C. Brench, *The Novelist's Inheritance in French West Africa*, London, OUP, 1967, p. 48.

23. *Secret Lives*, London, Heinemann (AWS 150), 1975, p. 130. Westpost, Connecticut, Lawrence Hill, 1975.

24. ibid.

25. J. Caseley-Hayford, *Ethiopia Unbound* (1911), 2nd edn with a new introduction by F. Nnabuenyi Ugonna, London, Frank Cass, 1969.

26. R. E. Obeng, *Eighteen Pence* (1943), Accra, Ghana Publishing Corporation, 1971/2.
27. 'Sol Plaatje's *Mhudi'*, *Journal of Commonwealth Literature*, VIII, 1, June 1973, 1–19; Sol T. Plaatje, *Mudhi* (1930; 1957; 1970), introduction by Tim Couzens, Johannesburg, Quagga Press, 1975. London, Heinemann (AWS 201) 1977. Westpost, Connecticut, Negro Universities Press, 1974 (reprint of 1930 edition).
28. John Okparocha, *Mbari: Art as Sacrifice*, Ibadan, Daystar Press, 1976, p. 9.
29. *Voices of Silence*, New York, Doubleday, 1953, p. 334.
30. ibid., p. 15.
31. Frank Willett, 'Ife and Its Archaeology', in *Papers in African Prehistory*, ed. J. D. Fage and R. A. Oliver, Cambridge, CUP, 1970, p. 306. New York, CUP, 1970.
32. Donatus I. Nwoga, 'Plagiarism and Authentic Creativity in West Africa', *Research in African Literatures*, VI, 1, 1975, 32–9.
33. S. K. Date-Baah, 'The Law of Copyright in Ghana', *Okyeame*, 5, November 1972, 97.

Modern African Poetry: The Domestication of a Tradition

D. I. Nwoga

P oetry has always been a major component of African imaginative activity. The range of poetry extends from the single phrase filled out with grunts and developed through repetitions, composed and performed to ritual; through the most sophisticated phrasing of language; to the development through exploration of images relevant to a theme. The occasion for poetry extends from pure entertainment; through the expression of emotion about the various universally shared aspects of life – sickness, marriage, love, death; to ritual incantations made to bring about changes in life or changes in relationship between the living and the dead or between man and the supernatural. In all this activity, one thing that is most common is the factor of poetry being a communal event, something performed before an audience, aimed at persuading and entertaining, enlightening the people who are there before the poet and reacting to his words and to his general performance. To that extent the composer of oral poetry had to be conscious of this audience, to aim his language at its level and to be sure he followed canons established in the tradition to which his audience belonged. Whether he was proposing new ideas or whether he was agreeing with generally accepted ones, he had to be relevant to justify his performance and to retain his audience.

What I have described is what one would consider the basic African poetry and there are large amounts of this, as has been revealed by the extensive research going on now both in universities by students and staff and outside by interested ethnographers. Much of the oral poetry has now been published. I think it is legitimate to point out at this point that African poetry as defined above does constitute the major part of the poetic activity that still goes on at the moment. The 'modern' in my title is therefore not a time adjective. Traditional oral poetry still flourishes side by side with poetry written in African languages.

By 'modern' African poetry in my title I am referring to the work which is being written in the language derived from the colonial experience. This is not poetry of any long timespan though there are samples of it that appeared before the turn of the century. I am developing my theme on the basis of poetry which dates from about 1957 when Gabriel Okara's poems first appeared in the first issue of *Black Orpheus*. Before then of course existed what I have referred to elsewhere as 'pioneer poetry'. Among the pioneer poets there had been a consciousness of poetry, there had been some writing aimed at declaring popular stands on various issues, like the poetry of Dennis Osadebey and Azikiwe which appeared in newspapers and were broadcast on the radio and even published in anthologies; there had been poetry of personal opinions on national issues and on the matter of the racial position of the black man, like the poetry of Armattoe and Gladys Casely Hayford; there had even been experimentation with language and Crispin George and Gladys Casely Hayford of Sierra Leone had written in Creole. The poetry of Armattoe and Hayford had remained valid because of their clarity of perception and statement. But the poetry of Okara suddenly made public a new direction, a new intensity, a new vigour which did not exist in any of the poetry in English that preceded it.

Basically then this essay seeks to explore the trends of poetry in the twenty years since Okara first appeared in print. Obviously written in a language which limited the possible audience because of the problem of literacy and the foreignness of the language, his work opened up for others the possibility of either developing towards privacy or achieving the kind of context and audience and validity which existed in traditional poetry. In other words I want to look at the major influences on poetry within the last twenty years. What have been considered the roles which poetry could play? What has been the result of the influences on the style of writing and the language, the imagery, the poetic structures? How have the poets reacted to the various changes that have taken place in the sociopolitical context and what relationships have existed between the poetic period and the type of poetry that was written? Finally, I will hazard a proposition as to whether, as a result of all these activities, one could say now that poetry in foreign languages, particularly English, has developed into a domesticated tradition.

I will resist the temptation of trying to treat every poet and restrict myself to those who have broken new ground and who have tended to establish a reputation and an influence over other poets.

In any people's poetry, there are always those poets who achieve a sort of easy and fluent ordinariness in their subject and style, a humour that is pervading but not poignant, a style that is interesting and pleasant but not strikingly original. An example of this is 'A Nigerian Death Ride' by Thomas Chigbo.[1] The poem is enlightening and interesting reading about the road habits of Nigerian drivers. It could have been written at any time by anybody and so he does not belong in a study which tries to explore the changes that have taken place towards the development of a tradition.

The Impetus to Modernity

Though there is a growing tendency in criticism towards the study of national literature[2] and even more specifically the literature from ethnic groups,[3] there are still many issues of literary importance which one can best speak of in the larger terms of African literature. I believe the development of and change in literary tradition belong to this more generalized perspective. In this connection, it is useful to note that the Mbari poetry competitions of the early 1960s were Africa-wide in perspective and the prizes were won in 1962 by two South Africans and a Nigerian. In 1962, the Conference of African Writers of English Expression in Kampala brought a close contact between the writers and critics of all Africa and even artists from the African diaspora. That first contact has led to a continuing consciousness of Africa as a unified literary scene. Lewis Nkosi compared the West African scene with the South African when he wrote in 1962 about the relationship of literature and life in those communities;[4] Taban lo Liyong, complaining about the dearth of creativity in East Africa, contrasted this to the West African situation.[5] That contact has continued and been deepened through exile and travel. Its results in terms of the changes in literary practice make it possible to talk in this essay about the overall development towards domestication of a tradition of modern African poetry in English.

The year 1960 can be used as a significant period marker for the appearance of a new type of poetry in Africa. A more accurate detail would be 1957 when *Black Orpheus* first appeared in Ibadan with the poetry of Okara. But that first whisper of modernity did not become a loud statement till the appearance of the various publications that Mbari, Ibadan, brought out between 1962 and 1964. The six poets published then were from West and South Africa:

Christopher Okigbo (Nigeria), J. P. Clark (Nigeria), Okogbule Glory Nwanodi (Nigeria), George Awoonor-Williams (Ghana), Lenrie Peters (Gambia), and Dennis Brutus (South Africa).

This was new poetry. In contrast to the relaxed, gentle efforts of the earlier writers like R. G. Armattoe and Dennis Osadebey, this was the work of people who came to poetry writing with deliberate conscious concern for the poetic processes. Paul Theroux chose an effective title for his study of that early work of the six poets: 'Voices Out of the Skull'[6] Though they formed no school of literature – and could not have formed one since they were so scattered geographically and by their own specific experiences – there is a major factor which provided a common impetus to their individual brands of modernity. That was a new awareness of the details of international literary creativity and criticism, especially among those first graduates of university courses in English and classical studies.

There was an overwhelming enthusiasm which took many directions. One of these was a tendency to see art as capable of absorbing all the impact made on the writer and therefore a sometimes staggering ability to borrow from the world. Dennis Brutus and Christopher Okigbo are prime examples of this all-embracing receptiveness to influences. The record is sometimes unbelievable. In an interview in 1962 Okigbo admitted that when he was working on *Heavensgate* he was under the spell of the Impressionist composers of music – Debussy, César Franck, Ravel – and he was also able to define the quality of their music which affected the quality of his poetry as follows: '... as in the music of these composers who write of a watery, shadowy, nebulous world, with the semitones of dream and the nuances of the rainbow, there isn't any clearly defined outline in my work: this is what happened in my *Heavensgate*'.[7] In the Introduction to his *Labyrinths*,[8] which he wrote in 1965, he presents the influences on his poem 'Lament of the Silent Sisters': 'The Silent Sisters are however, sometimes like the drowning transition nuns of Hopkins's "The Wreck of the Deutschland", sometimes like the "sirènes" of Debussy's *Nocturnes*'; the motif 'No in thunder', he claims, is taken from one of Melville's letters to Hawthorne, and 'this motif is developed by a series of related airs from sources as diverse as Malcolm Cowley, Raja Ratnam, Stephane Malarmé, Rabindranath Tagore, Garcia Lorca and ... Peter Thomas'. Hopkins comes in again with the motif of 'carrion comfort'. The poem itself is patterned like the Greek ode with strophes. Before we reach the end of the Introduction other facets of inter-cultural borrowings are identified: 'Babylonian capture', Palinurus, the helmsman of Aeneas's ship, 'Ishta's lament for Tammuz', and many such others: a staggering concatenation of poems, names, and places.

Dennis Brutus's interview in Texas in 1970 also shows to what extent the world and its literature had been a major force in the forming of his poetic tendencies and consciousness. Talking about his poem 'The Sibyl' he acknowledged first of all that he adopted that title from the Greek name for the old woman of the oracle, the old woman who made prophecies of doom, in order to project his own prophecy about the inevitable bloody destruction that would result from the politics of South Africa. He revealed that he structured his poem 'A Troubadour' with a consciousness of all the types of the disciplining sonnet form, his intention being to create a form even tighter than the Petrarchan. Talking about the influences on his earliest poems of the 1950s, in particular the poem 'So, for the moment, Sweet is peace', he claimed that Hopkins was the strongest influence in his life then but that that period had also been influenced by John Donne, Browning, Eliot, Ezra Pound, Patchen, Rexroth, and Wallace Stevens; he took his half-rhyme schemes from Wilfred Owen and Gibson; he took his images from English poetry of Swinburne, from the Latin poetry of Thomas Aquinas in which he compares Christ to the pelican, and took the word 'Sweet' from another of Aquinas's Latin hymns.[9]

Interviews with other poets reveal the same, openly acknowledged, tendency to be influenced mainly by poets of the European tradition:

> The echoes of the African tradition come to me subconsciously, I hear them, and perhaps that is the only African part – or influence – that I can confess to; otherwise, I think the technical part of it is entirely conditioned by my experience with reading European literature.[10]

> I was particularly interested in and probably much influenced by one poet in particular – Gerard Manley Hopkins. His energetic, innovative, highly revolutionary use of the language, his wonderful concatenations of rhythmic patterns, strike strong sympathetic vibrations within me.[11]

Another area of this enthusiasm was in the experimentation with forms, with words. This experimentation was part of the practice of their mentors, but was also a result of a liberating conception of poetry which no longer saw it as a stereotyped activity in which words had specific poetic values and forms were rigid structures into which experiences had to be fitted. Poetic experience was a liberation of perception and a liberating medium had to be found for the expression of the experience. Above all it was on the quality of experience that this enthusiasm achieved its greatest impact. The environment favoured this liberating quality of perception. Whether the experiences themselves were favourable or harsh, there was a sense of being in a vortex. Politics was flamboyant. Expectations were heady. There was the electric convergence of the modern and the traditional without the acerbity of later attempts to cope with this modernity. The learned could see the wisdom of the old without yet experiencing the inadequacies of tradition, and the emptiness of modern expectations had not yet become evident. The environment was therefore conducive to all varieties of experiences and perceptions. The wicked colonial fact was about to be discarded. Everything was set for a new world.

In retrospect, it is possible to assess the depth to which any of the poets experienced their environment by how much their poetry sang; by the level of exuberance with which they played with their words and forms; by how vividly and with what metaphysical and spiritualist mystery they invested their perception of their environment; by how much they allowed metaphysical reality to impinge upon the ordinary physical personal and political issues with which they were involved in their poetry. Life was heady and full and only poets who could get beyond surface realities could give expression to the spirit of the period.

The themes were public themes. But to a large extent public events were seen from the personal angle and within an overall intellectual liberalist framework. The overwhelming impression one receives from Brutus's early poems, for example, is not one of the obvious and loud expression of white wickedness but of a consistently perceived dignified human existence with all the affections and all the actions that belong to this quality, and the implied inhumanity of a system which made it impossible for a man to live a dignified life. Echeruo's statement that 'In those early years [1961–5] I sought to understand myself and human life'[12] is another expression of the general tendency.

There were of course varieties of this kind of search for the meaning of self and life. The individual, depending upon his experiences, sought the meaning of life in his reactions to the environment, his reactions to political events, his reactions to human relationships. The beginning of modern African poetry, then, produced a poetry of individual search mingled with political or public statement.

The result of this kind of intensive personal search through the labyrinths of public experiences could be poetry of terrible complexity, terrible privacy, and near meaninglessness to an audience that had not shared the immediate personal situation of the poet. On the other hand it could lead to poetry of great intensity and mental, emotional, psychological, and literary joy, like Okigbo's 'Watermaid'.

It is not surprising then that poetry of the older generation had as its audience a largely international community. As Nadine Gordimer says about the first generation of black South African writers: 'Subconsciously their writings were aimed at white readers and were intended to rouse the white consciousness over black frustration.'[13] In West Africa, the idea of course was to give expression to a new sense of culture which was to be a contribution to international world culture. The implication of these aspects will be assessed later in this essay but I think it is fair to summarize now and say that this was a movement generated independently in South Africa and West Africa, a movement to modernity propelled by a greater and more meaningful contact with the literary activities of a wider world, received consciously as possible guides to new creativity in the African environment.

The Influence from the Past

The second major movement in the development of a tradition of African poetry originated from East Africa. Of course, it sounds slightly preposterous to have to talk about phases of development in such a short literary history. But there certainly is an identifiably different impetus from what has been discussed so far behind the poetry that came from the pen of Okot p'Bitek. Whereas the impetus for the majority of poets of the earlier discussion arose out of contact with the outside world, Okot p'Bitek fed his creativity from the impact of his culture on his imagination. In all he has written and said, one sees a strong sense of cultural nationalism and his continuous reaction against the overwhelming presence of European culture. His own mother was a great poet and thirty-four of the songs he presents in *Horn of My Love* came from her; his father was a good storyteller and 'very witty in his use of proverbs'. Thus, when Okot was in school and was being taught English literature, he kept reacting with a consciousness of his own literature and a will to make it as strong and as valid as what he was being taught from another culture. It is in this way that he derived influences from Longfellow's *Hiawatha*, the story of Ulysses and the books of the Bible, especially the love songs of Solomon.[14]

As is usual in literary history, it is possible to look back through the poetry of West Africa and see that what Okot p'Bitek achieved so dramatically in 1966 had been attempted in little snippets by other poets. The poets of the Nsukka tradition, especially Egudu, Okogbule Wonodi, and Pol Ndu, had always, in their poetry, shown a consciousness of the Igbo tradition of religion, speech, and poetry, had shown a consciousness of the mysticism of African traditions. But the overwhelming Ibadan tradition had swamped their production. And in any case they had never produced anything comparable with Okot p'Bitek's *Song of Lawino*.[15]

In many ways then, Okot p'Bitek himself was the culminating point of an earlier tradition of African poetry, a tradition in which one would group Kofi Awoonor, some of J. P. Clark's work, and certainly the Nsukka poets mentioned earlier.

The Domestication of a Tradition

The Critical Argument

After twenty years and a lot of poetry in Africa it is valid to discuss to what extent it can be claimed that the African poet has established for himself a language and a form to give genuine effective expression to the realities of his experience. The argument has indeed raged towards this establishment.

There has of course always been a strong tradition of criticism within the African poetic tradition. After M. J. C. Echeruo had won the poetry first prize with his poems which were later published in *Black Orpheus*, 12, in 1963, Okigbo said in an interview that he found Echeruo's poetry somewhat academic and did not find sufficient feeling in it, whereas he found Dennis Brutus a very sensitive poet.[16] Echeruo himself, talking about J. P. Clark's poetry in 1973, said, 'I think *Casualties* is a disaster. It is sheer journalism. There is absolutely nothing in it, nothing that's good enough as poetry',[17] an opinion echoed later the same year by Mr. Kalu Uka who said 'I think *Casualties* is rubbish'. Uka went further to criticize Clark's poetry as betraying too many European influences: 'you can see him overdoing Hopkins and one or two other echoes'.[18] Kole Omotoso, talking about English departments and the production of poets, said of the English department at Ibadan that the only poet it had produced was 'possibly Samson Amali and I think he is a really bad poet ... yet this is their only product, an artist who is a total disaster'.[19] Okot p'Bitek in a recent interview complained about the new direction of East African writing and said that most of the works were light-hearted and they seemed to be replacing the popular things which came from Europe – the James Hadley Chase kind of books – and he would like to see more serious works, works which 'deal with the ills of our society seriously'; and he thought writers in East Africa were growing timid 'because they know that the hawk is flying over them'. (On the other hand he complained about Soyinka because 'I cannot follow him at all'.)[20]

These are criticisms of individual poets and criticisms of particular periods but there are major general issues which have come into the critical discussion in Africa and they include the problem of obscurity, the problem of relevance, and the problem of a tradition of poetry.

One of the most determined critics of the poetry produced so far in terms of all these aspects has been Chinweizu. In 1973, he opened his attack with the article 'Prodigals Come Home'.[21] In association with Onwuchekwa Jemie and Ihechukwu Madubuike he carried on the campaign under the title 'Towards the Decolonization of African Literature' published in Okike, 6 and 7,[22] re-published in Transition, 48.[23] In his reviews published in Okike, 9 and 12,[24] he took up the same issues; and much more recently, in association with O. Jemie, he has concluded with a quite effective, angry and sarcastic attack, entitled 'The Hopkins Disease'.[25]

Put quite simply, the point Chinweizu is making is that the poets and critics of Nigeria and Africa, like Africa's politicians, intellectual élite and development planners, are poor, misguided, imperialist, neo-colonialist, brainwashed slobs. As such, the poets are producing work which does not qualify as 'modern African poetry' but should really be called 'modern poetry in Africa' – a type of poetry which is a tired and ineffective imitation of the traditions of the West. The result of this imitativeness of the wrong models is that, contrary to the genuine African oral traditions, the poets engage in the exploration of their puny egos instead of being the voice of their communities in their quest for development values; moreover, instead of pursuing the simple clarity of traditional verse the poets use obscurity to keep the public away from their élitist but misguided irrelevant trivia. The critics who should have warned and cajoled the poets away from their faulty and culturally dangerous misconceptions are unfortunately themselves the products of the same neo-colonial brainwashing and they are corrupted into participating with the poets in the futile and 'elaborate and obvious con game of puzzling out gratuitous conundrums'.[26]

Chinweizu is very convincing in many points of his presentation. In one of his more detached pieces of criticism, for example, he argues that Okigbo's 'Path of Thunder' is his best achievement which is attributable to 'his consciously working within African traditions and of his bringing to his work valuable lessons he had learned from other traditions, Western Modernism not excluded'. His highest praise goes to 'Elegy for Slit-drum' which 'though written in English, owes nothing to modern European sensibility: a poem at the third transmuted corner of a cultural triangle at whose other corners stand the African Traditional and the Modern European sensibilities, but still a poem whose African lineage is beyond dispute'.[27] This is a firm statement of the generally accepted critical stand in Africa that the successful African poem must be the work of a poet with a sensibility well grounded in African traditions who also has available to him techniques of development derived both from Africa and from other traditions. Indeed, in his book, *The West and the Rest of Us*, he states this moderate view in italics:

> We should all heed Césaire's warning that merely copying our past is not enough. We should also realize that a sterile worship of any tradition, not excluding the modern European, will bring cultural death, not renaissance.[28]

The excitement which Chinweizu has created has been partly the result of his impressive overwhelming sweep of mind which can be dangerously persuasive, but more of his conception of genuine African traditions and of the relationship between modern Africa and its traditions and the West. One has the impression that Chinweizu, deliberately, perhaps, for polemical purposes, but dangerously because it can deceive, overstates his case. Otherwise one is distressed by his presentation of the African poetic landscape 'with its flora and fauna', especially when he talks in the late twentieth century of 'native eyes to which aeroplanes naturally appear as iron birds; a landscape in which the animals behave as they might behave in African folk-lore, of animals presented through native African eyes',[29] because, obviously, it would be naïvely atavistic for even a villager now not to see the aeroplane as an aeroplane, a machine made by man for travelling through the air.

In their essay 'The Decolonization of African Literature', Chinweizu *et al.* continue to attack by relating modern practice to traditional literature. Their conception of traditional poetry is one which attributes to it clarity as its major characteristic and gives to the poet the role of communal voice. Here again is that slight overstatement that ruins a case. The pitch of emotion attached to the literary argument is alarming and I believe most statements are made for shock effect, for example, 'as a result of their addiction to archaisms, the poetry of the Ibadan/Nsukka poets tends to be craggy, lumpy, full of obstructions, unnecessarily and artificially difficult; simple ideas are often deliberately clothed in esoteric idiom'.[30] Indeed the tone of total condemnation of the Ibadan/Nsukka poets and critics robs the Chinweizu trio of the possible contributions they could have made to the ongoing shaping out of aesthetic criteria. Theirs was just one voice among those who were saying that overcomplication of statement and self-centredness of theme were damaging to the genuine growth of poetry. In 1974, Ogungbesan tracing Okigbo's achievement, said of the last phase that the enormity of the crisis of 1965–6

> reached behind the mask in which Okigbo had earlier insulated himself from his society, forcing him to discard the cloak of mythology in which his earlier poetry had been suffocating ... The simplicity, energy and assurance of 'Path of Thunder' come from a complete identification with the communal experience. Because national events had such a direct impact on his sensibility, Okigbo authentically assumed the collective role of 'town crier'' and moaned of the impending tragedy of a society that had failed to heed the warning of the gods.[31]

This independent praise of 'Path of Thunder' as the peak of Okigbo's poetic achievement is not very different in its tone and reason from the trio's

> Through most of his career, Okigbo indulged himself in writing cap-tivating nonsense, developing his voice. But luckily for him, just before his death, events gave him public occasion to use that voice. This obscurantist 'poet's poet' was jolted off his elitist clouds. He found matter for his manner, and became a candidate for greatness.[32]

Central to their critical viewpoint is the rejection of 'privatist' poetry – not merely in terms of stylistic presentation (which is acceptable) but even the exploration of personal states, thoughts, and emotions as an act of poetry. This is certainly a great limitation to the scope of poetry which, in a situation of moral and cultural transition, uses the individual consciousness as the theatre in which an understanding of the most intimate meaning of cultural disorientation or confusion can be displayed. The call for commitment in the poets is however justified – though the claim that this commitment does not exist is only expression of a preference for a certain type of commitment.[33]

The call for clarity is also obviously overstated, and is usually joined with a charge of neo-colonialist 'obscurantism' which cannot be substantiated:

> anybody who can read what is popularly known as Onitsha Market literature, or ... to use non-Nigerian examples, Okot p'Bitek's *Song of Lawino* ... should be able to read whatever our other poets write in English. This simple literacy test should define the African writer's primary audience and community.[34]

The call for a conscious revival of an African base for literary as well as other facets of African development is firmly and vigorously stated in all of Chinweizu's writings. Unfortunately one is distressed by the polemical stance which makes Chinweizu's contribution to the search for an African poetics sound like frustrated crying over spilt milk. At some point someone must say boldly and clearly that, while acknowledging the viciousness of the forces of colonial exploitation, a victim stasis can be unproductive and, even worse than that, retrogressive. Africa has been shoved into the twentieth century like a non-swimmer into deep water and it has either got to learn to cope with it or become perpetually irrelevant except for further and more complete decimation.

Soyinka's reaction to the Chinweizu troika was unfortunate in its violence but perhaps it was a valid over-reaction to overstatement.[35] What is clear in all the discussion is that the apprehension of traditional literature varies and I recognize greater validity in the Soyinka analysis. Moreover, one acknowledges that the attempt to decree one type of African poetry is premature and inelastic and would do great harm to the growth of that activity.

There have been other critics, and the issues of obscurity and commitment have featured more recently, especially in Nigerian criticism.[36] But at this point, it is necessary to look at the changes which have taken place in the poetic tradition and how these have tended towards or against the domestication of a tradition of modern African poetry.

Domestication in Practice

The acerbity of the critical argument has obscured the progression of modern African poetry for the period, though short, has had its changes which make invalid any criticism which tries to span the whole output. The existence of generations is becoming an accepted stand in modern African poetry and creative artists have also spoken of the changes created in them by time and events. Gabriel Okara, for example, has indicated that when he writes again there will be a change in his mode. His future poetry may be 'a bit political in tone ... What will preoccupy my thinking will be the effects of politics on our society.'[37]

In defining the generations, the crisis and the resultant civil war have been recognized as creating a new urgency in Nigerian poetry. Both Echeruo and Kole Omotoso in 1975, and Gerald Moore in 1977, have spoken of these generational changes and, to a large extent what they have said would apply to the whole of Africa. Echeruo speaks of 'the greater conviction among the writers that their mission is clearly defined', Kole Omotoso of the social attitude of the younger 'Particularists' as against the older 'Universalists' which makes them 'believe that they have to address first of all those who live in their street, in their towns and cities, in the countries', and Gerald Moore generally of the growing explicit leftist ideological commitment of the poets.[38] In East Africa, too, as far back as 1968, Ali Mazrui had depicted a progression in four movements in East African writing from the theme of praise of the heroes of the independence struggle, through 'the defence of tradition against modernity', and the literature of political 'empathic identification with others abroad' as in Vietnam and Angola, to the taking up of issues of 'national corruption and coups'.[39]

The maturing of African poetry, the clear change in its states, its domestication in both intended audience and stylistic conventions, is a phenomenon which can be traced both in individuals who have written over a long period, and in the difference between the older generations and the younger writers.

The Choice of Tradition

One major fact of this domestication is the localization of the influences that now impinge on the poets. Quite early in the 1960s the poets had taken into account in the maturation of their talents the impact of the growing study of their own traditions. One important local influence is, of course, the traditional literature. Most African writers have said that in the process of finding their own voice they have had to go back to their roots to the point where the external influences have become mere catalysts to self-discovery.

David Rubadiri was saying in 1966, 'And so I begin to write more like ... myself as an African who's got roots or beginning to get them, as opposed to the young student who had to live between two worlds, as it were, two values of life'.[40] Kofi Awoonor at the same time was speaking of an earlier imitativeness of foreign influences and the development of his own voice from the resources of the oral traditions, and in his opinion 'none of us, if we are good writers, are in any way diminished by being influenced. We have achieved what we have done, through English writers, not with them.'[41]

Research in oral literature was growing. Courses in African oral literature were being taught. Kalu Uka, who teaches at Nsukka and admits that he himself has not been influenced by the oral poetic tradition except for its music, acknowledges that the younger poets of Nsukka 'now feel closer ties to local poetic traditions'.[42] The extent of the prevalence of this can be seen from the poems in a recent edition of *Omabe*, the poetry magazine of the department of English at the University of Nigeria, Nsukka. It contains an excerpt from the poem *What the Madman Said* by Obiora Udechukwu, a promising but non-prolific poet although a prolific artist.

> How many baskets of water can mould a block?
> How many he-goats can guard a yam barn?
>   And we talk of yam-masters
>   But their sons eat alịbọ.
>
> Fish that lives in the ocean
> That same fish washes with spittle.
>   And you talk of hell
>   Does it need death to arrive?
>
> The question looms in the evening cloud
> It hangs so it's now part of the sky
> The question their chiefs do not want to see
> The question that questions their stools.[43]

The debts to Igbo oral traditions here are many, mainly to the proverb tradition. Throughout the poem one hears the echoes of proverbs like: 'You do not fetch water with a basket'; 'you do not give yams to goats to protect'; 'the son of a yam-master does not eat alịbọ (a yam flour that is made into dark foo-foo; good yam foo-foo is pounded from fresh boiled yam); 'one who lives by the river does not wash his hands with spittle'. The last stanza derives its meaning from the Igbo tradition that the only justification of leadership is the fulfilment of the role to the satisfaction of the ruled; a chief whose people receive no amenities has no right to his stool. In the same issue, a poem by Pat Nwoga, who is Irish by nationality but has lived in Nsukka for sixteen years, contains the following image obviously taken from the local traditions:

> Anklets of ivory have become plastic
> As men dance to a discordant tune.[44]

conveying the impression of the debasement of values in a dying environment. Charles Ezeonwu's title 'Blowing the Ivory Horns' and much of the following poem on the failure of universal primary education in Nigeria show a borrowing of concepts and images from the same tradition:

> Ivory horns across
>   nineteen and one royal mouths
>   talk of – yu pee ee.
>
> Regal steps. Legs of anklets;
>   digging dance acknowledging
>   adulation over – yu pee ee ...[45]

I have presented here a local example of a major phenomenon in modern African poetry. And I have used unacknowledged poets even though the trend was established by the major poets. As will be shown later, this activity goes far beyond the use of traditional images and symbols, and involves an adjustment to the imaginative processes.

It has to be pointed out, incidentally, that the use of images and other facets of oral tradition does not lead immediately to easy comprehension and appreciation of the poetry. It does help to elicit the emotions and wider allusions from those readers from whose traditions the borrowings have been made. However, every teacher of African poetry knows how images like Okot p'Bitek's 'Do Not Uproot the Pumpkin' and Kofi Awoonor's 'We Shall Sleep in Calico' hold up the uninitiated till much cultural exegesis has been done. The advantage, however, of the continuation of this tradition is that progressively the private ethnic images and symbols will become more and more available to the wider African audience leading to the creation of a general African sensibility.

In addition to the development of closer ties with the African traditions of poetry, there has also been the situation that younger poets have used the older African poets as their models. The influence of Otok p'Bitek has been very strong in East Africa. Okello Oculi acknowledged this and explained that they found that he had 'hit exactly on the kind of nerve, at the tissue, of the [African] system'. They became disciples of Okot – Oculi patterned his *Orphan* and Buruga his *The Abandoned Hut* on *Song of Lawino* – because, like Okot, they 'were responding to intrusions into our environment. We were responding to the needs of our people – their political and social aspirations. We were responding to their cultural outrage.'[46]

Of all the major poets, however, it would appear that Christopher Okigbo has been the most influential on the younger poets. In spite of the difficulty of his poetry, he has fired many imaginations. At least thirty poems by about twenty poets have been written to his memory. Echoes and images have been taken from his poetry, his tradition of complex Christian imagery has been parodied and copied, his lyric cadences have been reproduced. Jared Angira of Kenya is an enthusiastic disciple of Okigbo and in quite a few of his poems either mentions Okigbo or takes phrases from his poetry or simply imitates him. Here is a short example:

> Chris found a powder
> at the gates of Enugu
> and powdered the yam
> and the palm
> till they all went crimson mad
> and began somersaulting
> as Chris had done
> to heavensgate.[47]

Another poem opens with

> That chloroform sleep
> woke me up
> in dream
> only to find
> Ramogi under siege,[48]

and here there are strong echoes from Okigbo's 'Distances'.

In Nigeria, Okigbo's influence has been very pronounced. Tunde Adeniran, then a scholar in international relations who had an interest in poetry, explained in 1975 how he wrote his poem 'The Town-Crier' because of a vivid dream he had of Christopher Okigbo. The poem itself drew its title from Okigbo's reference to himself as 'town-crier' in 'Path of Thunder'[49] and is a dirge heavily influenced by the sounds and structures of Okigbo's poetry, incorporating the titles of Okigbo's poems in its statement.[50] Many poems in *Okike*, *Omabe*, and *The Muse* at Nsukka, *Idoto* at Ibadan, and *Sokoti* at Ife, show this influence. The cadences, units, and repetitions in Chinweizu's 'Fine Laughter'[51] bear witness to a definite impact from Okigbo's 'Path of Thunder'. Young unknown poets continue to battle with the Okigbo image.[52]

Audience, Language, and Theme

S. O. Duodu, in his review of *No Time to Die*,[53] presents an ironic literary fact. Kojo Gyinanye Kyei and Hannah Schreckenbach produced *No Time to Die* by travelling through Ghana, collecting the down-to-earth philosophical statements of the folk as presented in the slogans on mammy lorries. They interviewed the drivers, mates, and lorry-owners. They then wrote the poems in a language which was a mixture of standard English, pidgin English, and the local language. The book was directed at and dedicated to the common people and launched at the Accra Arts Centre in 1976. But 'although the book is dedicated to all mammy lorry drivers and their mates, not one of them was at the Accra Arts Centre on the day this humour-packed collection about them was launched!'[54]

It might be ideologically appropriate to talk of 'the average African reader' and 'comprehension by anybody who can read' but it is unrealistic to presume that there is such an audience waiting for the poets to write for them. I would imagine that if one went to the places where the drivers and their mates drink their beer and palm wine after work, one would find that they engage in their own poetic activities which are perhaps more vigorous than written verse by the educated. It is to some extent insulting to their sensibilities to presume that watered-down verse in English is what they hope for as their imaginative entertainment. The strategy for communication with the masses has to be more subtle than that.

All the same, the wish to communicate with 'the masses' has had a salutary effect on modern African poetry. One effect is the determination to work for greater clarity of expression; and this is no new phenomenon resulting from the anger of self-righteous critics. Dennis Brutus has described how, during his period of solitary confinement in a South African prison for anti-apartheid activities in 1963, he decided that style and language had to change towards greater ease of communication. In an interview in 1966 he presented the idea[55] and expanded on it in a 1972 interview:

> The first thing I decided about my future poetry was that there must be no ornament, absolutely none. And the second thing I decided was you oughtn't to write for poets; you oughtn't even to write for people who read poetry, not even students. You ought to write for the ordinary

person: for the man who drives a bus, or the man who carries the baggage at the airport, and the woman who cleans the ashtrays in the restaurant. If you can write poetry which makes sense to these people, then there is some justification for writing poetry.

And therefore, there should be no ornament because ornament gets in the way. It becomes too fancy-shmancy; it becomes over-elaborate. It is, in a way, a kind of pride, a self-display, a glorying in the intellect for its own sake, which is contemptible.[56]

The effect of this determination on Brutus's poetry has been commented upon by critics. Ezekiel Mphahlele writes in his review of *Strains* (1975), of Brutus's 'phase of loaded rows of epithets ... some of which epithets were thick plaster' and adds that 'the epithets became sparser as we move to the 1970s ... When the verbs do more work, when the epithetical plaster is knocked off, there is more energy in the poem.'[57] John Povey, along the same lines, while admitting to 'the extraordinary lyricism of *Sirens, Knuckles, Boots*, speaks of the 'dense, over-clever, quite unpronounceable' lines of some of its poems like 'A Troubadour', but of the later poetry in *Letters to Martha* says that 'the language no longer exhibits that clever ingenuity of word choice; it is now honed into an efficient directness'.[58]

This development in a single poet is duplicated in the new generations. There is no doubt that the poetry of the 1970s does not share in all the devices of complication which featured in the 1960s. This is partly the result of contact with black American poetry as in the case of Keoropatse Kgositsile and Oswold Mtshali of South Africa and Chinweizu of Nigeria, and partly the result of greater control of style as in the major poets like Brutus, Soyinka, and Kofi Awoonor. For all, there was also the sense of a greater urge to communicate. This urge has also come out of a more positive social commitment in the poets. There has indeed been a pervasive influence from Marxism and its variant through Franz Fanon, and this has given a forthright tone of conviction to new African poetry. The achievement of this determined socio-moral stand by the poets has its dangers—the danger of oversimplifying issues into absolute black and white categories which blunt judgement;[59] the danger of losing the basic human sympathies in dealing with characters in crisis situations like the South African situation.[60] But it has the major advantage of strengthening the tone of the poets and saving them from the need to stay with self-exploration longer than necessary. It gives them a focal point for the gathering of their best impulses; it provides them with a non-mystical myth to give consistency to their attitudes.

The Return to Orality

The more determined moral stance, the call for action through poetry of greater simplicity, is one result of the return to the African audience. Another result, which to some extent operates with a different strategy, is the return to the oral medium and its implication in incomprehension in the poem as printed. One obvious example of this is the poetry of Atukwei Okai of Ghana. Atukwei Okai intones, chants, dances, and drums along with his recitation. Amanor Dseagu, introducing *Lorgorligi Logarithms and Other Poems*, comments:

> The dissociation of dance and song which has taken place in Western lyrical poetry must ... not be carried over into modern African poetry. In this respect, the poetry of Atukwei Okai must be seen as being in the very mainstream of African poetry ... The kind of poetry we should encourage, then, should be that which makes a more conscious use of imagery, that which is more symbolist than illustrative ... The image should be both sensuous and intelligent, archetypal and specific and above all surrealist because that is how African poetry works.[61]

Other poets too have adopted this strategy – Oswald Mtshali performed his poem 'Carletonville'[62] on stage in Austin, Texas, in 1975; Lari Williams of Nigeria has performed several of the poems in his *Drum Call*[63] on a number of occasions.

I have not seen other poets perform but it is clear that many are now affected by the tendency towards performance, like Barry Oduor-Otieno whose poems appear in *Okike*, 10, and young Odia Ofeimun of Nigeria in his poems that appear in *Idoto, Ibadan Journal of Creation*, 1 and 2. And all this tendency can be related to the growing concept of *poetry as ritual* which is becoming a feature of the African critical consciousness.[64]

Poetry of this tradition often appears formless and illogical on the printed page. Its success for the listener and conscious reader derives from the poignant imagery, symbolism, vibrant diction, incantatory rhythmic flow, alliterations that help to make the poem fit the drum and chant medium. Into those images the clever poet can put his theme in capsules of affective sense. Repetitions of phrases and lines help to grind the intended meaning into the consciousness of the reader. And irony, in particular, towards the chosen targets of criticism, appears to be a very common attitude quite often emerging through this medium.

The Proverb as Paradigm

Domestication, which has led to addressing a home audience, and adopting the tone of oral communication, has also confirmed one trend in poetic method – the parabolic stance. Poets have used traditional proverbs in their poems. But this is more an act of memory than creativity. By the proverb as paradigm, I am referring to that technique by which the poet, instead of giving the details of the physical event or situation, engineers the reaction appropriate to the pattern set by the event. This is beyond the mere act of metaphorization – a structure is set up parallel to that which is the subject of the poetry and the mood and reaction is thereby generated to the pattern and the original situation which the wise can interpret. This was an important strand in the poetry of Nsukka, especially in the work of Pol Ndu whose 'Eagle Dance'[65] is an incantatory narrative of fear suitable as a response to the pre-war mood of Nigeria; it is the strategy of Okigbo's 'Path of Thunder'. Soyinka's 'Conversation at Night with a Cockroach' and 'O Roots!' (*A Shuttle in the Crypt*) also adopt this method of creating meaning.

The best example of this kind of poetry among the youngest poets is in the work of Odia Ofeimun. Ofeimun has only become prominent in the last two years, though his first poems appeared in 1970[66] and he published poems again in *Okike* 1, 3 in 1972. His poem 'The Campus Philosophers'[67] declares in its title the subject matter but the rest of the poem uses a ritual parallel to create the appropriate response in the reader towards the intellectual élite who are effete; in the poem 'The Messiahs' he ironically shows up the similarity with variation of the new rulers to those they replaced. The title-poem 'The New Brooms' will serve to illustrate the ironic proverbial stance of Ofeimun's poetry and the strength of language and moral stance of this young poet:

> The streets were clogged with garbage
> the rank smell of swollen gutters
> claimed the peace of our lives
>
> The streets were blessed with molehills
> of unwanted odds and bits
>
> Then, they brought in the bayonets
> to define the horizons of our days
> to keep the streets clear
> they brought in the new brooms

To keep the streets clear
they brought in the world-changers
with corrective swagger-sticks
they brought in the new brooms
to sweep public scores away.

But today listen today
if you ask why the wastebins are empty
why refuse gluts the public places unswept
they will enjoin you to HOLD IT:
to have new brooms, that's something.

And if you want to know why
the streets grunt (now)
under rank garbage
under the weight of decay, of nightsoil
more than ever before
they will point triumphantly, very triumphantly
at their well-made timetable:

'We shall get there soonest
nightsoil clearance is next on the list.'

Conclusion

Written poetry does not have a large audience in Africa. This is
partly the result of the oral habit of our culture, partly because
poetry in the written as against the song form has always been an
élite form (except, incidentally in its narrative forms in which
Byron did well in nineteenth-century England and Maillu is now
doing well in East Africa – giving their moral injunctions in light-
hearted verse with a touch of obscenity). Towards its domestication, appeals have been made for simplicity of style in the tradition
of Africa's indigenous literature and for intense moral commitment
in the poets who should be the voices of the common people and
call them to action to improve their circumstances. This call, valid
to some extent but misguided in certain particulars, is part of a total
process in which both critics and poets are joined towards making
poetry in English serve a useful socio-political purpose. Towards
this end, the major poets, as they develop more maturity in their
chosen styles, have also redirected their techniques and themes to
suit a wider local audience. The search for an African authenticity,
however, has not had one-directional effect. Along with simplicity
of diction have come strategies of orality and proverbalization
which do not accept an obvious linear statement.

Domesticated African poetry in English is that which talks to as many Africans as possible about issues of greatest relevance in Africa's ongoing development, both in the public management of affairs and in the maturation of human persons through the emotions and values of life: love, laughter and sorrow, spiritual growth. Though its language is English, the elements of its background are the total environment of today's Africa; its tradition is a convoluting mixture of the basic African origins and the inspiring catalyst of borrowed models. It is poetry which is not a repetition of the past, but is adequate for today because, though based on the past, it is using all the techniques offered by a wider world to cope with the sensibilities generated by Africa's history. Its success depends on its ability, to end with a cliché, to educate and to entertain.

NOTES

1. *A Festac Anthology of Nigerian New Writing*, ed. Cyprian Ekwensi, Lagos, 1977, pp. 48–52.
2. Theo Vincent, 'Two Decades of Nigerian Literature', *Oduma*, II, 2, Rivers State Council for Arts and Culture, Port Harcourt, Nigeria, 1975, pp. 57–67.
3. For example, Emenyonu writes consistently about the traditions of Modern Igbo Literature and Bernth Lindfors has written on the distinction between Yoruba and Igbo purse styles in *Black Orpheus*, II, 7, Mbari, Ibadan, 1972.
4. He made a comparison between the nostalgic attitudes of West African writers as against the South African's realistic exploration of the crude realities of the time (*Home and Exile*, London, Longman, 1964).
5. *The Last Word*, Nairobi, East Africa Publishing House, 1968.
6. *Introduction to African Literature*, ed. Ulli Beier, London, Longman, 1967, pp. 110–31.
7. *African Writers Talking*, ed. Dennis Duerden and Cosmo Pieterse, London, Heinemann, 1972, p. 138. New York, Africana.
8. *Labyrinths*, London, Heinemann, 1971, pp. xii–xiv. New York, Africana.
9. *Palaver*, The University of Texas at Austin, 1973, pp. 25–36.
10. David Rubadiri, 1966, in *African Writers on African Writing*, London, Heinemann, 1973, p. 122. Evanston, Northwestern University Press.
11. Kofi Awoonor, *Transition*, Accra 41, 1972, p. 42.
12. *Dem Say*, The University of Texas at Austin, 1974, p. 12.
13. 'English-Language Literature and Politics in East Africa', *Aspects of South African Literature*, ed. Christopher Heywood, London, Heinemann, 1976, p. 111. New York, Africana.

14. 'An Interview with Okot p'Bitek', by Bernth Lindfors, World Literature Written in English, XVI, 2, The University of Texas at Arlington, November 1977, pp. 281–99.
15. East Africa Publishing House, Nairobi, 1966.
16. African Writers Talking, op. cit., p. 140.
17. Dem Say, op. cit., p. 14.
18. ibid., p. 72.
19. ibid., p. 50.
20. World Literature Written in English, XVI, 2, p. 294.
21. Nsukka, Okike, 4, December 1973, pp. 1–12.
22. Okike, 6, December 1974, pp. 11–27, and Okike, 7, April 1975, pp. 65–81.
23. Transition, IX(v), 48, Accra, April/June 1975, pp. 29–37, 54, 56–7.
24. 'African Literary Criticism Today', a review of African Literature Today, No. 7: Focus on Criticism and The Benin Review, No. 1 (Okike, 9, December 1975, pp. 87–105); and 'Giant Breasts', review of Awoonor's The Breast of Earth, Giant Talk, ed. Troupe and Schutle, and Obiechina's Culture, Tradition and Society in the West African Novel (Okike, 12, April 1978, pp. 80–8).
25. Okike, 12, April 1978, pp. 40–6.
26. ibid., pp. 45, 46.
27. Okike, 4, p. 5.
28. New York, Vintage Books, 1975, p. 303.
29. Okike, 4, p. 5; The West and the Rest of Us, p. 320.
30. Okike, 6, p. 12.
31. 'Nigerian Writers and Political Commitment', Ufahamu, v, 2, University of California, Los Angeles, 1974, p. 23.
32. Okike, 6, pp. 25–6.
33. Charles Nnolim calls the call to community of forms and themes 'barefaced platitudes' and goes on to charge that 'since the troika speak with dead seriousness, one is bound to conclude the troika are uninformed, for the present study will demonstrate that African literary artists are the most committed in the twentieth century' ('An African Literary Aesthetic: A Prolegomena' Ba Shiru, VII, 2, University of Wisconsin, Madison, 1976, p. 58).
34. Okike, 7, p. 76.
35. First in 'Neo-Tarzanism: The Poetics of Pseudo-Tradition', Transition, 48, pp. 38–44 and later in 'Aesthetic Illusions: Prescriptions for the Suicide of Poetry', The Third Press Review, I, 1, Sept./Oct. 1975, pp. 30–1, 65–8. His conclusion is that 'What the neo-Tarzanists preach is a statist contextualism, the poetics of itemization within narrowly defined areas, the separation of experience from experiencing, of matter from perceiving, of thought from reflecting. It is the poetics of death, and mummification, not of life, renewal and continuity' (p. 68).
36. Kole Omotoso: 'The artist has to be able to reach the average man in Africa who can read' (Dem Say, op. cit., p. 56); Ozzie Emekwe: 'Any

work of fiction or poetry whose words are too obscure for the so-called simple but literate audience is not suitable for human consumption, except, perhaps, as a riddle' (*Okike*, 9, p. 76); Femi Osofisan: 'The often decried "difficulty" of our writers, their obtuseness and elliptical styles, are in fact not accidental or gratuitous affectations as critics seem to think, but rather, inevitable eruptions of a deeper malady. In a context where the notion of culture has frozen into a fetish, art cannot but be degraded into the practice of KAYEFI, the display of cleverness without vision, of craftsmanship without depth, a fatuous weaving of barren imaginations' (*Afriscope*, Pan Afriscope (Nigeria) Ltd., Lagos, VII, 1, January 1977, p. 23).

The discussion has not been completely one-sided though. Against the implications of the above charges of obscurity, one has to state that there is a relative value here as some perceptions might require more complexity in statement than such direct clarity. Cf. Theo Vincent's 'Two Decades of Modern Nigerian Literature' and Odia Ofeimun, 'Criticism as Homicide': 'Much as I agree that there is need to cultivate a healthier reading public I think it amounts to gaming for artistic suicide when a serious writer begins to water down his perspective and style, scrambling for a Hadley Chasean-type audience in the name of reaching the people' (*Afriscope*, VII, 6, June 1977, p. 32).

37. *Dem Say*, op. cit., p. 46.
38. M. J. C. Echeruo, 'Publishing and Writing in Nigeria', *Afriscope*, V, 6, June 1975, p. 45; Kole Omotoso, 'Ritual Dreams of Art', ibid., p. 40; Gerald Moore, 'Against the Titans in Nigerian Literature', *Afriscope*, VII, 7, July 1977, pp. 19, 21–2, 25.
39. 'The Patriot as Artist', *Black Orpheus*, Ibadan, II, 3, 1968, p. 23. Thomas Knipp has also written of a new age of West African poetry in which militancy and irony predominate, *Ba Shiru*, VIII, 1, pp. 43–55.
40. *African Writers on African Writing*, op. cit., p. 121.
41. *Transition*, 41, p. 44.
42. *Dem Say*, op. cit., p. 73.
43. Nsukka, *Omabe*, 25, ed. Pat Nwoga, April 1978, p. 25.
44. ibid., p. 18.
45. ibid., pp. 20–1.
46. *African Writers on African Writing*, op. cit., pp. 128–30.
47. From 'Me and Chris', *Silent Voices*, London, Heinemann (AWS 111), 1972, p. 37. New York, Humanities.
48. 'The Siege of Ramogi', ibid., p. 61.
49. 'Hurrah for Thunder' concludes, 'If I don't learn to shut my mouth I'll soon go to hell,/I, Okigbo, town-crier, together with my iron bell' (*Labyrinths*, op. cit., p. 67).
50. *Transition*, 49, September 1975, p. 6.
51. *Okike*, I, 2, December 1971, p. 1.
52. See, for example, 'To I.C., A Plea for Understanding', by Hyginus O. Ekwuazi, then a first-year English student in Ibadan, in *Idoto*, Ibadan, 3, April 1976, p. 8, which has lines like:

but the apocalypse will come
when truth shall ride on seven horses
and this poem will be finished.

53. Accra, Catholic Press, 1976.
54. *Afriscope*, VI, 4, April 1976, p. 37.
55. *African Writers Talking*, op. cit., p. 58.
56. *Palaver*, op. cit., p. 29.
57. *Okike*, 9, p. 118.
58. 'Three South African Poets', *World Literature Written in English*, XVI, 2, pp. 266–7.
59. Echeruo, in 'Publishing and Writing in Nigeria', *Afriscope*, V, 6, June 1975, talks of the danger of this oversimplification of the moral stance, p. 46.
60. In his review of Keoropatse Kgositsile's *The Present Is a Dangerous Place to Live*, Third World Press, Chicago, 1974, Mphahlele regrets the absence of 'warmth and compassion for human beings' and warns of the danger of the protest stance cutting the poet off from all humanity which is the basis of his protest (*Okike*, 9, December 1975, p. 120).
61. *Lorgorligi Logarithms and Other Poems*, Accra, Ghana Publishing Corporation, 1974, pp. xv-xvi, xviii.
62. *South African Voices*, ed. Bernth Lindfors, Occasional Publication No. 11 of the African and Afro-American Studies and Research Centre, Texas, 1975, pp. 7–8.
63. Enugu, Nigeria, Fourth Dimension, 1978.
64. Soyinka talks of the relationship between ritual and some kinds of poetry in his comment on the demand for literal linear meaning by some critics (*The Third Press Review*, Sept./Oct. 1975, p. 66). Mphahlele, complaining that the South African writers in exile cannot be heard because of censorship, uses the image 'we outside echo like voices from hill to hill, and this knocks the bottom out of *poetry as ritual*, that is, an act in which there are voices and appropriate responses' (*Ba Shiru*, V, 2, 1974, p. 27). Kofi Awoonor compares the poet to the priest, especially with regard to the votive element – a combination of ecstasy, prophecy, and mystery, and 'taking upon himself all the burdens of his people', so that when 'he runs himself into a state of trance ... in the clear-eyed singular moment, the god of sense descends and communion takes place' (*Transition*, 41, p. 44). Kole Omotoso entitled his statement on the role of the artist in African societies 'Ritual Dreams of Art' (*Afriscope*, V, 6, June 1975, p. 38).
65. *Songs for Seers*, New York, NOK, 1974, pp. 10–12.
66. Lagos, *Nigeria Magazine*, 104, March/May 1970, pp. 68, 73, 75. This incidentally corrects the note on Odia Ofeimun in *Okike* I, 3, September 1972, p. 63 which claimed that Ofeimun's poems on pp. 17–19 of that issue constituted 'his first appearance in print'.
67. This and other poems referred to here were published in *Idoto*, Ibadan, 2, University of Ibadan, Ibadan, 1976, pp. 7–14.

Trends in African Theatre

Michael Etherton

Introduction

I t is difficult to determine what constitutes African theatre. In the first place, the more regionally or ethnically based the theatre becomes, that is, the more essentially African, the less accessible it is to other parts of Africa. Conversely, the more exportable the theatre is within Africa, in terms of the use of English or French, recognizable situations, and common contemporary themes, the more it becomes like any other international theatre. Because of this contradiction, it would seem to make more sense to consider theatre on the African continent in discrete ethnic categories, such as Yoruba theatre and Akan theatre, or in language categories such as Swahili theatre or Hausa theatre, rather than to talk about it as a whole, as African theatre. This, however, runs absolutely counter to cultural aspirations in Africa which still tend towards pan-Africanism as a rather generalized cultural ideology.

The move towards an internationalized theatre in Africa leads to the rapid transformation of performing arts into literature. It is another paradox. The status of genuinely African performing arts is conditional upon their being converted into literary texts. Every discussion ultimately devolves upon a consideration of those texts, which form the basis of university syllabuses in the performing arts and which constitute what we describe as the corpus of African drama. Even this article is itself part of the literary process, despite the fact that it will be critical of it.

In the following overview of current trends in African theatre and drama I shall attempt, first, to describe the dichotomy facing the playwright in choosing between an ethnic or an international drama; and then to describe the process of turning the drama into literature, which includes also the process by which history itself is made the subject of drama. Drama as literature manifests itself as theatre in specialized theatre buildings; and I shall try to summarize the arguments which oppose the provision of the many new, expensive structures for theatre recently built. I will then consider who pays for theatre, and what the relationship is between patrons and audience, including – because it seems to me to be relevant – the phenomenon of the popularity of the Kung Fu and Indian love films, and also the drama on radio and television. This leads into an analysis of popular theatre: that which is improvised and not written at all; that which also exists as literature; that which is purely escapist; and that which has specific community development goals.

We cannot get away from the curious paradox that uniquely African performance skills can no longer serve as the art forms for mirroring contemporary society. Instead they are transformed into borrowed literary forms, despite the intention of African governments to the contrary and their endless promulgations designed to revive the traditional culture.

The Concept of African Drama: Ethnic Drama and International Drama

The problem facing the cultural ministries of the new African governments of how to hold together the traditional forms of the culture, particularly the performing arts, in the face of rapid urbanization and radical social change, is mirrored in the problem facing the individual playwright in Africa of how to use the traditional performance modes organically both as form and content, in developing the new drama, rather than as mere exoticism and superficial decoration. A play by an increasingly respected Ugandan playwright, Nuwa Sentongo, recently published under the title *The Invisible Bond*,[1] indicates clearly the nature of this dilemma. It was produced in Uganda in English where it was most enthusiastically received by large Ugandan audiences; but when it was produced in Nigeria to predominantly student audiences it left them puzzled and bemused. Nuwa Sentongo shows the way in which the metaphysical world of the Baganda can be used to explore moral behaviour quite independently of Western liberal thought.

The central character, Kibaate, is lumbered with an animated corpse whom he has rescued from the hands of the Night-dancers, a secret society, members of which rob graves for cannibalistic feasts. Almost in a trance of death, which he eventually retreats from, shamed, Kibaate attempts spasmodically to shake off the endlessly insistent corpse. It is soon clear to the audience that the corpse is Damulira, whom Kibaate has killed by juju because he was the lover of Kibaate's young wife. Kibaate remains ignorant of the corpse's identity until the end of the play; and towards the end he is forced by the latter to confess his guilt:

Kibaate: Damulira must die. The Diviner has given me the medicine to kill him.

Corpse: You told me you love human life.

Kibaate: Of course I do. I love human life very much but I must safeguard my interests. I love the woman. I can't allow anybody to take her away from me.

Corpse: Doesn't Damulira love her?

Kibaate: What does it matter if he loves her? What matters is me. We all love ourselves. We are selfish. I am a victim of human nature, I can't help it. I'm not ashamed of it and I am not going to hide anything. Damulira must die.[2]

The moment of recognition comes shortly after this exchange, and it is for the character the moment of complete nihilism. The Night-dancers come in with the corpse of Kibaate's wife; she identifies the other corpse as Damulira and gives him expressions of her love. 'Stop that,' the Night-dancers tell the pair, ignoring Kibaate. 'Damulira and you are both corpses and we are going to eat you!'[3] Kibaate's over-riding fantasy of self-interest is framed by his society's amoral metaphysical world, peopled by the Night-dancers and the dead whom they devour.

One of the problems indicated by the fact that the play was not as well received in Nigeria as in its country of origin is that the ethnic background of African drama does not allow for the inter-changeability of drama on the African continent, even though this drama may be rooted in common African experiences. The language of the Ugandan play – a standardized English – is only part of the process by which the dramatist attempts to convey his meaning to his audience. The major part in the communication process is played by the images themselves. The visual references of the forms, like the choreography of the dancers, the masks and the rituals, as well as of the substance, like the religious beliefs and the rites of passage, may be hopelessly inaccessible to people living on the other side of the continent. No Igbo-speaker[4] who did not know Nyanja[5] well would dream of saying that he understood a play in Nyanja. There is no reason why he should automatically find meaning in the Nyau dance[6] of the Zambian-Malawian borders in the same way as a Chewe man does who regards the dance naturalistically, rather than stylistically, so well does he know the conventions by which the dance is staged, and the symbolic imagery through which a deeper understanding is achieved.

It is only when the drama moves away from the particularized African references that it becomes more internationally acceptable on the African continent. It is the internationalized performing arts of the world, characterized by the techniques of production of the developed industrialized world, which in fact provide the basis for an exchange within the continent of Africa. What ethnic quality survives in this internationalized art is there for its exotic value. It is itself no longer the medium for communication.

The serious African playwright who wishes to convey meaning through a particular African culture, a particular traditional African art form, must inevitably address himself to an ethnically limited audience. The composers and producers of Yoruba folk opera[7] understand this very clearly. They perform in Yoruba. The drumming and the dancing – the stage media – are slick and professional and conveyed in a sort of musical shorthand, making use of the Yoruba musical references well known to the audience. The Yoruba cosmogeny, and their myths and legends, are moderated to give new and often quite contemporary insights. All these elements make up the performance to appreciative Yoruba audiences wherever they may be concentrated, in or out of Nigeria.

If the pan-African voice eludes the serious dramatist, so also does the national voice. The composer of Yoruba folk operas is not addressing a Nigerian audience. This is evident from the very homogeneous nature of the audience at, for example, Duro Ladipo's performances. This may be primarily the result of a language barrier; but it is also true that a Moslem Hausa audience will have an antagonism towards the masks, the drumming, the dancing, and the overtones of pagan worship in a Yoruba folk opera. It is of course, this last, the tribal pantheon, which specifically conveys a metaphysical exploration, which can also alienate non-initiates, or make the analysis in the play incomprehensible.

Drama as Literature: 1. Transpositions and the Poetic Drama of Myth and Legend

Behind the problem of finding a national or pan-African voice from an ethnic base lies the concept that the development of the performing arts must culminate in the writing of a play.

The development of theatre as literature is conscious and deliberate, and is the result of the clear goal of raising the standard of drama, that is, of making it capable of conveying insights and perceptions which we associate with all great literature. Initially, two methods can be discerned for creating literary dramatic work. The first is a transposition of an enduring – and therefore successful – play-text from another culture, another literary tradition, into the specifics of the African milieu. *Edufa* by Efua Sutherland,[8] based on Euripides' *Alcestis*,[9] and *The Gods Are Not To Blame* by Ola Rotimi,[10] based on Sophocles' *King Oedipus*,[11] are two thoroughly transposed African plays enjoying wide performance.

The other method is to re-create on the stage the creation myths of African cultures, including their moralities, allegories, and folk stories, and to render arcane and dying rituals in a renovated popular story form acted out on stage. Examples of this genre are many. The Yoruba pantheon has been the most extensively treated: Duro Ladipo's *Oba Ko So*[12] and Ijimere's *The Imprisonment of Obatala*;[13] Ijimere's *Everyman*[14] and Ladipo's *Eda* (Everyman),[15] both of these being transpositions from the work of the German playwright von Hofmannsthal;[16] Wale Ogunyemi's *Eshu Elegbara*.[17] Plays from other African cultures are not quite so specific in the relationships between the gods and between the gods and man. Instead, they refer to a time when the world was young: the *Anansesem* – stories extended into plays (which Efua Sutherland calls *Anansegoro*) based on the trickster figure of the Akan-speaking people; Elvania Zirimu's *When The Hunchback Made Rain*,[18] part allegorical, part absurdist; *Ozidi*, the re-creation of a Ijaw festival by J. P. Clark.[19]

Interesting developments of this genre can be seen in two notable new plays, *Mutu* by the Ghanaian Joe de Graft,[20] premiered in Kenya in 1974 and shortly to be published; and *The Bacchae*,[21] Wole Soyinka's version of Euripides' play.[22] *Muntu* is a drama generating a creation myth, which is used as an allegory of the emergence of the new Africa. It was produced in 1974 for the World Council of Churches' Congress in Nairobi and so, by inference, manifests a religious rather than a political overview. It is a lot sparser than Soyinka's *Dance of the Forest*[23] with which it can be compared, the latter being also a metaphysical exposition of the birth of the new African state carrying forward its past. *The Bacchae*, basically a religious play which *The Dance of the Forest* is not, is Soyinka's re-working of Euripides' play for the National Theatre in London and its predominantly white audiences, and is an attempt to show how important the new god Dionysus was for the urban poor of the Greek city states (and, Soyinka adds, for the slaves which made the rise of those states possible). Soyinka also wants to show that the contradictions embodied in the person and godhead of Dionysus have a meaning today for the etiolated West. Soyinka forges an equation between Dionysus and the Yoruba god Ogun, both in the introduction to the play and in other critical pieces which he has recently published.[24]

Both plays are extremely literary in their initial conceptions, Soyinka's being based on what is possibly Euripides' most literary work written at the end of his life in self-imposed exile, and de Graft's being based upon a form of stage writing which enables the stage to be bare except for symbols which the poetic dialogue alone imbues with life. Soyinka's stage images too, in The Bacchae, are sustained by very literary poetical utterances.

Although the process is overwhelmingly literary in its approach to developing theatre, there are some exceptions: plays which work away from their literary sources and are not easily rendered in the form of a play-text. Two examples of this contrary trend to the general process of literarization may be quoted. The first is Obaluaye[25] by Wale Ogunyemi, which was performed at the Ife Festival of the Arts in 1971 with a detailed musical score for the whole play by the Nigerian composer-musician Akin Euba, who also directed the production. The play is about religious syn-cretism (not unlike de Graft's Muntu) and concerns a Christian Bale who is punished by the Yoruba orisa for being a Christian and for being vaccinated, particularly by Obaluaye, who is Sompona the smallpox god, and who acts as the agent of retribution for the other gods. The cast includes some of the Yoruba gods, as well as ghosts, gravediggers, dancers, drummers, the vaccinated Bale, and other humans. Akin Euba, in his introduction, is at pains to point out and stress the non-literary nature of the production: 'In fact, what is attempted in Obaluaye is a five-dimensional presentation, con-sisting of music, dance, drama, design and lighting, in which these elements are given equal emphasis'.[26] Although the text has been very well prepared for publication as a dual text in both English and Yoruba, it still is an unsatisfactory record of what was accom-plished in that production, because the text cannot hope to repro-duce the richness of the music or the choreography.

The second play which suggests a contradiction of its literary origin is Moremi by Duro Ladipo.[27] Joel Adedeji points out that Ladipo has considerably revised his production from the version which was published in Ulli Beier's translation some years ago, a version which was largely derived from Samuel Johnson's *History of the Yorubas*.[28] Professor Adedeji states that it is now much closer to the actual festival which is presented in the area.[29] However, these plays represent the exceptions to the general process of making the drama literary.

The literarization of theatre comes not only from stylized and poetic sources, but also from quite a different source – naturalism.

Drama as Literature: 2. Naturalism

The naturalistic play has a close relationship with the naturalistic novel – indeed the development of social consciousness in European theatre in the twentieth century was initially generated in the 1880s by playwrights in Europe who attempted to follow Emile Zola's commitment to showing a 'slice of life', however sordid and hypocritical that life might be, and to do for the theatre what he and his followers were doing for prose fiction. Naturalism is therefore a literary movement primarily; that is, the writer is concerned to forge new literary conventions in order that his literary art may more closely reflect society as it is and not as it should be. Naturalistic novels and plays have frequently been accused of abandoning art; but the reverse is true rather, because naturalism has enabled the writer to convey in his prose fiction, or his dramatic prose, a critique of his society. He no longer has to work through outmoded conventions which refer to another age; he can face and transform his own age directly.[30]

The implications of this for the development of African theatre are immediately apparent, and it is to my mind significant that many of the most recently published plays are basically naturalistic in conception, that is, they attempt to show a 'slice of life', show their societies as they are, and not avoid criticism of them. An example of a play which does reflect this is Rahseed Gbadamosi's *Echoes from the Lagoon*[31] which attempts to show the rich and the poor living side by side in Lagos on the edge of the lagoon – written, Gbadamosi claims, from direct experience in an attempt to evoke on stage the situations which he saw with the eyes of his youth and modified by what he sees now. The play is intended as a dramatic critique of the increasing economic and social inequalities in Nigerian society, and was viewed and read as such by the audience and critics. However, like many naturalistic plays, from Africa and elsewhere, the play is unsuccessful, finally, as a critique of society, because it fails to penetrate below the surface so carefully observed, and analyse the wider social forces and social relations.

A second example of naturalistic drama, which in this instance does try to get below the surface and show clearly and simply the inner workings of the society, is a collection of plays by the Tanzanian playwright Mukotani Rugyendo. The three plays in the collection which has just been published, The Barbed Wire, And The Storm Gathers, The Contest,[32] show a range of stylistic experiment. And The Storm Gathers presents an analysis of a coup wholly from the point of view of a rural peasant community. Rugyendo also appears to be writing the play for them. As he allows the situation to unfold, so he widens the audience's understanding of the significance of the events; in the end the whole situation is clearly transformed by a deeper awareness of the forces operating. The external recognition by the audience of the characters becomes an internal recognition of how people operate and interact with each other.

Another interesting naturalistic play is Amavi by the Ghanaian Jacob Hevi.[33] The play is rural in setting, showing the life over twenty years of a girl married off by her father to a young farmer who takes her to a rough mountainous area near an alien village to farm cacao. She has children, works hard on the land; but is eventually ousted after about eighteen years by a new young wife who has the man throw her out one night. She falls down the mountain; her youngest child is killed and carried back dead, strapped to her back, to her aged father who impotently blames himself for forcing her on to this husband so many years ago. It is fascinating to compare this play with some of the 'eternal triangle' love-story plays which will be described later and to see that it contains all the elements of those plays: the forced marriage; the escape to the bush by the new lovers; the use of juju to destroy genuine love; the tragedy; the repentant, erstwhile tyrannical, father. However, the writer's absolute determination to be true to his characters and their contemporary rural life transforms all these elements from the superficially romanticized view into a social awareness of considerable depth: the forced marriage is to a strong and loving young farmer; the lovers, starting their marriage in virgin territory, make the land productive, in the process of which their affection for each other grows; the juju is accepted by all parties but in fact works circumstantially rather than by actual magical potency; the tragedy is a messy accident and concealed; the repentant father is useless and unable to obtain any sort of retribution. Characterization is complex: over the years people change and their dominant traits emerge. The final impact of the play is of an overwhelming desolation.

Naturalism is seen as a means of gaining wider audiences for theatre. By showing things as they actually are – apparently – people can see their lives in the drama as though in a mirror. It is not surprising, therefore, that naturalism is the automatic mode of presentation for most theatre groups in Africa who develop plays for public performance on the basis of improvization.

African History as Drama

The process of making drama literary, and particularly the writing of literary play-texts which seemingly show life as it actually is lived, have also encouraged the writing of literary play-texts which bring the past to life. The starting point for the historical play is the same as for contemporary naturalistic drama: the movement away from the poetic drama of myth, legend, and creation. It is a shift from the re-creation of oral traditions in dramatic terms to the re-creation of a past contained in written histories. It is concerned with the colonial period; and also with the immediate pre-colonial period and with those once powerful and extensive African empires like Benin which have an indigenous chronology of rulers giving some access to a more remote past. Examples of drama dealing with pre-colonial history are *Kurunmi* by Ola Rotimi;[34] the play on the same personality and events by Wale Ogunyemi, *The Ijaye War*;[35] Ogunyemi's *Kiriji*[36] about events in another Yoruba civil war which took place shortly after the Ijaye war, from 1877 to 1886; and a play on an incident in sixteenth-century Benin's history, *Imaguero* by Evinma Ogieiriaixi.[37] Examples of plays about the colonial and immediate pre-colonial history are, from Nigeria, *Ovonramwen Nogbaisi* by Ola Rotimi;[38] from Ghana, *The Mightier Sword* by Martin Owusu;[39] from Zambia, *The Lands of Kazembe* by Andreya Masiye,[40] about the first encounter whites had with the hinterland tribes of present-day Zambia and Mozambique during the Lacarda expedition from Beira to the interior in 1798; and, also from Zambia, Kaabwe Kasoma's *Black Mamba* trilogy,[41] which deals with the life of Kenneth Kaunda and the struggle for Zambian independence.

There is from Kenya, the important new play by Micere Mugo and Ngugi wa Thiong'o, *The Trial of Dedan Kimathi*,[42] which is concerned with the heroism of the Mau Mau freedom fighter of the title; and from Tanzania there is *Kinjegetile* by Ebrahim Hussein,[43] about the Maji Maji uprising in Tanganyika at the turn of the century. There is a distinction to be made between these plays about colonialism, in which the focus is on the struggle with the whites, and plays like Wole Soyinka's *Death and the King's Horseman*,[44] and *Anowa* by the Ghanaian playwright Ama Ata Aidoo.[45] Soyinka is at pains to point out that his play is only incidentally about the colonial presence: the colonialists are only catalysts and not antagonists in the metaphysical conflict which takes place between the Elesin and his fellow Yorubas. Aidoo's play is a detailed study of the role of women in late nineteenth-century Ghanaian society and of Ghanaian involvement in slavery. It shows an interaction of Ghanaians, of ideologies in conflict, to which the European is incidental. Another play in this vein which has just recently been published is *The Old Masters* by Sonny Oti[46] in which a conflict between members of the slave caste in a village community and the young aspirants to leadership amongst the freeborn is played out, despite the attempt at intervention on behalf of the slaves by the colonial administrator and his missionary colleague. In these plays, and others like them, the colonialists and their interventionism are seen as part of the background, of secondary importance to the drama being played out between opposing African forces. These plays do, however, tend to be fewer in number than those which deal directly with the conflict between the extending colonial influence and the threatened traditional African societies. A brief comparison of *Ovonramwen Nogbaisi* with *The Trial of Dedan Kimathi* will indicate the qualities which these sorts of historical drama embody, as well as the literary nature of the work. The authors themselves, Ola Rotimi on the one hand and Ngugi and Mugo on the other, have mounted highly praised productions which are clearly seminal, at least in the case of the latter play,[47] to the development of African theatre, and so have extended the impact of their plays beyond the publication of texts.

Ovonramwen Nogbaisi was premiered at Ife in 1971. In the published version the play is subtitled 'an historical tragedy in English'. It concerns the fate of the Oba of Benin, whose name gives the title to the play, who finally capitulated to the British in 1897, and who then saw them occupy his capital and dismantle his empire. The history of the period is complex. Ovonramwen himself has been consistently portrayed as cruel and brutal – though obviously, until quite recently, accounts of the conflict have tended to be from colonial sources and so are inevitably one-sided. Rotimi

finds it necessary to describe Ovonramwen as '. . . a man long
portrayed by the biases of colonial History in the mien of the most
abominable sadist, but in actuality, "a man more sinned against
that [sic] he ever sinned",'⁴⁸ Rotimi's play, therefore, describes how
Ovonramwen tried to hold his kingdom together in the face of, first,
secession by the outer lands of the empire, aided by the whites who
were attempting to extend their coastal trading practices into the
potentially lucrative interior; and, secondly, by powerful reac-
tionary chiefs within the palace, hostile from the start to the rule of
the new Oba and watching for any weakening of his authority. The
prologue and opening scene show Ovonramwen's punishment of
one such faction. The condemned chief of this faction however
warns Ovonramwen: 'Indeed, the whiteman who is stronger than
you will soon come.'⁴⁹ And the oracle at Ife, when consulted,
confirms the prospect of bloody civil war, and advises caution. The
words of the Ifa priest continue as a leitmotive, over stage ampli-
fiers, right through to the end of the act. The warnings clearly
express Ovonramwen's fears. The characterization of the first act is
sustained throughout the whole play. Ovonramwen urges caution
in dealing with the whites, but his chiefs and generals deliberately
misunderstand his instructions, disobey him, and butcher several
whites. Ovonramwen is shown to be horrified by the action of his
generals. There is preparation for a war which is subsequently
fiercely fought but ends in the defeat of the Benin forces and the
flight of the Oba from his palace to a hiding place in the city.
Eventually he is persuaded by the surviving chiefs to give himself
up; but in the peace negotiations the conditions imposed on him
conflict so fundamentally with the religious taboos surrounding
his kingship that he escapes into hiding again rather than sign.
Faced with the threat of severe reprisals if Ovonramwen does not
give himself up, the chiefs reveal his hiding place to the British
army of occupation. He is recaptured but not killed. Nor does he,
like Kurunmi, commit suicide. Ovonramwen leaves the stage,
finally, with a sarcastic remark which he makes to his British
captors – 'Tell Queen Victoria that at last the big pot of corn has
been toppled; now mother hen and her children may rejoice!'⁵⁰ – a
reference to the trading profits which the British would gain by the
elimination of an independent Benin. The play ends with an epilogue which exactly echoes the prologue and shows the British
treating their prisoners in exactly the same way as Ovonramwen
treated his at the height of his authority.

Rotimi clearly wishes to make of Ovonramwen a tragic hero,

perhaps even a national, Nigerian, hero. However the play shows
the problem of trying to make an heroic figure out of a failure. The
religious sanctions and beliefs which hedged about the Benin
throne proved ineffective in the face of the secular might of the
European invaders. The divine office of king no longer retained its
validity; and to argue, on the basis of cultural identity, for a return
to, or support for, such an unsuccessful ideology, an ideology
which has already failed, seems to betray once again the mass of the
people, whose ancestors bore the brunt of the British invasion and
occupation. Whether Ovonramwen was cruel or not is not the
point; the fact is – he lost. And he brought his kingdom down with
him. Rotimi tries to show that Ovonramwen was not cruel. In the
process, however, he shows, even more clearly, how he is rendered
ineffectual by the very religion, ideology, value system, which he
seeks to uphold and perpetuate. As far as the inhabitants of his city
and empire were concerned, his ineffectuality is as much a vice as
his supposed cruelty. It is very difficult to see him as a tragic hero;
and in his position as leader of his people it is impossible to see him
as a folk hero.

The play which sets out to delineate the true folk hero is *The
Trial of Dedan Kimathi* by Micere Mugo and Ngugi wa Thiong'o.
Kimathi, one of the most important leaders of the guerrilla war for
independence in Kenya, called Mau Mau, has been the subject of a
number of books, including an inadequate play by Kenneth
Watene,[51] but none has been written with such intense political
commitment, as well as a commitment to make Kimathi's life and
death meaningful for modern Kenya, as Mugo's and Ngugi's
imaginative play. The focus of the drama is Kimathi's trial; but the
play ranges freely forwards and backwards in time in order to
contain in the first instance the story of how a female peasant
activist, simply called 'woman', attempts to help the imprisoned
Kimathi and in the process wins over to the cause of freedom two
young people who in the final scene of the play make their brave
act of commitment. In the second place the play contains the
temptations of Kimathi. The Indian banker, the Kenyan business
executive and politician, the priest, all try to bribe him, in various
ways, to give up the struggle, and are, to a certain extent, symbolic
of the Kenya which has emerged since independence. Finally the
play also deals with the heavy burden of responsibilities which the
leader of a popular revolution has to face – in this case, the punishment due to Wambararia, Kimathi's younger brother, who had
attempted to negotiate behind the latter's back. The woman is

called to speak and she sums up the revolutionary attitude:

> ... Brother, Uncle, kinsman, clansman ...
> When will you learn?
> We shall continue to suffer
> Until that day
> We can recognize our own
> Our true kinsman
> When we can correctly
> Identify our enemies
> What is this superstition about
> Kindred blood even when it
> Turns sour and treacherous
> To our long cherished cause?...[52]

But despite this impassioned plea and a painful discussion after-wards, Kimathi refuses to execute the younger brother and his comrades – to his own cost later. The scene is reminiscent of Brecht's powerful Lehrstück, *The Measures Taken*,[53] and is obviously crucial to the relevance of the play for contemporary southern African liberation movements.

The play as a whole weaves these various strands together, culminating in a climax which is so theatrically effective that at its first performance in Nairobi the audience at the end are reported to have danced out of the theatre into the street. There can be no doubt that the play is very effective in the theatre. It has moved away from naturalism, employs music, dancing, and singing, as well as the use of light and blackout to great effect; and makes a determined effort to bend all the resources of the modern theatre to the aim of political awareness and commitment. The one problem is that the play may be trapped within the well-equipped modern theatre. In terms of its substance it should be possible for it to be performed in the southern African guerrilla training camps as well as in the theatres of Africa's cosmopolitan capitals.

Despite the successful theatricality, the play is still basically literary in its conception; and its social commitment is also a literary commitment – as the authors indicate at the end of their preface:

In this we believe that Kenyan literature – indeed all African Literature and its writers are on trial ... African Literature and African Writers are either fighting with the people or aiding imperialism and the class enemies of the people.[54]

This literary commitment extends to the theatre, particularly a theatre staging the plays of writers:

> We believe that good theatre is that which is on the side of the people, that which, without masking mistakes and weaknesses, gives people courage and urges them to higher resolves in their struggle for total liberation. So the challenge was to truly depict the masses (symbolised by Kimathi) in the only historically correct perspective: positively, heroically and as the true makers of history.[55]

This view of the nature of historical theatre contains an explicit criticism of an historical theatre which eulogizes the generals and ancient traditional rulers – the romantic heroes like Chaka and Kurunmi – as much as of the theatre which deals naïvely with the colonial period.

It suggests a way forward, by means of literary drama with all its potential élitism, to a theatre which manages to address the mass of the people. In Mugo's and Ngugi's own terms, 'good theatre' is not necessarily performed inside well-equipped theatre buildings.

The Provision of Theatre Buildings

Specialized theatre buildings are, however, being abundantly provided. The most spectacular development has been in Nigeria which has seen the completion of five multi-million-dollar theatres[56] and which is no doubt contemplating the building of more. Ghana has been planning a national theatre for Accra but has not had the money to build it. The francophone states have had theatres provided in the capitals for a decade or more; and in East Africa, highly technical, well-equipped intimate theatres,[57] provided by the white colonial population for their own communities, have been taken over by African companies. These are all buildings which are purpose-built, providing stages with elaborate stage machinery and in some cases the latest in advanced stage technologies. Whereas the stages and their equipment conform to a fairly standardized concept of international theatre performance, the auditoria of these theatres and their relationship to their stages have become the subject of discussion about the nature of a specifically African type of performance. The Ibadan-based theatre designer Demas Nwoko, who is the architect not only of the massive Benin and Ibadan theatres but also of his own experimental theatre in Ibadan and a new theatre in Lagos (not yet built) for Hubert Ogunde, is concerned to reflect the true nature of African performance as he sees it in the design of a modern and well-equipped theatre. On the other hand, the National Theatre in Lagos is simply a replica of a Bulgarian model.

Governments and the universities have tended to provide auditoria which can be used for high-level conferences, lectures, assemblies, films, debates and union meetings, as well as for theatrical performance. Unfortunately, their use as theatres is limited: they do not have the technical facilities necessary for staging elaborate shows well – very often the stage is too narrow and there is no back-stage support area for a large cast – and the auditoria are too large for modest dialogue dramas such as those usually staged by student theatre groups.

However, the building of these large, expensive theatres and quasi-theatres has not gone unchallenged. Many of the most committed playwrights have perceived that the provision of elaborate facilities and plush buildings is not the *sine qua non* of good theatre, that plays come before stages and audiences before auditoria. Indeed, some would go so far as to say that the provision of these theatres inevitably means the exclusion of the vast mass of the population from the development of theatre. The modest Ibadan University Arts Theatre, the Ori Olokun Theatre of Ola Rotimi at Ife, the Mbari Club at Oshogbo – all in Nigeria – and the Makerere Travelling Theatre and Zambia University's Chikwakwa Theatre in East Africa have all had a commitment to travel and work outside the towns and in the rural areas.

In Ghana there has been a commitment since the days of Nkrumah to place both traditional and contemporary performances where they belong, namely, in the very midst of the people. This has led to the University of Ghana's Institute of African Studies establishing the *Kusum Agoromba*, a touring company performing plays in English and other Ghanaian languages; and *Kodzidan* in Atwia-Ekumfi, a centre for musical and dramatic performances, built by community effort under the inspiration of Efua Sutherland and Nana Okoampa VI, the Chief of Atwia.

In order to allow for the emergence of a local style in the architecture and a local identification with the place of performance, the drama studio at Ahmadu Bello University, Zaria, in the north of Nigeria, is built in mud – mud walls, mud arches, and mud domes – in the style of a traditional Hausa public building.[58] It is also this determination to provide a beautiful theatre cheaply in the midst of the people which informed the so-called Poor Theatre in New Gourna in Egypt, which was designed by the Egyptian architect

Hassan Fathy and built in local materials using traditional forms and designs.[59] Both these last two are examples of buildings serving as theatres and laboratories for experimentation in the development of new theatre forms within an existing cultural framework.

Theatre Patronage and Cinema, Television and Radio

It is clear, on the basis of even the most casual observation (and in fact there has been little or no research done in this field in most African countries), that there are already larger audiences for drama on television and much larger audiences even for films at cinemas than there are for live performances of plays. And while the vast majority of live theatre performances in Africa are plays acted by Africans and concerned with problems from an African point of view, the films are almost entirely imported, having been made in Hong Kong, India, Italy, or North America, with no concession whatsoever to their African consumption. The films are in languages which are quite incomprehensible, and even if there are subtitles in English or French these will be meaningless to those who cannot read English or French.[60] Many of the Asian films are shown on television, as are, of course, the popular adventure and crime detection series from the UK and the USA. But most television stations in Africa do attempt to produce local plays and many of these are very popular indeed.[61]

Yet in Nigeria the nightly consumption of Kung Fu and Indian love films is probably larger than the audiences for local television drama, though in the absence of viewer research it is very difficult to estimate correctly. If we consider the actual films themselves we can see that they are fictional performances wholly devoted to fantasies of the self, of the ego triumphant and indulged. They are never given a wider social overview, because there is in fact no society to which these films properly relate. The popular response to these endless permutated images of fighting and of romantic love seems to indicate that the audiences themselves are to a greater or lesser extent socially uncritical.

These films are without doubt commercially viable; they have no government or quasi-government patronage, and yet they make their producers, their distributors, and the cinema-owners rich. This drama, this example of the performing arts, has become a commodity. It is produced, sold, and bought in response to a need;

and this need has been largely created in a system in which economic inequality is increasing, and there is a desire to escape from the reality of suffering generated by that very system.

Unlike these films, neither African drama on television and radio nor live theatre in Africa yet has an economic independence. Nor does either have the popularity which the films have. Theatre patronage, that is, the source of funds, is generally not from its consumers, the audience, but from the universities, the broad-casting corporations, and the government directly. All agencies for the disbursement of funds are concerned to promote national unity and cultural identity. Their sponsorship of culture is keyed into the general rhetoric of cultural nationalism. Money is made available for traditional performances, and, in the universities, for the development of academic drama, either as performing arts, or as a branch of English, or in a research institute or in a faculty of education. Far from criticizing the African state, the performing arts, whether in the live theatre or on the broadcast media, develop on the basis of a consensus about the ideals of national unity, about social and economic development, and about the liberation of the whole continent from white domination. The availability of funds from governments to the universities and the broadcasting cor-porations for the performing arts can only be justified in terms of priorities on the basis of an endorsement of the ideology of nation-alism. But an involvement in the local culture cannot be allowed to conflict with the goal of national unity, though in a country which is ethnically diverse it is difficult to avoid this antagonism. Thus an ethnic cultural identity is modified by the desire for a national cultural identity.[62] Research is desperately needed into the dynam-ics of this process. So much historical and sociological research stops short of an analysis of training and the creation of jobs in the area of cultural development, and of the discrepancies between stated cultural policy and subsequent practice. Nevertheless, it seems clear that the process by which the ethnic view is exoticized to fit the requirements of international art is itself the mirror of the process by which that same ethnicity is made acceptable nationally – and ultimately locally. In other words, the basis of the cultural revival in the performing arts is denied by its very aim. In this situation it is very easy indeed for theatre to become a medium of superficial entertainment.[63]

Winning Against the Odds: the Drama of True Love

The fantasies of coming out on top, of coping successfully with the urban rat-race, reflect the consumer images of success which themselves contribute to that rat-race. Violence and love are treated superficially and usually in terms of wish-fulfilment. The easy solutions to the problems raised by tensions and conflicting relationships cannot be real because the wider social causes of the tensions are seldom analysed.

Although there is not yet any African drama based on social violence, war, spying, or syndicated crime,[64] and very little violence is shown on-stage, there is a growing body of drama concerned with the theme of romantic love and offering wish-fulfilment and self-indulgent solutions to the inevitable problems posed.

Utisi by the Kenyan playwright John Mike Kibwana,[65] staged at the National Theatre, Nairobi, in 1973 is typical of many in this genre. Described as the 'eternal triangle' it is a typically African one: the village beauty loves the handsome village boy who is now an engine-driver on the railways, but she is married off by her acquisitive father to a wealthy old man. The girl's rebellion is squashed by the father; but unknown to him she is pregnant by the boy. She is – quite literally – carried off to the old man's house where she maintains her sullen unco-operative behaviour. The old man discovers the source of the pregnancy and sends the girl back to her father claiming the return of all the bride-price. Miraculously the boy is found to be able to pay; the father repents of his hardheartedness; and the boy and the girl are happily wed.

'Zulu Sofola's play *The Wedlock of the Gods*,[66] which has been produced many times in Nigeria since it was first published in 1972 and is always popularly received by student audiences, shows a tragic rather than a happy conclusion to the path of true love. In this play the girl is married to a man she dislikes. He dies, and she ignores the customary mourning period by moving in with her true lover by whom she becomes pregnant. The families of the three – the dead husband, the wife, and the lover – are all outraged to varying degrees. In the end, their love only manages to unite them eternally in death. In a recent critical study of Sofola's work, Iyorwuese Hagher points to the confusion in this play concerning the social and religious references within it.[67] The gods whom the lovers claim have sanctioned their union cannot be the traditional village gods whose very taboos they have broken. However much the play may overtly refer to traditional precepts in its support for the lovers, the values of this couple are unmistakably the values of the 'Great Tradition' of Western culture – even to their tragic deaths. The relationship is romanticized in terms of individualistic values beyond those of the traditional society. The tragic conclusion, with its 'catharsis', indicates the playwright's somewhat illogical support for the lovers' stand.

'Laolu Ogunniyi is much more direct in describing the modern urban basis on which his characters reason about their sexual mores, social behaviour, and attitudes towards love and marriage. In his play *Riders on the Storm*,[68] broadcast on Nigerian television in 1974, he considers the eternal triangle in the persons of Dolu the husband, Dayeo the wife, and Tola who is Dolu's liberated mistress, and suggests that it ought not to be a problem. This view is maintained in the play by Tola, and also by Dr Wahabi, a psychiatrist, and – to a certain extent – by Dolu's mother, Dr Faula, whom we first meet at the tail-end of a tutorial she is giving a student on Kafka and Sartre. Tola, Dr Wahabi, and Dolu rationalize the outdatedness of monogamous marriage, but not on the basis of traditional African polygamy. Both Dolu's wife and his sister, Bimpe, forcefully express the notion that a married man and woman belong to each other; and it is this concept of possession which the others attack.

Tola: ... They will tell me I've become an article of derision ... marriage breaker, parlour mistress.

Dr Wahabi: The other woman.

Tola: Yes.

Dr Wahabi: We still have a long way to go.

Tola: You're telling me! ... What irritates me most is that with the spate of new ideas some people can still go to the altar and really promise to love one person from wedding day to eternity.

Dr Wahabi: It is a heartless moral code.[69]

Tola later says:

I can't bring myself to undergo a process whereby I become the possession of a man. And secondly, marriage as we know it is asking the law to come license your relationship with your partner. Isn't that stupid?[70]

However, the play ends ambiguously: a reconciliation between Dolu and his wife – which seems to leave him in possession of both ladies. The budding affair between Tola and Dr Wahabi is actually nipped in the bud by the playwright, so he is saved from showing us how Dolu might react to the concept of extending the same rights to his women which he is demanding for himself. The play attempts an analysis of relationships in a contemporary urban middle-class milieu, but avoids a wider analysis of the issues in terms of the outcome of events in the play, in favour of a somewhat indulged romanticized ending. Nevertheless, when compared with *Wedlock of the Gods, Riders on the Storm*, which is contemporaneous with it, shows the range of social and ideological values which currently informs drama in Africa: on the one hand there is a plea for romantic love based on the monogamous marriage and personal choice; on the other hand, a plea for romantic love on the basis of the rejection of the monogamous marriage as a metaphysical concept. This transition has taken several centuries in Europe, yet in Africa both views are simultaneously applicable, and manifest in the drama of romantic love.

There is always, when confronted by problems of socialization and true love, the escape into the bush. The bush is symbolic of a purer state of being, less compromising, and a retreat as much for those already in the village as for those in Lagos, Lome, and Lusaka. The Nigerian film *Amadi*, made by Ola Balogun,[71] is about the retreat of the hero of the film from Lagos to his village in the East, and then into the bush. In the end, however, there is a Faustian compulsion to transform the bush, to make it productive; which is not the case in an early radio play by Wole Soyinka, *Camwood on the Leaves*,[72] broadcast by the BBC in 1965, in which the boy, still a young adolescent, tries to escape from his reverend father's Christian and supposedly civilizing influence. He takes his young girlfriend into the bush; their relationship is their first experience of romantic and physical love. Quite naturally, their perception of the issues is idealized and simplified. The playwright's solution to the young ones' conflict with their parents is a tragic one. It is similar to Sofola's conclusion, though the values of the conflicting groups are reversed: in *Wedlock of the Gods* the lovers have opted for their own individualist choice and individualist morality – they themselves are the arbiters of what is right or wrong – and this is an echo of the ideology of Western liberalism, which opposes traditional beliefs and the taboos of the village. In *Camwood on the Leaves*, it is the lovers who seek to return to and revive in themselves the traditional Yoruba beliefs, against the boy's father's emasculating and conformist Christianity, as a means of achieving autonomy, the freedom to make one's own choice. The bush for the boy, Isola, is a place of retreat, but it is very much a fantasy and part of his image of self-fulfilment; and what Eldred Durosimi Jones describes as its unsuccessful symbolism[73] is indulged by the playwright in the tragic conclusion, as is the marriage of Sofola's lovers in heaven.

There is no retreat to the bush in Khayalethu Mqayisa's *Confused Mhlaba*,[74] a Port Elizabeth black ghetto love-story which is wholly formed by the racial degradation of black people in South Africa. Banishment to the rural areas is the methodology of apartheid, and the emphasis on ethnic cultural identity is the means by which both intellectual and economic growth is denied blacks by the whites. No one in the play has any fantasies. There is no way they can beat the system. Their conflict with the state questions its very existence. *Confused Mhlaba* tries to show a man, freed after many years of political incarceration on Robben Island, finding a way to live with a woman who herself has fought for her own personal independence. He wants to love the woman, have some residual self-respect, and not fall foul of the ever-vigilant white authorities. The rejection of all the values of the white state is total; every line conveys it, no matter how much the playwright may have modified his stand in order that the play might be permitted performance in South Africa. It was not. Inevitably it was banned, and the playwright was persecuted by agents of the Special Branch.[75]

Theatre and Community Development

Theatre in Africa which consciously perceives a political role is complemented by another sort of performance which is emerging in some African states. This is a theatre which helps community development projects.[76] These may be in the urban areas but are more likely to be rurally based and designed specifically to improve the lot of peasants. The guiding aim is to improve the quality of village life in order to halt the flight from the land into the already overcrowded towns. The projects are concerned with agriculture; with health – both preventive and curative medicine; with local organization such as the establishment of co-operatives, local councils, and local courts; and with literacy, adult education, and rural primary education for children. The most forward-looking of these projects are not in fact based on goals such as higher yield from the land or universal inoculation, but on specific community goals – like enabling farmers to analyse and solve their problems for the good of the whole village community. This latter view does not believe in making the land more productive merely to raise even further the comparatively high standard of living in the towns. Its aims are always to encourage rural participation and rural self-reliance, no matter what group of people are being involved in the community development work; and it is increasingly being realized that in order to involve local people it is necessary to use the local mass media. Drumming, dancing, storytelling, the masquerade, and the festival are the traditional means by which all rural communities – and particularly in Africa, still – communicate their awareness of their social problems and their moral philosophy within the framework of which their problems can be solved. Admittedly, rural communities in Africa are not entirely untouched by the contemporary mass media of industrial societies – radio, for example, is already very important in most areas – but it is still the so-called folk media that can make the message meaningful, that can encourage people to participate in new projects, and that can teach self-reliance.

These folk media themselves are extended into new dramatic forms, the most obvious of which is the introduction of spoken dialogue together with individualized, rather than stereotyped, characterization. This may grow out of the masquerade, or develop from the story told or sung by the griot. Efua Sutherland the Ghanaian playwright has recorded in a published play-text, The Marriage of Anansewa,[77] the development of the traditional anansesem and mbogua (obliquely satirical songs) into a series of spoken dramas with extensive contemporary characterization, and with contemporary situations wryly observed. This is part of a much wider Ghanaian concern to make a very thorough formalistic reorganization of traditional performing arts into modern theatre.

In Botswana this extension of folk media into contemporary dramatic modes is not so much for its own sake, that is, not so much a conscious artistic development, as a means to encourage rural Tswana to get together and set about discovering what their problems are, and how to solve them. The particular theatre project, now entering its fourth year, is called Laedza Batanani,[78] which translates as 'The sun is already up. It's time to come and work together'. The elements of popular theatre, described in the context of the project as 'representations of local social reality through drama, puppetry, singing and dancing, using local languages and idioms, to large, often open-air audiences not limited by class or education',[79] were employed to stimulate discussion and then to take collective action on such issues as cattle thieving, immigrant labour, government land reforms, VD and sex education, vegetable production, and sanitation. The most significant aspect of this work is that the villagers themselves suggest the content of the plays. Community workers then develop the material to the point of problem solving. At this point fiction merges with reality; and then tackling the real problems takes over, the villagers having been entertained and enlightened by the dramatized social models.

Similar work, following in the wake of the highly successful *Laedza Batanani*, is now beginning in Zambia in the *Chikwakwa* movement ('grass-roots theatre').[80] in Ghana in the use of the 'concert party' form for community development, and in Nigeria in the *Wasan Manoma* project ('plays for farmers').[81] The funding for this sort of project may be indirectly from governments, but it is likely that funding may also come from international agencies. Whatever the source, this sort of community development drama fails if it merely becomes part of the social rhetoric of governments. To succeed, the plays must take the part of the local people. They should reflect life from the viewpoint of the villagers themselves; and they should not avoid articulating criticism of government policy which is inadequate. Thus, although they may initially set out to be less than political in their aims, these plays may end up as the most politically active of all African theatre.

Conclusion

There is perhaps a growing awareness of how the national idealism of drama is increasingly used by corrupt regimes merely as an extension of their own rhetoric. In some countries the intelligentsia, as well as large sections of the rest of the populace, feel that these regimes must now be resisted; and some begin to see theatre as not merely critical but subversive. However, the fact that the live theatre is not commercially viable in a market economy, and is so dependent on government subsidy, makes it vulnerable and jeopardizes its growth. Already some university drama specialists, notably in Ghana, are actively exploring ways of making a serious, critical, and entertaining theatre pay. It is not too difficult to see how the issues of cultural identity, which previously absorbed playwrights and their patrons alike, now begin to give way to issues of political identity. In so far as these issues begin to attract larger audiences to live performances, governments dispensing patronage begin to get less than enthusiastic.

This political identity is not defined solely within the context of the individual nation because of the importance for everyone, over the next ten years, of the liberation of southern Africa from minority white control which will mean an increasing involvement – directly and vicariously – by African peoples in other countries. The transformation of internal policies of African countries by the southern African struggle can already be seen in the so-called front-line states: Zambia, Mozambique, Botswana and Tanzania. The significance of this for dramatic performance (either in live theatre or on television) is not in terms of the number of plays about the racial conflict *per se*, but whether or not those involved in developing theatre have the vision and the energy to generate a new and vital function for theatre in their own countries in response to social upheavals from whatever source. Theatre has had a role in the process of cultural revival after political independence had been achieved – the establishment of university theatre departments and the development of high-level manpower is evidence of this. The question now is whether these departments and government cultural agencies, and their personnel, can transform themselves into agencies which can develop theatre in the new and much more difficult phase. It is possible that the subsidies may dry up. Will these departments and cultural agencies then wither away? Or simply lose their independent point of view? Or will they help develop a relationship between drama and society which is new for Africa?

NOTES

1. Nuwa Sentongo, 'The Invisible Bond', in Michael Etherton (ed.), *African Plays for Playing*, Vol. 1, London, Heinemann (AWS 165), 1975. New York, Humanities, 1975.
2. op. cit., p. 43.
3. ibid., p. 44.
4. Igbo is the dominant language of south-eastern Nigeria.
5. Nyanja is the main language of eastern Zambia and along the Malawian border. The Chewe are one ethnic group which speak Nyanja.
6. See W. H. J. Rangeley, 'Nyau in the Nkhota Kota District', *The Nyasaland Journal*, Blantyre, II, 2, July 1949, 35–49; and III, 2, July 1950. Also Mapopa Mtonga, MA thesis on *Nyau*, University of Ghana, Legon; and introduction in James Gibbs (ed.), *Nine Malawian Plays*, Limbe, Malawi, Popular Publications, 1976.
7. Duro Ladipo's company; Alawada Group International; Hubert Ogunde Theatre; Ogunmola Travelling Theatre.

8. Efua Sutherland, *Edufa*, London, Longman, 1967. New York, Longman, 1973.
9. Euripides, *Alcestis and Other Plays*, translated by Philip Vellacott, Harmondsworth, Penguin, 1965.
10. Ola Rotimi, *The Gods Are Not To Blame*, London, OUP, 1973. New York, OUP, 1971.
11. Sophocles, *King Oedipus*, in *The Theban Plays*, translated by E. F. Watling, Harmondsworth, Penguin, 1947.
12. Duro Ladipo, *Oba Ko So, The King Did Not Hang*, transcribed and translated by R. G. Armstrong, Robert L. Awujoola, and Val Olayemi, Ibadan, Institute of African Studies, 1972.
13. Obotunde Ijimere, *The Imprisonment of Obatala and Other Plays*, English adaptation by Ulli Beier, London, Heinemann (AWS 18), 1966. New York, Humanities, 1968.
14. op. cit.
15. Duro Ladipo, *Eda, Everyman*, transcribed and translated by Val Olayemi, Ibadan, Institute of African Studies, 1970.
16. Hugo von Hofmannsthal, *Jedermann*, written in 1912 and derived from the Medieval morality play *Everyman*. Ulli Beir, who greatly assisted the development of the Ladipo theatre, introduced the playwright to the modern German version of the old morality.
17. Wale Ogunyemi, *Eshu Elegbara*, Ibadan, Orisun Acting Editions, 1970.
18. Elvania Zirimu, *When The Hunchback Made Rain*, manuscript.
19. J. P. Clark, *Ozidi*, London, OUP, 1966. New York, OUP, 1966.
20. J. de Graft, *Muntu*, manuscript.
21. Wole Soyinka, *The Bacchae of Euripides: A Communion Rite*, London, Eyre Methuen, 1973. New York, Norton, 1974.
22. Euripides, *The Bacchae and Other Plays*, translated by Philip Vellacott, Harmondsworth, Penguin, 1954. Soyinka acknowledges his debt to the translations by Gilbert Murray, London, Allen & Unwin, and New York, OUP, 1904, and William Arrowsmith in Grene and Lattimore (ed.), *Euripides Five: Three Tragedies*, Chicago, University of Chicago Press, 1959.
23. Wole Soyinka, *A Dance of the Forests*, London, OUP, 1963. New York, OUP, 1963.
24. Wole Soyinka, *Myth, Literature and the African World*, Cambridge, CUP, 1976, pp. 12, 13, 26, 27. New York, CUP, 1976.
25. Wale Ogunyemi, *Obaluaye*, translated into English by the author, Ibadan, Institute of African Studies, 1972.
26. op. cit., the introduction.
27. Duro Ladipo, *Moremi*, in *Three Nigerian Plays*, ed. Ulli Beier, London, Longman, 1967.
28. The Rev. Samuel Johnson, *The History of the Yorubas*, London, G. Routledge, 1921. New York, Routledge & Kegan, 1969.
29. Information given by Professor Adedeji, Head of Theatre Arts Department, University of Ibadan, in conversation.

30. Wole Soyinka's 'elaborate metaphor' for post-nineteenth-century literary movements (Myth, Literature and the African World, pp. 37, 38) is misleading about naturalism which he describes as a manifestation of 'period dialectics'. The bulk of drama on television and film today, anywhere, including Nigeria, is unconsciously naturalistic; and an analysis of this phenomenon, particularly in Nigeria, is likely to reveal a great deal about the dynamics of Nigerian culture which contradicts the rather romantic notion of a total cultural identification in Africa today.
31. Rasheed Gbadamosi, Echoes from the Lagoon, Lagos, Onibonoje Publishers, 1973.
32. Mukotani Rugyendo, The Barbed Wire and Other Plays, London, Heinemann, (AWS 187), 1977. The Contest, the earliest written of the three, is not in fact a naturalistic piece at all; though in its political intent it relates very closely to the other two plays. It shows that Rugyendo has discovered in naturalism a form of drama which helps him to communicate to the mass of the people an acutely perceived critique of his society.
33. Jacob Hevi, Amavi, in African Plays for Playing, Vol. 1, op. cit.
34. Ola Rotimi, Kurunmi, London, OUP, 1971.
35. Wale Ogunyemi, The Ijaye War, Ibadan, Orishun Acting Editions, 1970.
36. Wale Ogunyemi, Kiriji, Lagos, African Universities Press, 1976.
37. Evinma Ogieiriaixi (elsewhere spelt Enwinma Ogieriaikhi), Imaguero, Benin City, Emotan Publishing Co., 1972.
38. Ola Rotimi, Ovonramwen Nogbaisi, Benin, Ethiope Publishing Corporation, and London, OUP, 1974.
39. Martin Owusu, The Mightier Sword, in The Sudden Return and Other Plays, London, Heinemann (AWS 138), 1973. New York, Humanities, 1974.
40. Andreya S. Masiye, The Lands of Kazembe, Lusaka, National Education Company of Zambia, 1973.
41. Kaabwe Kasoma, Black Mamba Plays, Lusaka, National Education Company of Zambia, 1975. Black Mamba Two is published in African Plays for Playing, Vol. 2, Michael Etherton (ed.), London, Heinemann (AWS 165), 1976. New York, Humanities, 1976.
42. Ngugi wa Thiong'o and Micere Githae Mugo, The Trial of Dedan Kimathi, Nairobi and London, Heinemann (AWS 191), 1976.
43. Ebrahim Hussein, Kinjeketile, Dar-es-Salaam, OUP, 1969. In the introduction to the play, Hussein moderates the historical detail of the period in favour of the issues he wishes to explore in his play.
44. Wole Soyinka, Death and the King's Horseman, London, Eyre Methuen, 1975. New York, Norton, 1976.
45. Ama Ata Aidoo, Anowa, London, Longman, 1970. New York, Longman, 1970.
46. Sonny Oti, The Old Masters, Ibadan, OUP, 1977.

47. *The Trial of Dedan Kimathi* was first performed in Nairobi in 1976 and then taken to Lagos for FESTAC in February 1977. *Ovonramwen Nogbaisi* was premiered at the Fourth Ife Festival of the Arts in December 1971, at the Ori Olokun Theatre, and this performance is written up, with photographs, by Samuel O. Asien, 'The Tragic Grandeur of *Ovonramwen Nogbaisi*', *Nigeria Magazine*, 110–12, 1974, 40–50.
48. 'Background', p. xi, *Ovonramwen Nogbaisi*, op. cit.
49. op. cit., p. 6.
50. op. cit., p. 78.
51. Kenneth Watene, *Dedan Kimathi*, Nairobi, Transafrica Publishers, 1974. Ngugi's and Mugo's play was written partly as a contradiction to this play.
52. *The Trial of Dedan Kimathi*, pp. 73, 74.
53. Bertolt Brecht, *The Measures Taken*, translated by Eric Bentley, in *The Jewish Wife and Other Short Plays by Bertolt Brecht*, New York, The Grove Press, 1965.
54. Preface, *The Trial of Dedan Kimathi*.
55. ibid.
56. The National Theatre, Lagos; the Lagos University Theatre; the Arts Council Theatre in Benin; the Arts Council Theatre in Ibadan; the Ife University Theatre.
57. For example, the Donovan Maule Theatre in Nairobi; the National Theatre in Kampala; and the intimate theatre club theatres in Lusaka and, on the copperbelt, Zambia.
58. S. Ehrlich and M. Etherton, 'Mud Brick Theatre', *Architecture Design*, December 1976.
59. Hassan Fathy, *Architecture for the Poor*, Chicago, Chicago University Press, 1973.
60. An interesting interim report has just been published (October 1977) by the Department of Mass Communications, University of Lagos, on the *Workshop/Seminar on: The Nigerian Film Industry and National Cultural Identity* held recently in Lagos. At the workshop/seminar papers were presented by Alfred Opubor, Onoura Nwuneli, Onuma Oreh; Adegboyega Arulogun; Wole Soyinka; Frank Aig-Imokhuede; Edward Babatunde Horatio-Jones. The workshop made recommendations under four headings, namely, production, distribution, exhibition, and audience, of which the distribution is the most interesting for this paper:

    DISTRIBUTION
    – Destruction of foreign distribution monopoly
    – More stringent enforcement of indigenization decree
    – Introduction of quota system for importation of foreign films
    – Vigorous market study of opportunities in Nigeria and West African region, as well as overseas markets for Nigerian films
    – Establishment of necessary business and cultural agreements to ensure worldwide distribution mutuality.

A more detailed *Proceedings* is in preparation by the Mass Communications Department, University of Lagos.

61. In Nigeria, for example, the Hausa plays of Kasimu Yero, which are regularly transmitted over Kaduna television in the north of Nigeria, are very popular. They are basically domestic satire, and are often critical of the mores of Hausa society. They and Yero himself deserve a separate detailed study.

62. An interesting example of a television series which attempts a criticism – albeit usually very mild – of the national army from a regional base is the Nigerian drama series *Samanja*, whose eponymous hero, played by the author Mallam A. Pategi, is an NCO in the Nigerian army. The series, which began on Kaduna television and which uses a mixture of Hausa and English, is reported to be popular with the army as well as with the Nigerian public.

63. This assumes plays broadcast by the authors' local radio and television stations. The BBC Africa Service, however, broadcasts plays on a regular basis by African writers, the selection of which is in London and not in the writer's home country. To a much lesser extent plays by non-national Africans are broadcast by African broadcast stations. Once again, the size of the audience for these and the BBC plays is not accurately known.

64. There is, however, a trend in this direction in Black American films.

65. J. M. Kibwana, *Utisi*, Nairobi, Comb Books, 1974.

66. 'Zulu Sofola, *The Wedlock of the Gods*, Nigeria, Evans, 1972.

67. Iyorwuese Hagher, *The Contribution of Women to the Development of Contemporary Theatre in Africa*, MA thesis, 1977, Ahmadu Bello University, Zaria.

68. 'Laolu Ogunniyi, *Riders on the Storm*, Ibadan, Onibonoje Press, 1975.

69. op. cit., p. 47.

70. op. cit., p. 48.

71. Ola Balogun, *Amadi*. Director: Ola Balogun; produced by Afrocult Foundation Limited, 1975. This film made cinema history in Nigeria by being the first feature film recorded in a Nigerian language, namely Igbo.

72. Wole Soyinka, *Camwood on the Leaves*, London, Eyre Methuen, 1973. New York, Third Press.

73. Eldred Durosimi Jones, *The Writing of Wole Soyinka*, London, Heinemann, 1973, p. 56.

74. Khayalethu Mqayisa, *Confused Mhlaba*, Braamfontein, South Africa, Ravan Press, 1974.

75. *Index on Censorship*, Winter 1976 (21 Russell Street, Covent Garden, London, and 156 Fifth Avenue Room 221, New York, NY10010).

76. One of the most significant and sustained experiments is described in R. Kidd and M. Byram, 'Laedza Batanani, Popular Theatre and Development: A Botswana Case Study', in *Convergence* (International Council of Adult Education Journal, Spring 1977). A more extended

write-up of the project (printed by Botswana Extension College, June 1976) gives information of other similar projects such as the following:

(i) International Planned Parenthood Federation, *Folk Media and Mass Media: Their Integrated Use in Communication Programmes for Social Development and Family Planning*, London, IPPF, 1974.

(ii) Allan P. Liu, *The Use of Traditional Media for Modernization in Communist China*, Cambridge, Mass., MIT Press, 1965.

(iii) Bro Russell, *Community Education Through the Arts: The Fun Bus*, Non-Formal Education Center, Center for International Education, University of Massachusetts, 1975. Russell has also been involved recently (December 1976–August 1977) in community development through a detailed programme of popular drama in southern Ghana.

77. Efua Sutherland, *The Marriage of Anansewa*, London, Longman, 1975. New York, Longman, 1975.

78. *Laedza Batanani, Popular Theatre and Development: A Botswana Case Study*.

79. ibid.

80. Fay Chung (ed.), *Chikwakwa Reports: 1971, 1972, 1973, 1974*, Literature and Languages Department, University of Zambia, Lusaka, Zambia.

81. B. Crow and M. Etherton, 'Wasan Manoma: Community Theatre in the Soba District of Kaduna State', forthcoming in *Savannah*, Ahmadu Bello University, Zaria.

The Missing Link in African Literature

Juliet I. Okonkwo

T he phenomenal growth of West African written literature in the last two decades has had considerable impact on the contemporary international literary scene. When teachers, writers, and critics gathered at conferences in Freetown (Sierra Leone), and Dakar (Senegal), between March and April 1963 to consider the relative merits of African writing, African literature was still a timorous applicant to the honoured body of subjects approved for the syllabuses of schools and universities.

In general, the conference displayed throughout a deep concern with the place and value of literary studies. There was widespread agreement that the case for the introduction of African literature rested, if on nothing else, upon its *relevance* to the experience and interest of African students. In other words it was not essentially different from the case for starting students off on modern European writing rather than on *Beowulf*.[1]

Now, however, African literature is studied seriously, for its own sake, in many universities of Africa, Europe, and America, at both the undergraduate and postgraduate levels. This recognition of the intrinsic worth of African literature has grown partly because of its improved quality, its greater variety, and the increased volume of writing available. From the mostly anthropological documentations of Nzekwu, Nwapa, and Munonye, the novel has undergone immense technical experimentation in the hands of Soyinka (*The Interpreters, Season of Anomy*), Awoonor (*This Earth, My Brother*), Ouluoguem (*Bound to Violence*), Okara (*The Voice*), Ayi Kwei Armah (*The Beautiful Ones Are Not Yet Born, Fragments, Why Are We So Blest?, Two Thousand Seasons*). Themes have proliferated from the communal protest over cultural conflicts to individual perceptions of truth and reality.

In poetry, the simple, direct declamations against colonial impositions and cultural assertions of the negritude and African personality schools have given way to the complexities of Chris

Okigbo's *Labyrinths*, Soyinka's poetry or Echeruo's *Mortality*; and the ritualistic torrents of West African drama have thrilled and astonished audiences in many parts of the world. But perhaps the seriousness with which African writing is now received is due to the new horizons which it is opening to alternative views of life and culture that have hitherto been denied validity or relevance. It is indeed a great triumph for the cultural nationalistic movement which gave this writing its birth and a part of which it is. What politics achieved in the colonial sphere, African literature has achieved in the field of culture.

Such an impressive output by West African writers has often inspired comparisons with the exuberant literary activities of sixteenth-century Elizabethan England, as this critic suggests:

> Several critics in recent times have compared West Africa with England's sixteenth-century 'nest of singing birds'. While this might be regarded as somewhat exaggerated at this stage, there was some truth in it because not only was there in West Africa the ever-increasing quality of writing characteristic of that period in England, but novels and poetry and plays were (and are) being written freshly and eagerly with much to say, and untainted with the incessant navel-contemplation of contemporary European and American writers.[2]

One such critic is Professor Eldred Jones who has attempted to establish some parallel features of both periods. He attributes this similarity to something more fundamental – a social condition that is common to both:

> A favourite comparison of mine is that of the contemporary literary scene in West Africa with the literary ferment of the Elizabethan era in England. Both have comparable background features that have produced similar results. An almost explosive contact between Africa and the rest of the world has been one of the results of the struggle for, and the achievement of independence.
>
> West Africans are savoring at first hand the thoughts, the ways of life, of peoples all over the world; and many of our writers, actual and potential, have travelled in what are for them new areas like Russia and South America while their traditional contacts with Britain and America have deepened and widened. Even those who stayed at home have been involved in a revolution of ideas, the dramatic impact of which is apparent not only in West African dress, religion, architecture and political systems, but inevitably, in West African writing. At the same time, the sources of traditional inspiration for those who wish to draw from them are far from dry. West Africa is therefore capable of producing a whole gradation of types and standards of literature, for the new influences touch life at all levels.[3]

A closer look at the literary activities of these two beginnings will disclose that although they are both characterized by a sudden burst of increased literary productivity, the impulses which directed them, and consequently their subsequent lines of development, were different. The similarity of increased literary output itself is a very slight one. The Elizabethan writers inherited a much longer tradition of formal education and of written literature which went back to about the sixth century AD when England was converted to Christianity and, simultaneously, introduced to writing. Many more people, therefore, possessed the educational background, and were acquainted with the basic prerequisites, for literary endeavour. Their own flood cannot be compared seriously with the initial trickle in West Africa. A more significant divergence, however, is in the texture and development of these national literatures.

Eldred Jones sees the influence of external factors as contributory to the quickening in thoughts, attitudes, and imaginative response of a people to their environmental phenomena. Elizabethan and West African responses to external ideas are divergent. The overwhelming attitude of the Elizabethans to the discovery of classical thought and literary forms (even when they came via Italy and France) was one of open admiration, imitation, and absorption. They proceeded to transplant what they admired into their own culture through the literary medium.

> The recognised method of mastering the new techniques was 'Imitation', a term familiar to poets and rhetoricians since classical times. The writer turns to his chosen model but without the obligation to reproduce it faithfully which belongs to the translator. Du Bellay defines the method in his *Defence*: the imitator must project himself into the situation from which the original poem sprang, and then develop it in the same way and with the same degree of detail, but in terms of his own personality and background – what Du Bellay calls 'devouring ... digesting ... converting into blood and nurture'. Imitation thus transfers a literary form out of one civilisation into the terms of another without destroying the original pattern.[4]

'Imitation' made accessible to the Elizabethan all the various forms of literature by the ancient Greeks and Romans, the more recent Italians, and the French. The Elizabethan writer, therefore, had a great variety of forms to assimilate; and, in this way, the ode, the elegy, the sonnet, the satire, the eclogue, the epigram, and the heroic poem were all absorbed into the English literary tradition. The concepts and ethical principles of Plato, Aristotle, Seneca,

Cicero, and other 'ancients' formed the basic subject matter of their literature. The Elizabethans copied, adapted, and translated Greek and Roman literature into their own native vernacular so that they became part of the English literary heritage.

On the West African front, the political, social, and economic situations at the period militated against a comparable response to influence, literary or otherwise, from Europe. After an initial flaccid acquiescence, as seen in the poetry of writers like Dennis Osadebey or Gladys Casely-Hayford, the nationalistic movement for independence favoured an aggressive rejection and suspicion of cultural influences from Europe. The ideology of negritude and allied concepts like African personality or pan-Africanism which inspired most of the literature of the period under review prevented the open absorption and imitation of foreign models in the Elizabethan manner. The need to reassert the traduced cultural values of Africa and to exonerate her from the subtle propaganda of colonialist calumny became one of the formative influences on the nature of West African literature. According to Abiola Irele:

> The literature of negritude is dominated by the collective consciousness of the black writer as a member of a minority group which is subordinated to another and more powerful group within the total political and social order.[5]
> Negritude in fact appears as the culmination of the complete range of reactions provoked by the impact of western civilization on the African, and of the whole complex of social and psychological factors that have gone to form black people's collective experience of western domination. Its roots thus lie far down in the total historical experience of the black man in contact with the white.[6]

Negritude nourished much of the creative genius of West Africa, especially among francophone writers. Even though the doctrine made little headway in anglophone West Africa, the writers' emphasis on the dignity and integrity of ancestral African culture produced the same effect. Rather than absorb, therefore, West Africa rejected. Because of this more immediate need to employ literature in the service of cultural nationalism, African literature failed to draw as much material from European thought as the Elizabethans did from the Greeks and Latins. A few poets such as Chrisopher Okigbo, Wole Soyinka, J. P. Clark, and M. J. C. Echeruo imitated some of the stances and techniques of the so-called 'metaphysical' school (the metaphysical school, even then, stands outside the mainstream of European literary tradition), but their preoccupations were still culturally biased.

The consequence of this has been to limit West African writing to a severely circumscribed subject matter. Since its effort is to illuminate what is peculiarly African, with the exception of a few specially gifted writers who manage to make their themes and characters transcend the entirely local, what most of the literature has done is to fill a gap that was ignored by Europeans. It presents only a segment of life; according to a critic, it is 'a mere appendage to European literature'.[7] In addition to this limitation, the employment of colonial languages – especially English, French, and Portuguese – has exerted its own influences on the development of African literature. An important aspect of the literary ferment of Elizabethan English was the patriotic desire to refine and stretch the English language through its use in literature. Latin, the literary language of mediaeval Europe was employed by many English writers in some major works. But

> By 1500, however, the sterility of this aim had become apparent, and the writers sought increasingly to emulate in the modern vernaculars what the ancients had achieved in theirs. The new romantic epic of Ariosto and enormous popularity of Petrarch's vernacular love poems mark the change. In France Du Bellay's *La Defence et Illustration de la langue Francoyse*, which forms the manifesto of the Pleiade in the middle of the century, asserts the potential literary greatness of the French language and calls for the wholesale imitation of the classics in French ... [8]

Roger Ascham, tutor to the young Princess Elizabeth, had advocated the nationalistic use of the English vernacular as a means of polishing it and bringing it to the standard of the classics. One of the most memorable claims for an increased use of the English vernacular came from Richard Mulcaster (1530–1611), headmaster of the Merchant Taylors School:

> I doe write in my natural English tongue, because though I make the learned my judges, which understand Latin, yet I mean good to the unlearned, which understand but English ... For is it not indeed a marvellous bondage, to become servants to one tongue for hearing's sake the most of our time, whereas we may have the very same treasure in our own tongue, with the gain of most time? our own bearing the joyful title of our liberty and freedom, the Latin tongue remembering us of our thralldom and bondage? I love Rome, but London better; I favour Italy, but England more; I honour the Latin, but I worship the English.[9]

Indeed, the ubiquitous sonneteering of the Elizabethans was really useful in this way. Its subject matter was stereotyped and its form static; its real sphere of inventiveness was that of imagery and linguistic experimentation. Its equivalent in prose was the euphuistic style with its lexical and conceptual variations. Such a feasting in words can be illustrated when Shakespeare's Touch-stone addresses William in *As You Like It*:

> Therefore, you clown, abandon – which is in the vulgar leave – the society – which in the boorish is company – of this female – which in the common is woman – which together is, abandon the society of this female; or clown, thou perishest; or to thy better understanding, diest, or, to wit, I kill thee, make thee away, translate thy life into death, thy liberty into bondage. I will deal in poison with thee, or in bastinado, or in steel; I will o'errun thee with policy; I will kill thee a hundred and fifty ways, therefore tremble and depart.[10]

And the celebrated John Milton puts down his own resolve in 'At A Vacation Exercise':

> Hail native Language, that by sinews weak
> Didst move my first endeavouring tongue to speak
> And mad'st imperfect words with childest tripps...
>
> Here I salute thee and thy pardon ask,
> That now I use thee in my latter task.[11]

Very little of this linguistic consideration played any part in the literary activity of West Africa. Franz Fanon in *Peau Noir, Masques Blancs* had stressed the language aspect of cultural emancipation. The West African linguistic anomaly has engaged the attention of critics of African literature from time to time. But in spite of the obvious contradictions, the mutilations of English by Amos Tutuola were considered far more tolerable than outright ver-naculars. The reason for this situation once more goes back to African history – colonialism and cultural domination by Euro-peans – and to the circumstances under which modern West Afri-can literature emerged. On the one hand, the colonizers had done their best to replace the people's culture, including language, with their own; on the other, since the first writings by Africans were directed to the Europeans in the battle against colonialism, they necessarily had to be written in European languages.

It has meant that African writing has been denied some of those activities which accelerated the mastery of literary techniques and which helped to enrich and expand the scope of Elizabethan litera-ture. Translation was one of the methods through which the Elizabethans realized the dual aims of their literary renaissance: to bring home to their people the best that had been thought in Greek and Latin; and to refine and enrich their language, both lexically and grammatically. Adaptations of subject matter and theme, imitations, paraphrases, borrowing of literary forms and devices, were other methods. Through them, most of those important concepts which have contributed to the foundations of modern civilization were transmitted to the ordinary people who could neither read nor write Latin. This activity was possible because of the difference in the literary languages of borrower and creditor. Since English has already absorbed from Greek and Latin, and the West African is writing in English (or French), he can only operate on the periphery, filling in gaps that were omitted by European writers. With the exception of a few university graduates (especially of the arts faculties) the vast majority of the populace is ignorant of the basic requirements of literary practice. So, apart from the culturally determined differences which appear in West African writing, one must also take into account the vast amount of bad writing which has resulted from ignorance in techniques.

It would appear, therefore, that the cultural nationalism of West African literature is incomplete, and even contradictory. Eldred Jones's claims that 'the sources of traditional inspiration for those who wish to draw from them are far from dry' is applicable to the vast majority of West African writers; but that 'West Africa is therefore capable of producing a whole gradation of types and standards of literature, for the new influences touch life at all levels' is true for only the very select few. In an article entitled 'Difficulties of Cultural Emancipation in Africa', Gerhard Grohs discusses the varying levels and types of cultural emancipation attained in the different parts of the African continent. He sees in the work of the Historical Association of Tanzania possibilities for a conscious emancipation from cultural colonial traditions.

> ... If similar groups are constituted to promulgate Swahili literature, a cultural emancipation on the lines of the nationalistic movements in Europe ... could begin to take root. Several moves in this direction are evident in school-theatre competitions, where pupils write and perform plays in Swahili, and in the large number of poems sent to – and sometimes published by – the local newspapers.[12]

For the West African literary renaissance to be complete, it has to be extended to the language domain.[13] One reason for this is political, what Gerald Moore considers 'properly the concern of journalism'. However, literature, especially renaissance literature, has always been a close ally of nationalism and the need for the establishment of a specific individual identity. In the case of Africa as a whole, the need is even greater considering the special relationship that has always existed between the white and the black worlds, between the colonizer and the colonized. Ever since the initial contacts between the different races of the world a struggle for mastery and ascendancy over the destiny of the black race has characterized this relationship which manifests itself in multifarious forms. One critic has actually described the imposition of the colonial languages on the African peoples as 'a kind of unavowed cultural imperialism which strives to enlarge ever further one's cultural domain through absorption and annexation'.[14] This is implicit in the type of claim made by Adrian Roscoe in the introduction to his *Mother Is Gold* that 'If an African writes in English, his work must be considered as belonging to English letters as a whole and can be scrutinized accordingly'.[15] So, Achebe is seen as an extension of the Conrad–Hardy tradition; Christopher Okigbo as the inheritor of T. S. Eliot and Ezra Pound: J. P. Clark, Echeruo, and others as a revival of the 'metaphysical' school in combination with the Hopkins innovations; Soyinka becomes the disciple of the 'Brechtian drama of the absurd'.

One of the most sympathetic and objective expatriate critics of African literature, Gerald Moore, devotes a long section of the introduction to his *The Chosen Tongue* to a discussion of the anomalies attendant on the African's espousal of English and French for creative purposes. To him, one of the tragic inevitabilities is the predictable decay and extinction of African languages. He recognizes the legitimate fears of the coloured peoples in the ultimate consequences of their continued, passive acceptance of the cultural values (and language) of Western or Eastern Europe:

> Unlike the writers of the white dominions, those of Africa and the Caribbean are by no means convinced that they belong, spiritually and intellectually, to the West. The brilliant preaching of Frantz Fanon, powerfully reinforced by the practical example of Maoism and Castroism has imprinted upon many the concept of a third world, largely coloured and almost universally poor, whose interests and aspirations are inimical to those of the West and the Russian East, both envisaged as white blocs of immense military and economic power. This power they will use to keep the third world strong at present only in numbers, in a proper state of subservience.[16]

Of far greater consideration, however, is the effect of employing one language to communicate the culturally felt perceptions of a different people; for 'everyone knows that the merits of a people – moral, spiritual, and psychological are not readily transposed and find their truly appropriate expression only in the matrial tongue'.[17] As Professor Eldred Jones has pointed out, its inhibiting influences can lower or even block creativity:

> It takes a great deal of time, and effort to master a second language well enough to produce in it a work of art which is not at best a literary curiosity, tolerated because it is produced by someone from whom the world expected nothing and so is pleasantly surprised to get anything at all. This means that many artistically gifted persons may not have direct access to a world audience.[18]

On another plane, the product of such artistic endeavour necessarily depreciates its potential because of the mutations and approximations required to force the rich connotative implications of original concepts into an adopted language. Peter Young illustrates how this happens in the novels of Achebe, Amadi, Nwapa, Nzekwu, and others in his essay 'Tradition, Language and the Reintegration of Identity in West African Literature in English'.[19] The rendering of *dibia* as *medicine-man*, for instance, oversimplifies the functions and status of the *dibia* in Igbo traditional society. In the same way, some of the richness in the proverbs are lost in an attempt to translate them into idiomatic English.

The more combative pioneers in the West African literary endeavour recognized quite early the limitations implicit in their choice of language and considered it as a temporary necessity, dictated by the peculiar times and circumstances. To David Diop, the use of a foreign language shuts the door permanently on a new line of literary development which can be beneficial to the world as a whole.

> The African creator, deprived of the use of his language and cut off from his people, might turn out to be only the representative of a literary trend (and that not necessarily the least gratuitous) of the conquering nation. His works, having become a perfect illustration of the assimilationist policy through imagination and style, will doubtless rouse the warm applause of a certain group of critics. In fact, these praises will go mostly to colonialism which, when it can no longer keep its subjects in slavery, transforms them into docile intellectuals patterned after Western literary fashions which besides, is another more subtle form of bastardization.[20]

The adopted language, therefore, is used to fight the war of recognition and independence. Because the war is directed externally, an external language is more effective, but once that goal of independence and self-awareness is achieved, the searchlight should be internally directed. 'Surely', he declares, 'in an Africa freed from

oppression it will not occur to any writer to express, otherwise than
in his rediscovered language, his feelings and the feelings of his
people.'

The first phase of the West African literary movement has been
over for some time now and its objectives have been accomplished.
Those objectives have been variously expressed, but the most
memorable is set out by Chinua Achebe in 'The Novelist as
Teacher':

> ... to help my society regain belief in itself and put away the complexes
> of the years of denigration and self abasement ... You have all heard of
> the African personality, of African democracy, of the African way of
> socialism, of negritude, and so on. They are all props we have fashioned
> at different times to help us get on our feet again ... I would be quite
> satisfied if my novels ... did no more than teach my readers that their
> past – with all its imperfections – was not one long night of savagery
> from which the first Europeans acting on God's behalf delivered them.[21]

Achebe's *Things Fall Apart*, *Arrow of God*, and the great bulk of
those works published in the Heinemann African Writers series
more than achieve these aims. They succeed in re-creating the
pre-colonial African society, complete with legal, religious, and
social organizations which worked for order and equity. Thus the
positions of individuals in society, their beliefs, their relationships
to others, their anxieties, their aspirations, and their entire cosmic
world-views are illuminated. An alternative world-view, not
necessarily superior to but of equal validity with the European one,
is uncovered. A novel like *Arrow of God* goes even beyond this, for
over and above its ramifications about Ezeulu, his children, his
wives, the elders, their neighbours, and their God Ulu emerges that
eternal Yeatsian question which shows that the worlds
occasionally overlap:

> O chestnut-tree, great-rooted blossomers,
> Are you the leaf, the blossom or the bole?
> O body swayed to music, O brightening glance,
> How can we know the dancer from the dance?[22]

Wherein does ultimate power lie in Umuaro – in Ulu or in his priest
Ezeulu? In Elechi Amadi's *The Concubine*, the interrelatedness of
the worlds of man and of the spirit and the conflicts which exist
between them are dramatized in the tragedy of Ihuoma and
Ekwueme. Such works as Camara Laye's *The African Child*, Onuora
Nzekwu's *Blade Among The Boys*, Francis Selomey's *The Narrow
Path*, reveal the process of growing up in a west African situation.

In general, these works concentrate on the West African setting, West African characters, and West African concerns, and have helped to confer on the black man the humanity that has been deliberately withheld by European men of letters.

On the technical side, however, it must be admitted that except in the hands of master craftsmen like Achebe and Amadi, most of the writers have been so intent on their subject matter that style has suffered. A lot of it is pure narrative, interspersed with proverbs, incorporating folktales and rhetorical discussions without any conscious artistry in weaving them together into unified technical design.

Of greater dramatic impact is the poetry of assertion of the neg-ritude school – Senghor, Birago Diop, David Diop, and Tchieaya U Tamsi – who defy the exclusively Europeanized point of reference to posit an opposing African one for which they claim greater validity. Like Dadie's 'Allegiance to Africa' they ring with the joy, conviction, and vitality of discovery. The rounded wholeness of the African world-view, freed from the compartmentalizing propensities of Western civilization, gains reclamation:

> Africa of tom-toms
> Africa of laughing girls on the river bend
> I am true to you.
>
> Africa of joyous peasants working in unison,
> Africa of gold and diamonds,
> Africa of serene song-filled nights
> Hospitable Africa, I am true to you.[23]

One of these great discoveries is the innate beauty and warmth of the black woman expressed in Senghor's 'Femme Noire' but with greater concreteness in David Diop's 'A Une Danseuse Noire':

> Negress my hot uproar of Africa
> My land of riddle and my fruit of reason
> You are dance by the naked joy of your smile
> By the offering of your breasts and your secret powers
> You are dance by golden legends of bridal nights
> By new times and ancestral rhythms.[24]

An aggressive anti-colonialism lends great force to this poetry, exposing the hypocrisies and deceptiveness in the claims by the colonizers to altruistic civilizing motives. David Diop's 'To the Bamboozlers' is a good example.

> Cynical masters flashing cigars
> Riding on flights of orgies

And parading equality in an iron cage
You preached sadness chained to fear
Melancholy song and renunciation

And your mad mantises
Making death swoop on every summer born
Invented the nightmare of marching steps in negro circuses.[25]

The same exposure is contained in Oyono's *Houseboy* and Mongo
Beti's *The Poor Christ of Bomba*.

The reassertion of the African world-view, African values, the
denunciation of colonialism, with its cruelty of man to man, its
oppression, humiliating arrogance, greed and exploitation, its
thoughtlessness, hypocrisy, the idiocy of pride in civilization – all
those have been sung, and admirably. African personality, African
democracy, African socialism, negritude, have all had their day.
They produced such gems as Achebe's novels, the poetry of Senghor, Clark, and Diop, the satires of Mongo Beti and Ferdinand
Oyono', the ideological novels of Kane (*Ambiguous Adventure*),
and René Maran's *Batouala*.

Apart from introducing these new revolutionary and liberating
themes, these works injected fresh blood to the literary repertoire of
the times in the field of imagery which exploited the rich resources
of the African landscape and African life as a whole. Christopher
Okigbo writes:

Fingers of penitence
bring

to a palm grove
vegetable offering

with five
fingers of chalk[26]

evoking the African conception and practice of sacrifice. The
objects mentioned in the passage – 'palm grove', 'vegetable offering', 'five fingers of chalk' – are all employed during sacrifice and
therefore particularize this act of penitence, distinguishing it from
the Europeanized Christian convention. Gabriel Okara's lines

... jungle drums telegraphing
the mystic rhythm, urgent, raw
like bleeding flesh, speaking of
primal youth and the beginning
I see the panther ready to pounce,
the leopard snarling about to leap
and the hunters crouch with spears poised[27]

conjure up the institution of initiation through which every boy in traditional African society has to go. It is a process accompanied by pleasure and pain suggested by the 'mystic drums' and the discipline symbolized by the laceration of the 'bleeding flesh'. Echeruo's lines

> Now the sun goes down
> into the valley
> beyond the palms; the
> broods will be returning.
>
> soon the last cock will crow,
> the last clay-pot be stowed,
> And the fifth finger licked.
>
> sheep and dogs and kids
> beside the hearth
> sleep beyond all reproach[28]

celebrate some African scenes and habits in the 'palms', the 'clay-pot', the 'fifth finger licked'. Many words and concepts are suddenly familiarized through the allusions to them in African poetry. There are the inevitable 'sun-bird', 'weaver-bird', 'the palm', 'the oil-bean tree', and animals and flora of the African landscape. Perhaps J. P. Clark's 'Night Rain' is the best example of this complete suffusion of the world of poetry with African idioms and imagery.

> What time of night it is
> I do not know
> Except that like some fish
> Doped out of the deep
> I have bobbed up bellywise
> From stream of sleep
> And no cocks crow.
> It is drumming hard here
> And I suppose everywhere
> Droning with insistent ardour upon
> Our roof thatch and shed
> And thro' sheaves slit open
> To lightning and rafters
> I cannot quite make out overhead
> Great water drops are dribbling
> Falling like orange or mango
> Fruits showered in the wind[29]

The novels incorporate, in their manipulable form, the folktales, proverbs, and many other aspects of oral tradition. On the language arena, Achebe, Soyinka, Okara, Clark, and Awoonor have all approached the difficulty of communicating from one culture to another language in positive, imaginative (if limited) experimentations.

But, as Ben Enwonwu writes in 'The Battle for Cultural Freedom':

> The decades of the colonial past should no longer plague our minds. We have no need any longer to be reminded, nor to remind ourselves, of those decades. The advent of colonialism should be constructively placed in the annals of our history as museum pieces. Rather, we might be wise to remember and make use of those aspects of the colonial era that have contributed to our growth, including even the oppressive aspects which we can use to face the more aggravating oppressiveness of the subtle methods of neocolonialism.[30]

Soyinka, quite early in his literary career, divested himself of the preoccupations with the colonial encounter and his attitude to the negritudinist and allied ideologies speaks out in his much-publicized and much-misrepresented 'tigritude' outburst. His first major play, *A Dance of the Forests*, under the guise of resurrecting the past for the delectation of the nostalgic patriots, exposes the barbarity and the non-flattering aspects of that past, especially as illustrated in the court of Mata Kharibu. The Kadiye's unscrupulous parasitism in *The Swamp Dwellers*, the Baroka's fundamental antagonism to new concepts in *The Lion and the Jewel*, and the latter's life of destructive concupiscence debunk the excessive adulation of the past. Soyinka has of late clarified his position on the negritude issue in a recent essay 'Ideology and the Social Vision'[31] and his own relationship to the past finds expression in what can be regarded as his literary manifesto, 'The Writer in a Modern African State':

> The African writer needs an urgent release from the fascination of the past. Of course, the past exists, the real African consciousness establishes this – the past exists now, this moment, it is co-existent in present awareness. It clarifies the present and explains the future, but it is not a fleshpot for escapist indulgence, and it is vitally dependent on the sensibility that recalls it.[32]

Kofi Awoonor makes an almost identical statement on his own stand.[33] Together with Ayi Kwei Armah, Yambo Oulouguem (and Achebe in his fourth novel, *A Man of the People*), these second-movement writers focus their attention on the African present, occasionally revealing how the past has impinged on it but generally dissecting the malaise that has afflicted post-independence

Africa. The corruption, self-seeking, mismanagement, inertia, excessive materialism, moral laxity, violence, and other ills of modern Africa emerge as their dominant themes. Superficiality in values and the distortion of old traditions result in some comical yet tragic incidents in Ayi Kwei Armah's *Fragments* where a new baby dies because the parents are too impatient to collect the money expected from donations at his outing ceremony. Wastefulness in human and material resources characterize these societies as in Soyinka's *The Interpreters* where the talent and expertise of men like Sekoni and Sagoe are trifled with to make room for some director's propensity for selfish aggrandizement.

On the technical level, these new writers have absorbed the more eccentric, if brilliant, approaches of modern European literary practitioners, approaching their fictional experimentations on the 'stream of consciousness' technique of James Joyce, and more recently of Saul Bellow, or the parabolic symbolic presentations of Kafka. Individual rather than communal consciousness becomes the medium of their investigations. But, because of their very brilliance, ingenuity, and complexity, these writers can at best appeal to a 'select audience, yet few'. For this, they have attracted many adverse critics, notable among whom are the trio Chinweizu, Onwechekwa, and Madubuike (whom Soyinka in his defence calls 'The Troika').[34] Osmond Enekwe in 'Wole Soyinka as a Novelist'[35] attacks the language and style of Soyinka's *The Interpreters* and *Season of Anomy*. In general, these writers are termed 'difficult', or 'obscure', and charged with being too imitative of European literary fashions and of incorporating a great deal of allusions from the European mythological and literary arsenal. A writer can choose to limit his audience to a literary, sophisticated élite, but that course cannot serve the national objective of revolutionizing the consciousness of the people. Nor can such 'precious' writing prepare anybody except the already educated to try their own hands at writing.

West African literary practitioners have accomplished a great deal and made considerable impact on the world scene. They have at least compelled the cynics to have a fresh look at Africa and her differing world-view. The excessively individualized, mechanized, technological world is beginning to suspect that Africa could provide a new line of cultural and artistic development which may be more satisfying to the human spirit. All this is evident in the influence which African traditional art, African social organizations, African religions have so far wrought in some, especially artistic, European circles.[36] The fact still remains, however, that by adopting English, French, and Portuguese their literary products so far are extensions of the English, French, and Portuguese literary traditions. Moreover, a clearly defined limitation is imposed on their work since they can only supplement what these literary traditions have already accomplished in their own languages. One European critic is indeed astonished that Africans are very complacently 'conferring their genius upon the West by speaking and writing French and English'. He concludes:

> They may well put all their effort into writing in the national language, as seems to happen in Lesotho and Botswana today. They may put it into one of the great African currencies like Hausa or Swahili. If they decide upon English they will certainly be made by nationalists of one kind or another to feel out of tune; but they will win the widest circle of readers. And if we elsewhere in the English-speaking world hope they will write in our language, because we desperately need the freshness of their vision and purity of their passion, we ought to be humble enough to acknowledge that we are on the begging side.[37]

On the same issue, Jean-Paul Sartre, that French espouser of negritude, has some very penetrating remarks:

> The specific traits of a society correspond exactly to the untranslatable locutions of its language. Now that which dangerously threatens to curb the effort of the Negro to reject our tutelage is that the apostles of the new negritude are constrained to edit their gospel in French. Dispersed by the slave trade to the four corners of the earth, the blacks have no language common to them all; to incite the oppressed to unite they must have recourse to the words of the oppressor . . . it is in this language, for them half dead, that Damas, Diop, Lalean, Rabearivelo pour the fire of their skies and of their hearts. Only through it can they communicate; like the scholars of the sixteenth century who understood each other only in Latin, the blacks rediscover themselves only on the terrain full of the traps which white men have set for them. The colonist rises between the colonials to be the eternal mediator; he is there, always there, even though absent, in the most secret councils. And since words derive from ideas, when the Negro declares in French that he rejects French culture, he takes in one hand that which he has pushed aside with the other. He brands himself with the thinking apparatus of the enemy as with an embossment.[38]

The adoption of African languages for literary creation will open up many more fields of literary endeavour which will not only accelerate the rate of expansion of this literature, but also expose many more people to varied techniques developed by old and new. The vast area of translation has up to this time been generally neglected after the initial efforts of missionaries who translated the Bible and Common Prayer Book into African languages. Under inspired guidance, the relevant body of world literature, old and new, could be brought to serve the needs of the West African literary renaissance. When writers are transporting from one language to another, they are freer with 'borrowings'. Adaptations are fast ways of converting an important and relevant subject matter from one culture and language to another. Most of the literature produced under the negritude and allied banners has tended to emphasize mainly those things which distinguish ancestral Africa. In a modern and ever-changing world, even the most rabid nationalist will admit that Africa needs a synthesis of true values from her ancestry and those from ancient Europe in order to sustain stable and disciplined societies. Literature has always functioned as a subtle means of modifying the sensibilities of peoples. Africans are now 'on their feet again' and therefore need not have complexes about admitting that Africa can gain from an exposure to some selected European thought and literary techniques as long as a proper balance is maintained.

One valid reason for adopting the vernacular is that through its use in writing it will be strengthened. At the moment, both in vocabulary and in the expression of ideas (especially modern or philosophical and technological concepts), the African vernaculars are extremely deficient. But then so were English, Italian, French, and others before conscious programmes were designed to 'polish' them up by the leaders of their literary movements. It should be part of the undertaking of West African literary artists, through associations and in collaboration with linguistic and history experts, to help in the transformation of the chosen vernaculars into modern flexible languages which can cope with the complexities of the modern technological age. The example of how the Italian, the French, and the English accomplished this feat in their own time can serve as a useful guideline. The longer this necessary assignment is postponed, the more difficult and impossible it will continue to seem. It is an undertaking that will take generations and centuries to mature; and meanwhile, English, French, and Portuguese will continue to be used by those generations for whom it is too late to do otherwise effectively.

The question of readership which the non-vernacular advocates pose has never been a serious one. Literary works can always be obtained in translation, and even though Achebe wrote *Things Fall Apart* in English, it has already been translated into other European languages. There is no reason why works in African languages cannot similarly be translated if need be. The African writer should however be encouraged (he cannot be forced) to aim at a local readership who can be prepared for this new literature in the vernacular through the schools.

The final argument which the non-African language exponents always toss out like the apple in 'Atalanta's Race' is – 'which language?' While everybody is chasing the issue of 'which language?' the main proposition is forgotten. In a country like Nigeria, about two hundred and fifty languages have been identified by anthropologists. But for a very long time now, three languages, Hausa, Igbo and Yoruba, have been recognized and given prominence in official circles, and it would seem that most Nigerians understand at least one of them. These languages can be promoted into national languages in addition to English. After all, tiny Switzerland retains French, German and Italian. In other West African countries the situation must be simpler, and none can be as complicated as the Nigerian one; therefore, a solution is not impossible. Regional official languages can exist in Africa just as in Europe there is a multiplicity of languages. The Bulgarian writer writes in Bulgarian, the Pole in Polish, the Norwegian in Norwegian, the Swede in Swedish. Outstanding works in these languages are then translated into English, French and German. The same situation can exist in Africa. Africa is after all bigger than Europe.

In addition to these regional languages, it could be possible for all Africans to adopt and develop Swahili as a continental language which will help foster the spirit of unity and serve as a common language for all black people in Africa and in the Diaspora. Now, while African countries are embarking on the process of massive transformation of their societies from illiterate to literate, is the time to strengthen their neglected languages through schools and work out systematic programmes to encourage their use in writing.

NOTES

1. Gerald Moore (ed.), *African Literature and the Universities*, Ibadan, Ibadan University Press, 1965, p. ix. New York, International Publications Services, 1965.

2. Margaret Amosu, The Journal of Commonwealth Literature, 8, December 1969, 24.

3. E. D. Jones, 'Jungle Drums and Wailing Piano: West African Fiction and Poetry in English', African Forum, I, 4, Spring 1966, 93.

4. Maurice Evans, English Poetry in the Sixteenth Century, London, Hutchinson, 1969, pp. 27–8.

5. Abiola Irele, 'Negritude – Literature and Ideology', The Journal of Modern African Studies, III, 4, 1865, 499.

7. Obiajunwa Wali, 'The Dead End of African Literature', Transition, I, 10, September 1963, 13–15.

6. Abiola Irele, 'Negritude or Black Cultural Nationalism', The Journal of Modern African Studies, III, 3, 1965, 322.

8. Maurice Evans, op. cit., p. 25.

9. Richard Mulcaster, First Part of the Elementarie, 1572, p. 15.

10. William Shakespeare, As You Like It, v, i, 43–53.

11. John Milton, 'At a Vacation Exercise', 11. 1–8

12. Gerhard Grahs, 'Difficulties of Cultural Emancipation in Africa', The Journal of Modern African Studies, XIV, 1, March 1976, 77.

13. See Juliet Okonkwo, 'African Literature and Its Language of Expression, African Quarterly, XV, 4, 56–66.

14. Georges J. Joyaux, 'On African Literature', African Studies Review, XV, 2, September 1972, 307–18.

15. Adrian A. Roscoe, Mother Is Gold, Cambridge, CUP, 1971, p. x. New York, CUP, 1971.

16. Gerald Moore, The Chosen Tongue, London, Longman, 1969, p. xxii.

17. J. P. Makouta-Mboukou, Black African Literature, Washington, DC, Black Orpheus Press, 1973, p. 26.

18. E. D. Jones, 'The Decolonization of African Literature', in The Writer in Modern Africa, ed. Per Wastberg, New York, Africana Publishing Corporation, 1969, p. 71.

19. Peter Young, 'Tradition, Language and the Reintegration of Identity in West African Literature in English', in The Critical Evaluation of African Literature, ed. Edgar Wright, London, Heinemann, 1973, pp. 23–50. Washington, DC, Inscape, 1971.

20. David Diop, 'A Contribution to the Debate on National Poetry', in Hammer Blows and Other Writings, Bloomington, Ind., Indiana University Press, 1973, p. 59. Hammer Blows, London, Heinemann (AWS 174), 1975.

21. Chinua Achebe, 'The Novelist as Teacher', in Morning Yet On Creation Day, London, Heinemann, 1975. New York, Doubleday, 1975, pp. 71–2.

22. W. B. Yeats, 'Among School Children', 11. 61–4.

23. Bernard B. Dadie, 'Allegiance to Africa', quoted from Wilfred Cartey, Whispers from a Continent, London, Heinemann, 1971, p. 214.

24. David Diop, 'To A Black Dancer', in Hammer Blows and Other Writings, op. cit., p. 13.

The Missing Link in African Literature 105

25. David Diop, 'To the Bamboozlers', ibid., p. 17.
26. Christopher Okigbo, 'Lustra', in Labyrinths, London, Heinemann (AWS 62), 1971, p. 15. New York, Africana Publishing Company, 1971.
27. Gabriel Okara, 'Piano and Drums, 11. 1–8, in Modern Poetry from Africa, ed. Gerald Moore and Ulli Beier, Harmondsworth, Penguin, 1963, p. 121.
28. M. J. C. Echeruo, 'Lullaby', 11. 1–10, in Mortality, London, Longman, 1968, p. 21.
29. J. P. Clark, 'Night Rain', 11. 1–17, in Modern Poetry from Africa, op. cit., p. 112.
30. Ben Enwonwu, 'The Battle for Cultural Freedom', in New African Literature and the Arts, Vol. 3, ed. Joseph Okpaku. New York, The Third Press, 1973, p. 46.
31. Wole Soyinka, Myth, Literature and the African World, Cambridge, CUP, 1976, pp. 126–39. New York, CUP, 1976.
32. Per Wastberg (ed.), The Writer in Modern Africa, New York, Africana Publication Corporation, 1969, p. 19.
33. See Karen L. Marell (ed.), In Person, University of Washington, Seattle, Institute for Comparative and Foreign Area Studies, 1975, p. 148.
34. See Chinweizu's 'Prodigals, Come Home', Okike, 4, December 1973, 1–12. Also Chinweizu, Onwuchekwa Jemie and Ihechukwu Madubuike, 'Towards the Decolonization of African Literature', Okike, 6, 11–27. Soyinka replies in 'Neo-Tarzanism: The Poets of Pseudo-Tradition', Transition, 48, 38–44, and 'Aesthetic Illusions: Prescriptions for the Suicide of Poetry', The Third Press Review, I, September/October 1975, 30ff.
35. Onuora, O. Enekwe, 'Wole Soyinka as a Novelist', Okike, 9, December 1975, 72–86.
36. This view is expressed in a very illuminating article by George Woodcock, 'The Lure of the Primitive', The American Scholar, XLV, 3, 387–402.
37. Donald Stuart, 'African Literature III: The Modern Writer in his Context', The Journal of Commonwealth Literature, 4, December 1967, 114.
38. Jean-Paul Sartre, 'Black Orpheus', translated by S. W. Allen, in Présence Africaine (Paris), 1963, 21–3.

Influence and Originality in African Writing

Bu-Buakei Jabbi

The bond with the father, the imitation of the father, the game of being the father, and the transference to father-substitute pictures of a higher and more developed type – how these infantile traits work upon the life of the individual to mark and shape it! (Thomas Mann)

But there is a kind of critic who spends his time dissecting what he reads for echoes, imitations, influences, as if no one was ever simply himself but is always compounded of a lot of other people. (Wallace Stevens)

C laims of literary influence tend to generate considerable heat of emotion and distemper. Whether a critic is stridently dogmatic, merely depreciatory, or speculatively tentative in proffering a case of influence in some work or canon, another reader is always likely to decry the suggestion. Or, mere talk of influence may be impatiently cried down as lame criticism, a dull factualism, or as an attribution of literary origins or causation. Well known in established literary systems, this classic confrontation usually follows in the wake of influence itself; and, sooner or later, it may rear its problematic head in newer traditions of imaginative writing. Some would insist that such emergent systems are unavoidably influence-prone; more especially if, while they can boast of their own rich vibrant traditions of culture, they however seek expression in non-indigenous languages. Indeed, such a situation may only further complicate the nature of influences and their study in the new literature.

Literary influence, it would appear, can hardly be conjured out of the way in any widespread upsurge of creative activity, old or new. And if we are to assess its character and relevance dispassionately, it is necessary that the critic examine his own general idea of influence, and thereby hone well his power of analysis in response to its innumerable and subtle manifestations and also view its individual occurrences with a somewhat theoretic posture of mind. In a critique of literary influence we need to cultivate a frame of mind for making claims we might verify beyond a mere hunch, to

develop a predisposition for putting suspected or specified influences into due perspective; and, methodologically more important
perhaps, we must try to adopt a conceptual framework within
which discernible influences upon literary creation are not made a
blight or irrelevance by mere critical fiat. But such an approach, it
may be emphasized, should take care not to minimize the need to
judge relevance, degree, and significance, which are perhaps the
guiding criteria in such analyses.

The storm over Ouologuem's *Le Devoir de violence* (1968) on its
first appearance was an African instance of debate over literary
influence which revealed some of the main features of such
encounters. (For a bibliography and brief discussion of this
'Ouologuem affair', see Blair, pp. 305–10.) But presumably as
plausible evidence of African sources for African works continues
to come to light (e.g. Nwoga on Okigbo, Nnolim on Achebe), the
whole issue of sources and influences may be discussed without
the all too human feeling of embarrassment that benefactors
generally tend to be either non-African or only renowned literary
figures, or even both in one.

A number of reasons usually account for the heat on both sides of
the debate. For instance, influence may be construed on either side
as illicit dependence or passive imitation relieved by no adaptive
originality of usage. Such a conception may not always be an
accurate description of a particular instance of influence. But
where it is, the influence may be manifested in plagiarism or other
more or less direct forms of replication. In a slightly different sense,
a critic may infer a relatively mechanical idea of influence by
insinuating a closely imitative relationship between source and
manifestation when a less deterministic account might be nearer
the truth. Suggestions that a work or part of it was consciously
modelled on another may be inspired by such an idea. To view
literary influence as either illicit or mechanical imitativeness is apt
to be sweeping in its assessment, and may unwittingly blunt the
critic's percipience and fineness of discrimination. Another factor,
by itself less generative perhaps of emotion but equally mechanical
in procedure, may spring from the critic's execution of his analysis
rather than from his idea of influence as such. He may, for example,
proceed by a dull sequence of parallelisms and similarities which
declaim or imply indebtedness without attempting to assess the
extent and quality of the writer's responsive interaction with what
he himself has built into his work as an appropriate allusion or
plane of reference.

By contrast, but probably seeking at the same time to deflate controversy beforehand, a discussion may safely settle into a guarded comparatism which implies an influence without as much as suggesting some mode of contact between forces or writers in question (Oke on Oyono). Or, in spite of such uncommitted comparisons, it may still do some justice to the integrity and originality of a seemingly influenced writer (Jervis on Achebe). Such strategies may be induced by a writer's transmuting of influence almost beyond recognition or by his operating at a highly abstracted level of transfer. They may also arise from the critic himself being wary or afraid to risk overt attributions of influence, a hesitance that may itself issue from any of the ideas of influence already mentioned. A more brazen critic, apparently construing influence as a necessary virtue, may stake a boldly specified claim of influence which, on investigation, turns out to be a fanciful hunch or mere hairsplitting without much basis of truth (Howard on Ngugi and Fanon, pp. 112–17). Such a critic forgets that the respective historical circumstances of two writers may sometimes point more to affinities of circumstance, experience, or even sensibility, than to literary influence as such. Closer attention to biographical detail would be a main corrective here.

Sometimes, especially in cross-cultural analyses or in new systems of writing, a different factor may be involved in the debate: namely, a type of cultural nationalism with a wonted demand or assumption of a purity-in-isolation as a possible or ideal imaginative condition of the author or body of literature it would defend against an alleged influence. As Ali A. Mazrui observes in an interesting discussion of the influence of English literature in African politics, 'it is the nature of nationalism to be inhibited in acknowledging a debt to foreign inspiration' (Mazrui, p. 119). An extreme cultural nationalism, as a matter of fact, may not merely shuffle over a fact of influence. It could well be moved to deprecate all need of transcultural influences or even comparisons in a well-meaning but overzealous effort to save some authentic cultural identity or to cultivate integrity and originality in the writers of a new tradition (James, p. 151).

Generally speaking, however, a cultural nationalism may often have a more positive posture of objectives. Mazrui himself views African nationalism from such a positive point of view (pp. 107–8). It has manifested itself, he says, in three main forms since colonial times. (His evolutionist concept, 'phases', would not always reflect the truth in individual cases.) There was, he says, an initial attempt

to prove a capability to master Western culture; second, there was a
revivalist repudiation of the colonizing culture in order to unearth
and develop an indigenous heritage. Both these forms, however,
may not necessarily be accurate definitions of the character or order
of transition of African nationalism in the form of cultural
expression. But Mazrui's third form of nationalism is an interesting
conception.

> A third phase of cultural nationalism is the capacity to take pride in
> some aspects of African culture without feeling an urge to renounce
> Western [or any other foreign] culture at the same time. But when a
> cultural nationalist reaches this stage . . . [he] is beginning to accept the
> proposition that there is such a thing as a global pool of mankind's
> cultural achievements from different lands. (Mazrui, p. 108)

The scenario defined in this third form would at least commend an
eclectic perception of cultural identity, which is pertinent to the
question of literary influences in a cosmopolitan world. But Mazrui's brief account may also point to some of the general historical
explanations behind some of the traces of influence in African
writing.

But no cultural nationalism is necessary for the ambivalence of
attitude which may creep into separate discussions of influence
dealing with writers in isolation. And this is understandable, since
influence itself is generally a matter of degree and its assessment
also depends upon personal taste, a thing which enjoys a proverbial privilege of *non disputandum*. Such ambivalences would
seem to underline the need for a more self-conscious general idea of
literary influence, for then individual cases can be discussed without too obvious disparities of attitude in various comments by the
same critic.

Wole Soyinka, himself a writer of expansive sensibility and a
critic with fairly eclectic sympathies, affords a notable instance of
such ambivalence in commenting on influences in Camara Laye's
Radiance of the King (1954) and in Yambo Ouologuem's first novel
(Soyinka, 1963, pp. 387–8; 1976, pp. 98–106, 125). These two
novels seem to offer good material for studying influences sys-
tematically in African writing, especially influences from Western
literature. But Soyinka is almost dismissively unsympathetic in
one case and philosophically accommodating in the other, using
terms which can probably be swopped between the two works in
question. At any rate, his comments on Laye have been vigorously
controverted: 'In his novel, Laye has embodied a world which is not

only different from Kafka's world, but is almost diametrically opposed to it, and in using Kafkan elements he has consistently remoulded and re-organized them in such a way as to express this opposite vision' (Ita, p. 42).

Be that as it may, however, Soyinka's larger-minded later approach to Ouologuem's alleged plagiarism begins to trace in general outline a path which a systematic account of literary influence would probably adopt for a start. He points out the immediate but minor moral question of having to acknowledge one's debts and sources, especially where the borrowings are more or less direct and substantial. Many writers, however, do not bother with such acknowledgements, though obviously from no surreptitious motive but preferring instead to trust the good sense of the reader to place or cherish the allusions on detection. Soyinka hints at an even more important issue involved in the question of influences; that is, the philosophical issue of 'the principle of ownership of the written word' (1976, p. 99). He seems, however, to conceive of this 'principle' in a purely verbal or dictional sense, the sense of the actual words used in a piece of writing which would seem to exclude categories like plot or character. Otherwise, would not a conceivably *structural* aspect of this 'principle' apply as much to the so-called imitativeness of Camara Laye's characterization as its *dictional* aspect would seem to apply to Ouologuem's 'undeniably well substantiated' plagiarism (1976, p. 98)? It is such apparent bottlenecks in critical response that a general theoretic conception of influence can help to open and smooth out, though that would not mean undiscriminating approval or commendation of all instances of influence. By the way, Camara Laye had acknowledged the connection with Kafka nearly a decade before Soyinka's indictment. He did so in an epitaph to the French original of his novel and more explicitly in an article that followed it in January 1955. In the essay, Laye conceded only a limited extent of influence from Kafka. 'He limited it to one of technique, denying that his theme itself was associated with any Kafkaesque dilemma' (Blair, p. 197). The relationship of the Kafka epitaph to the themes of the novel has also been examined (Ita, pp. 19, 31–7).

But Soyinka's main theoretical emphasis falls in a third place, on a factor which has been at the core of virtually every significant influence study. This is the essentially literary question of 'whether or not we are confronted with an original contribution to literature, in spite of the borrowings' (Soyinka, 1976, pp. 98–9). And this is where the intractable question of the nature of literary originality comes into the consideration. It has to be tackled somehow, however cursorily or implicitly. But many a discussion of influence may find it more convenient to sidetrack this question. If one is to discuss influences profitably either in a specific context or in general terms, however, some rough and ready general conception of originality in literature would seem to be a necessary backdrop at the very least. A discussion of influence upon a certain work or author, that is, must ultimately consider to what extent the basic influences have been ingested into the work or the writer's outlook and also how they have been transcended by the writer in order to find a distinct originality of voice and aesthetic effect. Soyinka, on his part, sets out to answer his own question by analysing the satiric style and thematic concerns of Ouologuem's novel in the rest of his discussion.

But emphases can be dispersed differently in a less robust scheme like the conception of influence as causation. It is perhaps in the search for the origins of complex phenomena like literary forms that such a view is most likely to be found at work. For instance a critic may feel an imperative to decide whether 'the African novel *emerged* from traditional African sources *quite independent of* Western influences' (Palmer, p. 116). In their reform of Literature studies in Nairobi in 1968 Ngugi wa Thiong'o and his colleagues gave hint of one type of answer to such a question in their East African context: 'Its *roots go back to past* African literatures, European literatures, and Asian literatures' (Ngugi, p. 150). The change of metaphor and emphasis, as underscored in each case, is noteworthy. But before looking at some of the answers given at times to this question of origins (or backgrounds, to put it more neutrally), the character of the question itself may be briefly examined. For such a question could be trivial for a start or futile in the end, depending on its formulation. And yet it seems to broach an issue of crucial importance.

The climate and quality of a discussion can be radically affected by the way its central questions are posed. And certain questions may be essentially prejudicial in their very formulation. They unconsciously tend to take shape in non-starter form, manage to get going somehow and even perhaps evoke a good deal of enthusiasm, but nevertheless fizzle out in the end without much fruit of insight or discovery. Which came before the other, the chicken or the egg, the kernel or the palm-tree? These are merely more circular forms of prejudicial questioning, which in more direct form may determine their own answers in their formulation. A burning desire to decide conclusively whether the African novel originated exclusively from traditional indigenous sources or from the Western novel seems to be a variation of this prejudicial mode of inquiry.

But when considering the particular historical circumstances surrounding the emergence of modern African writing, is it really necessary to put one's foot down one way or another over such an issue? Are we not just looking for the roots that fed and still feed this newly grown tree, or is it supposed to have only one root? Would it not be more fruitful perhaps, for tree and question alike, merely to try and assess the nature and extent of the ways in which all historically valid backgrounds to African writing have respectively helped, or can still help, to shape the new literature? Any consideration or evidence that a critic can muster could still be turned up, though perhaps monolithic and arbitrary answers may be more nearly forestalled by the modification. But maybe for some minds the ultimate upshot of even such a modified inquiry would still be to determine finally whether some form emerged from one specific source 'quite independent of' other possibilities. We will have to operate with the very simplest units, which will necessarily be truncations in the case of the novel, if we want to answer such a question with any degree of relevant truthfulness; and even then the overall answer will not be uniform. Otherwise we can only simplify the issues and falsify the situation in the process. But, fortunately, the options and possibilities at work in such cultural developments are seldom so invidiously competitive or mutually exclusive in their functioning. A law of the excluded middle would thus be inappropriate to apply in a search for the sources and origins of the modern African novel as we really have it.

One may also observe that a critic's temptation conclusively to decide the question in one exclusive direction may stem from a more or less latent bias of knowledge or of sympathy. That is to say, more steeped or more knowledgeable perhaps in one relevant cultural system than in another (whether or not from such historical accidents as birth, schooling, education, or upbringing), a critic may be more inclined to see varying influences and relevances in African writing at the expense of similar things from the system of tradition in which his knowledge or sympathy may happen to be a little shorter. Thus a critic better informed in Western literatures than in traditional African forms may see modern African writing as emerging mainly from Western forms; another critic, more sympathetic or nostalgic towards African traditions, may alternatively see things the other way round. And both may fail to realize that their opposed preferences may not exhaust the possibilities. A third manifestation of this bias is the cautious critic who is hesitant to be caught in a false step. He may try to make up for his ignorance or indifference in some direction by making a blind claim of concession towards it, hoping it will coincide somehow with some significant truth which he vaguely apprehends as a possibility when things are viewed from the other angle. Considering our individual limitations in the presence of the vast complexity of cultural factors which generally inform the new writing, these are no despicable positions. One would only wish that they were all more consciously held in balance in the mind of the historian of roots, origins, backgrounds, and influences! Whatever its form, however, this bias of knowledge and sympathy will always involve a degree of hidden ignorance or indifference to certain relevant cultural phenomena and to facts or possibilities of some particular stamp or colour. African literature cannot afford such prematurely rigid alignments in criticism and scholarship during these early stages of its development.

And those who feel an urgency to write a comprehensive history already (whether tentative or final) of the rise of this new writing ought to remember that matters of verbal style, technical or generic form, or language of expression (the kinds of things one is likely to see more often invoked as evidence), are neither separately nor jointly adequate in themselves to settle questions of literary origins and developments. Major cultural developments tend to be more complicated in their motivation and factors of causation and growth. There is usually a wider ferment of culture and of history to be brought into the reckoning as well. A crucial question of such complexity should not be oversimplified either from an impatience for categorical solutions or from disinclination towards certain kinds of consideration and certain modes of questioning.

The supposed battlelines in settling the origin of the African novel have been plotted upon the following canvas of influence as causation.

The attempts [sic] by some critics to demonstrate that the African novel is a direct outgrowth of the African oral tradition borders [sic] at times on the ridiculous. Every minor feature with oral association, even if it only occurs in conversation, is pounced upon as evidence. Figures of speech such as similes, and the use of various rhetorical devices, are all adduced as examples of the influence of the oral tradition, as though similes and rhetorical devices only occur in oral literature and are confined to the African oral tradition. Of course such critics stress the importance of the proverb, especially in the case of Achebe, seeing it as the conclusive proof. But Achebe uses proverbs in order to give his conversations authenticity, not necessarily because he has been influenced by [the] folktale or oral tradition.

The fact is, that although a number of African novelists incorporated elements of the oral tradition into their works, their novels were not outgrowths of the folktale. Much as we would like to think otherwise, for nationalistic and other reasons, the novel, unlike poetry and drama, is not an indigenous African genre; the African novel grew out of the Western novel, and writers like Achebe, Laye, and Ekwensi were influenced much more by Conrad, Hardy, Dickens, and Kafaka than by the African oral tale. (Palmer, p. 117)

Neither the oral tradition 'champions' referred to here nor the sources of reference to their contributions are specified; so it is difficult to say how accurately they are being represented or how appositely they are being interpreted by this critic. Nevertheless, the resulting critical man-of-straw set up for poking is fairly clearly drawn and he is controverted with a zealous absence of any equivocation. From his own cut-and-dried answers and his consistent metaphor or 'direct outgrowth', however, it is obvious that the problem resides in this critic's own conception of influence as causation. For both his interpretation of the other critics and the attack he levels against them ride throughout on the assumption that an accepted influence upon a literary work or form is to be equated with the cause of its being, its direct or exclusive source of origin. The references he fails to supply might have clarified this point better. But there is a more general weakness which pervades the comment: a clanger of overassertion coupled with misplacings of emphases. As a result, quite a few important considerations are too hastily dismissed or some improbable assumption affirmed without weighing or sifting the available evidence.

There is, for instance, the use of elements of oral tradition in the novel; say, as exemplified in Achebe's use of proverbs. Achebe, of course, uses all sorts of oral elements in his novels: idioms, figures of speech, jokes and word-games, *blason populaire*, and the more often noted proverbs and folktales. They may occur in the conversations of his characters or in the narrator's free rendering of their thoughts or speeches into *erlebte rede*. They do even frequently occur in the purely narrative stretches of the novels, and also outside the novels in the comments and literary criticism of Achebe himself. But if he uses proverbs, for instance, in the dialogue of his characters *partly* for verisimilitude, can they not *at one and the same time* be an influence from Igbo oral tradition? From what source are they supposed to be flowing into his work then? And what about when he uses the same elements in the other modes of utterances or comment we have outlined, that is, not in the conversations between characters as such? Their aesthetic utility often transcends mere verisimilitude. And in any case how are we to account satisfactorily for them in his literary output without invoking the concept of influence at some stage? But by doing so, is one necessarily claiming that Achebe's entire style (not to mention the whole entity of the African novel in its much greater variety from writer to writer), is thereby a direct outgrowth from oral tradition? Again, an indication of his references might have enabled one to put his erroneous presumption at the door of critics other than that of Palmer himself. And the same would go for the additional presumption that the elements importing influences from oral traditions are generically unique either to oral expressivity or to African oral tradition.

One would have thought that in pointing to influences upon a work or body of literature, one is merely highlighting some of those factors which seem to have helped in shaping the character of that work or literature as we have it. One need not claim as a corollary that a whole tradition or even genre of literature has grown out of the specified influence. The Western novel, like the more indigenous cultural phenomena occasionally reflected in the modern African novel, is a crucial background influence upon the rise of the new form; but, again like those other phenomena, it is not an exclusive source of origin for the African novel. They are all contributory factors and forces in its emergence, and their relative ratios of influence or catalytic inspiration obviously vary too much from one writer or work to another for a categorical mensuration to be necessary in a general discussion of the African novel as a literary form. And there are still other generative forces and factors in the rise of the African novel beyond forms of African traditional expression and the Western novel.

In his main argument about applying relatively uniform critical criteria to both the Western novel and its new African cousin, Palmer devises the following interesting idea which he might have developed more provocatively in connection with the glib assumption that the novel is alien or 'not indigenous' to Africa.

> In fact it is a distortion to call these criteria Western criteria. If they have grown up alongside the development of the Western novel it is most probably because the Western novel was the first to be seriously discussed. They are probably the considerations that readers of novels everywhere will discuss in order to account for the impact of novels on their minds. (Palmer, pp. 118–19).

As a matter of fact, neither the novel itself nor its discussion as a form preening itself on social realism and psychological perspicacity in depiction of character can be said to have emerged first in the West. Centuries before such a literary form arose in late seventeenth-century Western Europe, that is by the time William the Conqueror had subdued England in 1066, the realistic novel had already emerged in the Far East. *The Tale of Genji*, by Shikibu Murasaki of Japan and written at the end of the tenth century or the beginning of the eleventh, 'is exactly what we mean by a novel' and also contains a discussion of the genre (Spearman, p. 123). 'Everyone is now aware that one book conforming to the descriptions and definitions intended to cover the novels of eighteenth- and nineteenth-century Europe appeared in eleventh-century Japan, and a considerable number in China from the fifteenth century onwards' (Spearman, p. 120). Historically, therefore, neither the form nor the critical criteria attendant upon the realistic novel are inherently or otherwise essentially Western. And since the form arose independently in the Far East and in Europe, there is no logical connection between its rise anywhere else and its known existence in other traditions.

Palmer might thus have gone the whole hypothesizing hog to pose the more radical question: what forms of prose fiction will emerge anywhere when a people, as they become more pervasively and more qualitatively literate in an increasingly technetronic era,[1] begin to afford persons of adequate talent who can also find ample time to write long fictional narratives about their own lives and times or about the general human condition and environment? Let it be taken for granted that such a people generally possess a basic sense of the flow of time and of their feelings or their experiences, that they have long traditions of other modes of prose or sung narratives – albeit unwritten – and that their raw experience of social interaction and of a few rich individual lifespans among them is in any case unimpaired. Would anything akin to the novel, as the world has known it in its various stages of development even during the last 300 years or so, be ultimately likely to develop among such a people whose writers of relatively capable talent continue to muse in their imaginative writings about their natural and socio-cultural environments?

It is in a hypothetical consideration of this general nature that Palmer partly seeks support for his welcome view that critical criteria are not necessarily Western because of their historical development. But if, in spite of their historical background, it is a 'distortion' to call critical criteria Western, why would one assume that the novel form itself (though it shares a similar background) is, however, Western? Or that its later development in Africa, as had been the case in Western Europe itself or in Russia, is nevertheless 'not an indigenous African genre; [that] the African novel grew out of the Western novel'? Why, anyhow, would verse and drama be more native to Africa than this essentially narrative form? Are African poems and plays today less infused with Western influences than African prose fiction? And granted the suppositions and assumptions of these rhetorical hypotheses, what element in the form of the novel remains culture-bound? Or is anything only indigenous to a culture if it was invented there? Dan Izevbaye compresses it all into a short, pithy question: 'Are cars and cameras alien to Japan because they were not invented there?' (Izevbaye, p. 5).

If one were to inseminate into the presumed answers to these questions both Mazrui's idea of 'a global pool of mankind's cultural achievements from different lands' and also a structurally expanded version of Soyinka's philosophical 'principle of ownership of the written word', one might then have much of the basic yeast of ingredients for a refutation of J. P. Clark's facile observation which Palmer would hand down. At any rate, more fruitful critical insights might emerge in the process. It must be noted that the novel was not born in the developed form that we have today, and that the West has not been the only active agency of change and development in the novel as a literary form.

The long and the short of all this is that we need to examine our critical assumptions a little more closely, to learn to make finer and more careful discriminations in the light of a fairly all-round awareness of all relevant cultural realities we have at our disposal, and also to know when to stop short of momentous conclusions for which our evidence may still be rather scarce. Perhaps, also, the criticism of a new literature may afford to extend its function to include the search for ways of stimulating that literature to grow into a strong and distinctly individual tradition of its own, in spite of its common sharing of a few characteristics with other traditions of writing. We will hardly be able to do this effectively if we cannot acknowledge plausible and potential sources of influence from indigenous African roots. Such a concession or recognition does not have to gell into an isolationist cultural nationalism or a nostalgic retreat into the past.

This brings to mind a common tendency in some commentaries

on 'oral' tradition. Whether or not well disposed towards its relevance and potential uses to the new writing, a good many critics seem to be aware more of 'oral' elements when they discuss the relationship between African literature and African traditional forms. And, unfortunately, even the scholarly attention which has recently begun to be given to general African folklore seems to have put out so far an initial foot of 'oral' emphasis (e.g. Dorson (ed.), 1972; Ben-Amos, 1975). Many critics accordingly talk of African traditional forms only in terms of an oral or verbal dimension, seldom giving as much as a hint of their awareness of a possible non-verbal dimension. And yet these forms are by no means exclusively verbal; the mouth and the ear are not the only active organs for creating or perceiving culture in traditional Africa. An exclusive verbalism of outlook can thus remain oblivious of active non-verbal aspects of traditional forms both in themselves and in their potentialities for the new writing.

Drama, since it is less dependent on vocalization and verbal structures than verse or narrative, may be the most obvious, but certainly not the only, mode of literary expression that can benefit from such non-verbal elements. (For a specific analysis of the relevance of a non-verbal traditional feature to modern African drama, see Ogunba, 1970, especially pp. 8–18, on 'the overall design of a festival' in some of Wole Soyinka's plays). Then, also, the affinities of verbality between the novel form and oral elements of tradition may be fairly obvious, because of the distinctly linguistic mode of realization and existence common to both. Nevertheless, both oral tradition and the novel itself do have features of a non-verbal nature, though these may be more obvious and more numerous in the former. The sequence and juxtaposition of incidents, for example, though usually given shape in verbal configurations in narratives, do not seem to depend on verbality alone for some of their more deliberate effects, as perhaps the broken chronology device in the modern novel may illustrate. A good deal of the power and effects of such devices of juxtaposition and sequence probably issue as much from their verbality as from their positional or structural manipulativeness. In addition, the non-verbal aspects of forms like ritual or the festival, say, their material symbolism and their processual structures, can conceivably enhance narrative procedures of structuration and communication to some extent. It is probably in such aspects of form, style, and technique that traditional forms can best contribute to the development of the new literature. One must, though, be always awake to the dangers of direct transfer from the traditional to a modern mode of expression.

But claims or suggestions like this suffer from one great draw-back: the critic, whether African or expatriate, may have no direct knowledge of the immediate African language or tradition upon which a writer may be drawing for such connections. Critical analysis of them may thus take some time before being aired, even though readers who share a common indigenous tradition with the writer may be aware of the connections from the start. Critics who happen to be more favourably endowed in this respect in relation to a specific writer can help to alleviate this drawback, which seems to be engendered by the cultural diversity in Africa. Meanwhile, disendowment or uncertainty on the part of other critics should not be allowed to lead to too final a foreclosure at this stage of the potentialities of traditional forms for literary creativity.

A shred of the plausibility of such possibilities may be seen in an unlikely quarter. In what may at first look like a wild *tour de force* of comparative analysis, Victor W. Turner, who has written copiously in the last twenty years on ritual among the Ndembu of north-western Zambia, has recently reported on an approach he has experimented with for a few years in tutorials on Dante, Blake, and Kierkegaard at the University of Chicago (Turner, 1976). He tries, that is, to apply his analyses of non-verbal symbolism in African rituals to certain texts of Western literature for possible illumi-nation. 'Both abound in symbols, but can ritual and literary sym-bols be meaningfully compared? . . . What highest common factors can we find? How may analysis of the former help us better to elucidate the latter and vice versa?' (Turner, pp. 45, 47). Turner's illustrative analysis of Dante's *Purgatorio* in terms of his lifetime's work on African ritual symbolism (pp. 64–81) is not, of course, our main point here. The point, rather, is that such a line of questioning could more generally have an applied significance for both writer and critic in the new African literature; symbolism or ritual need not be the only points of reference. Forms of traditional expres-sivity which may neither subsist in nor depend wholly upon words and vocalization could thus be an interesting area of experiment or speculation in creativity and criticism alike. A systematic account of influence in African writing would have to reckon with such possibilities, together of course with those from the oral domain as well, even if the modern literary art form under consideration may be more predominantly verbal in its mode of expression or existence. The new literature may be too young to preclude or renounce such possibilities out of hand at this stage.

It may be said, therefore, that the influences that have been or that might be brought to bear upon modern African writing emanate from both traditional indigenous and from non-African sources as well. A greater awareness of influence as a valid critical concept may thus be necessary. In fact, influence may be such a valid critical concept precisely because it is also a dynamic principle of creativity. Criticism should endeavour to be patient and dispassionate in analysing its manifestations within the textural and overall global aspects and contexts of the literary work or tradition. A new tradition of literature which would carry in its veins and on its face the distinctive marks and traces of its own sure instincts might utilize such a conception of influences with powerful effect in its creativity and criticism alike. And this would directly evoke the question of originality and its interplay with the legitimacy of influence. But it is perhaps clear already that influence and originality are not mutually exclusive in this conception; originality can in fact be achieved in the very moments and interstices of influence.

A writer of integrity seldom remains replicatively faithful to his sources, even in discernible cases of literary influence. He may, for example, conceive of a common theme in accordance with his own particular sensibility or vision, which could be completely different from those in his source. Or he may adapt a borrowed element to the exigencies and requirements of a specific context in his own work. Where two literary figures interact in this way, an influence may even sometimes be reflected in drastic, corrective reinterpretations of the precursor work or writer. Harold Bloom has mapped out a series of modes of corrective or adaptive interaction in cases of influence in his book entitled *The Anxiety of Influence*, though his conception of influence is rather psychologistic and also exclusively literary or aestheticized. But he puts his main point poignantly: 'Weaker talents idealize; figures of capable imagination appropriate for themselves' (Bloom, p. 5). The task of an influence study may then be the verification and assessment of these 'appropriations' in literary terms. And a successful or pertinent 'appropriation' would seem to be perfectly original in its context.

Vis-à-vis the possibility of an influence, then, literary originality seems to be a fairly expansive range of imaginative realizations and dispositions; one can hardly lay a finger on any one of its subtle prismatic shades or reflections to claim it as the sole essence of the thing. It can range from relative auto-suggestiveness to adaptive applications of hints, suggestions, or phenomena from other people, works, and modes of cultural expression. The realization of independent contextual effects, however, would seem to be a basic aesthetic requirement or desideratum. And that would ensure the conceptual flexibility the legitimacy of literary influence would seem to demand of creative originality.

This basic amplitude or flexibility is infused, for instance, into the following pragmatic conception of originality:

> ... that originality consists, not exclusively or even primarily in innovations in materials or of style and manner, but [equally as well] in the genuineness and effectiveness of the artistic moving power of the creative work ... What genuinely moves the reader aesthetically and produces an independent artistic effect has artistic originality, whatever its debts. (Shaw, p. 60)

Inclusive rather than exclusivist, such an accommodative view of originality seeks to embrace a good deal of that wide spectrum of creative potentialities that could be realized in a work of the imagination. Presumably, it entails no facile relativism which would relieve the critic of the duty to characterize and evaluate individual products of creativity as clearly and objectively as possible. Being matters of degree, quality, and manner, an ample conception of both literary influence and originality might not only underline, but also encourage, the need for fineness of discrimination in influence analysis and evaluation. The fact of influence becomes more meaningful in critical observation when its own mode and the corresponding responsive individuality of usage are respectively gauged and assessed.

NOTE

1. An era or society may be termed 'technetronic' according to the way it is 'shaped culturally, psychologically, socially, and economically by the impact of technology and electronics'; Z. Brzezinski, *Between Two Ages*, New York, Viking Press, 1971, p. 9.

REFERENCES

Dan Ben-Amos, 'Folklore in African Society', *Research in African Literatures*, 6, 1975, pp. 165–98.

Dorothy S. Blair, *African Literature in French*, Cambridge, CUP, 1976.

Harold Bloom, *The Anxiety of Influence*, New York, OUP, 1973.

Priscilla P. Clark, 'The Comparative Method: Sociology and the Study of Literature', *Yearbook of Comparative and General Literature*, 23, 1974, pp. 5–13.

Richard M. Dorson (ed.), *African Folklore*, Bloomington, Indiana University Press, 1972.

Michael J. C. Echeruo, 'Traditional and Borrowed Elements in Nigerian Poetry', *Nigeria Magazine*, 89, June 1966, pp. 142–55.

William R. Ferris, Jr., 'Folklore and the African Novelist: Achebe and Tutuola', *Journal of American Folklore*, 86, 1973, pp. 25–36.

Claudio Guillen, 'The Aesthetics of Literary Influence', in his *Literature as System*, Princeton, Princeton University Press, 1971, pp. 17–52.

Lee Haring, 'Ngugi and Gikuyu Folklore', *Keystone Folklore*, 19, 1974, pp. 95–112.

Ihab H. Hassan, 'The problem of Influence in Literary History: Notes Towards a Definition', *Journal of Aesthetics and Art Criticism*, 14, 1955, pp. 66–76.

W. J. Howard, 'Themes and Development in the Novels of Ngugi', in *The Critical Evaluation of African Literature*, Edgar Wright (ed.), London, Heinemann, 1973, pp. 95–119. Washington, D.C., Inscape, 1977.

Abiola Irele, 'Tradition and the Yoruba Writer: D. O. Fagunwa, Amos Tutuola, and Wole Soyinka', *Odu*, 11, 1975, pp. 75–100.

J. M. Ita, 'Laye's *Radiance of the King* and Kafka's *Castle*', *Odu*, 4, 1970, pp. 18–45.

Solomon O. Iyasere, 'Oral Tradition in the Criticism of African Literature', *Journal of Modern African Studies*, 13, 1975, pp. 107–19.

Dan S. Izevbaye, 'The State of Criticism in African Literature', *African Literature Today*, 7, London, Heinemann, 1975, pp. 1–19.

Adeola James, Review of *An Introduction to the African Novel* by E. Palmer, *African Literature Today*, 7, London, Heinemann, 1975, pp. 147–52. New York, Africana Publishing Company, 1978.

Steven Jervis, 'Tradition and Change in Hardy and Achebe', *Black Orpheus*, Nigeria, vol. 2, nos. 5–6, 1970, pp. 31–8.

Bernth Lindfors, *Folklore in Nigerian Literature*, New York, Africana Publishing Company, 1973.

Ali A. Mazrui, *The Anglo-African Commonwealth*, Oxford, Pergamon Press, 1967, pp. 107–13.

Ngugi wa Thiong'o, *Homecoming*, London, Heinemann, 1972. Westport, CT, Lawrence Hill, 1973.

Charles E. Nnolim, 'A Source for *Arrow of God*', *Research in African Literatures*, 8, 1977, pp. 1–26.

Donatus I. Nwoga, 'Plagiarism and Authentic Creativity in West Africa', *Research in African Literatures*, 6, 1975, pp. 32–9.

Oyin Ogunba, 'The Traditional Content of the Plays of Wole Soyinka', *African Literature Today*, 4, London, Heinemann, 1970, pp. 2–18; 5, 1971, pp. 106–15. New York, Africana Publishing Company, 1970.

Olusola Oke, 'Ferdinand Oyono's *Houseboy* and Gustav Flaubert's *Un Coeur Simple*', *Black Orpheus*, Nigeria, vol. 2, nos. 5–6, 1970, pp. 39–44.

Eustace J. T. Palmer, 'The Criticism of African Fiction: its Nature and Function', *International Fiction Review*, 1, July 1974, pp. 112–19.

John T. Shaw, 'Literary Indebtedness and Comparative Literary Studies', in *Comparative Literature: Method and Perspective*, N. P. Stallknecht and H. Frenz (eds), Carbondale, South Illinois University Press, 1961, pp. 58–71.

Austin J. Shelton, 'The Articulation of Traditional and Modern in Igbo Literature', *The Conch*, vol. 2, no. 2, 1970, pp. 30–52.

Wole Soyinka, 'From a Common Back Cloth: A Re-assessment of the African Literary Image', *The American Scholar*, 32, 1963, pp. 387–96.

Wole Soyinka, *Myth, Literature and the African World*, Cambridge, CUP, 1976. New York, CUP, 1976.

Diana Spearman, *The Novel and Society*, London, Routledge & Kegan Paul, 1966.

Victor W. Turner, 'African Ritual and Western Literature: Is a Comparative Symbology Possible?', in *The Literature of Fact*, A. Fletcher (ed.), New York, Columbia University Press, 1976, pp. 45–81.

An Approach to Ouologuem's Le Devoir de Violence

A. E. Ohaegbu

A lot has been said about the controversial Malian writer Yambo Ouologuem, and his novel Le Devoir de Violence translated in English as Bound to Violence.[1] But much of the argument tends more to generate heat than to shed light on the author's literary intentions and his vision of the world.

There is no doubt that Ouologuem's book is one of the best-written and most audacious novels that have ever emerged from post-independence Africa; it can even be said to be a shocker to the 'outward-looking' literary orthodoxy of pre-independence African writers in French. African readers and critics look at the book with rather unpleasant surprise, while some racially minded literary critics and reviewers of Europe and America easily succumb to the temptation of regarding it as the greatest blow that has ever been dealt to African life, tradition, and values by an African writer. It is the intention of this article to throw more light on the study of this novel by touching on some vital aspects of the book.

According to Hubert de Leusse,[2] Ouologuem is out to destroy a 'certain fictitious and idyllic image of Africa' presented by African writers and ethnologists. Considering the wave of violence which runs across the entire novel, this critic comes to the conclusion that 'Africa is in reality a land where violence is equalled only by the dread it called forth' – merely pushing the author's argument too far! Yves Benot[3] remarks that Ouologuem is a 'non-conformist' writer who does not believe that Africa had been oppressed and subjugated by colonization, and he goes further to say that 'this is a consoling and comforting book' to the French reading public. Obviously these critics imply that the reason behind the overwhelming acclamation of Bound to Violence by many Western critics, and their unanimity on the 'high quality' of the novel, is its attempt to destroy the image of Africa.

It appears to me that most critics are so carried away by the blanket of violence with which Ouologuem covers his Nakem

Empire that they tend to miss the over-riding message of the author – that man (not necessarily the black man!) has a violent nature which can be utilized to establish, sustain, and perpetuate political domination of a people. Gerald Moore has correctly remarked that

> Saif is offered as typical of oppression by which the 'notables' have always governed Africa; a system which, having survived the French conquest and the implantation of modern education, now hopes to manipulate even the nominal independence of Nakem to its advantage.[4]

To get this point across, the author has chosen some sensitive moments of the black man's history – feudalism, Arab invasion, slavery, colonization – which he exploits and manipulates to conform to his violent vision of the world. If this central theme is accepted, it has to be said then that the African reading public is only worried over the rather unsympathetically distorted, and of course 'unorthodox', use which Ouologuem has made of African history and material to prove his case. Why must the author use his own continent and people to create the hideous image of man? Does he feel so comfortable and safe in his borrowed garment of white civilization that he negates his past and forgets his own alienation? These are two of the questions which the uninitiated reader of *Bound to Violence* is prone to ask. But the subtleties of the novel have yet to be completely realized before full justice can be done to the book and its author.

It is true that Ouologuem is a hard-liner in his novel, but it has to be recognized that he works with a double-edged axe which spares neither the black man, nor the Western world, some of whose critics claim the novelist on their side. In fact one has to read in between the lines in order to understand that Ouologuem treats with equal contempt his Nakem Empire and the doomed colonial empire which the French had wanted to create in West Africa.

The story opens in a lachrymose and touching tone which indicates the subject matter, the time, and space of the novel:

> Our eyes drink the brightness of the sun and, overcome, marvel at their tears. Machallah! wa bismillah! ... To recount the bloody adventure of the niggertrash – shame to the worthless paupers! – there would be no need to go back beyond the present century; but the true history of the Blacks begins much earlier, with the Saifs, in the year 1202 of our era, in the African Empire of Nakem south of Fezzan, long after the conquests of Okba ben Nafi al-Fitri ... (p. 3)

As one can see right from the beginning of the novel, part of the grand design of Ouologuem is to show how the ruling moslem dynasty in the Nakem Empire has, from 1202 to 1947, consistently used violence and intimidation to control the destiny of the common man, referred to in the book as 'niggertrash' and 'pauper'. He is more concerned about the 'bloody adventure of the niggertrash' and the victimizer than with the so-called primitivism and barbarism of mediaeval Africa often harped on by critics.

Ouologuem's black man is synonymous with suffering and resignation; he is the 'worthless paupers', dehumanized and exploited for centuries by the Saifs and Arab notables, 'clubbed, sold, stockpiled, haggled over, adjudicated, flogged, bound and delivered – with attentive, studied, sorrowful contempt – to the Portuguese, the Spaniards, the Arabs (on the east and north coasts), and to French, Dutch, and English (west coast), and so scattered to the winds . . .' (p. 12). When French colonization came, it was the same 'niggertrash' who had to be victimized. For Ouologuem, both the black man and the white man have their share of the blame for the slave trade which depopulated Africa. Although he attacks the feudal system and its corollary, slavery, he does not seek to show that violence and oppression are consubstantial with the African; he rather attributes them to what can be called the general degeneration of the human kind of which the black man is only a part.

The mediaeval Nakem Empire which is the main theatre of action is supposedly located in western Sudan:

> The fame of that Empire spread to Morocco, the Sudan, Egypt, Abyssinia, and to the holy and noble city of Mecca; it was known to the English, the Dutch, the French, the Spaniards, and, it goes without saying, the Portuguese . . . (p. 3).

There is a strong temptation among critics to associate it with the Mali Empire of the thirteenth to sixteenth centuries. In fact nothing in the novel suggests that the Saifs who are of Arabo-Jewish origin are descendants of the ancient kingdom of Mali, nor can the 'well-beloved Isaac al-Heit', founder of the Nakem Empire and of the Saif dynasty, be compared to Sundjata, the great hero of the Mandingue epic so well celebrated by the famous historian Djibril Tamsi Niane of Mali. It is true that the author of *Bound to Violence* is a Malian and that he may have drawn from his experiences in his society to weave the intricate story of his novel, but this does not necessarily mean that this gruesome story of violence which he is telling is that of his country and people from 1202 to 1947 and even after; nor can it be said to be really and exclusively that of Africa. As Professor

E. N. Obiechina has well remarked: 'Africa there certainly is in the novel, but so also are Arabia and the Orient, France and Europe. To ignore this fact is to do less than justice to the novel and pander to age-old mystifications.'[5]

One fact which readers and critics of Ouologuem's book have to admit is that the writer, as an artist, is a universal observer whose experiences and imagination cannot be limited to a definite geographical area with mathematical accuracy. In this regard Ouologuem himself has been reported to have said that his searching and critical eyes extend to 'Africa of the great empires, the Congo and ex-anglo-egyptian Sudan', and that he has equally borne in mind Delafosse's account of the descendants of the Queen of Saba.[6]

Two great periods of violence are easily discernible in the novel. The first is the mediaeval period masterminded by the Saif dynasty with the complicity of the notables. Here violence is essentially associated with the feudal cruelties of the overlords on their innocent and 'bastardized' subjects who were often captives of war.

> In that age of feudalism, large communities of slaves celebrated the justice of their overlords by forced labor and by looking on inert as multitudes of their brothers, smeared with the blood of butchered children and of disemboweled expectant mothers, were immured alive ... That is what happened at Tillaberi-Bentia, at Granta, at Groaso, at Gagol-Gosso, and in many places mentioned in the Tarik al-Fetach and at the Tarik al-Sudan of the Arab historians ... (p. 4)

In trying to trace and deplore what he calls 'the bloody adventure of the niggertrash', Ouologuem calls to mind the atrocities of the feudal system in which the overlord arrogated to himself the right of life and death over his slaves. His argument is that 'forced labour', 'slavery', and the destruction of life and property which some African historians and politicians have often blamed on the advent of the white man in Africa already existed in 'the African Empire of Nakem south of Fezzan'. This reasoning leads the author to go to the extreme assertion that the French colonization of the Nakem Empire was in reality the 'beginning of decolonization':

> But to Nakem the colonial powers came too late, for with the help of the local notables a colonial overlord had established himself long since, and that colonial overlord was none other than Saif. All unsuspecting, the European conquerors played into his hands. Call it technical assistance ... (p. 24)

Although Ouologuem is quoted as saying: 'My aim is to do violence to the misconceptions of Africans so that we can see what the real problems are',[7] he seems to have retouched the problems to the point of unreality; his posture baffles those who know the reality and gives a measure of comfort and psychological satisfaction to the exponents of the *mission civilisatrice*.

An aspect of this mediaeval violence which has become a duty in Ouologuem's Nakem Empire relates to what the author describes as 'internecine rivalries and warring with one another for the imperial power ...' (p. 4). This type of violence persisted in the Nakem Empire and was about to result in a total disintegration of the empire and the people when French colonizers arrived and constituted a threat to the power of Saif and the notables who now 'diplomatically' became great nationalists and freedom fighters.

The second period of violence in the book covers the entire colonial occupation of Nakem up to 1947, the date of the first elections. In this part the author takes delight in offering us what really looks like a fight between two giants over the political control of the Nakem Empire; we have on the one hand the wicked Saif Ben Isaac al-Heit applying all the diabolical means at his disposal (fire, poison, assassination, asps, tricks, intimidation, etc.) to preserve his authority over Nakem; on the other hand the colonial administrators stand firm using the force of arms and also poison to eliminate Saif who constitutes a big obstacle to the effective installation of the colonial regime.

It is important to note that in both the mediaeval and colonial periods power and politics generate the violence which articulates the entire internal movement of the novel. In all cases the permanent victim is the people of Nakem – the niggertrash – whom Ouologuem presents as ignorant of their destiny and incapable of a veritable revolt, since centuries of unbroken servitude have transformed them into 'Zombies'.

This web of violence entangles not only the Saifs and their murderous agents, not only the colonial administrators who want to liberate the people of Nakem from the clutches of the Saifs and put them under a new form of domination, but it also involves Islam and Christianity which, under the cloak of spirituality, do violence to traditional art and culture.

A close study of *Bound to Violence* reveals three kinds of violence – physical, economic and cultural. Physical violence is a function of politics; it stems from man's irresistible urge to rule absolutely and exclusively – hence the seeming necessity to eliminate all potential threats. This explains the death of all newborn babies in the Nakem Empire under the rule of Saif Moche Gabbai of Honain:

> It came to pass that one day in the year 1420 Saif Moche Gabbai of
> Honain – after hearing the words of a soothsayer who predicted that he
> would be overthrown by a child to be born during the coming year in
> Tillaberi–Bentia, capital of the Nakem Empire – ceased to ignore the
> strange cravings of pregnant women. He consigned all newborn babes
> to the red death and lined their shrunken heads along the wall of his
> antechamber ... (p. 5).

It is for the same reason that Saif al-Haram usurped the imperial
throne from his brother, Saif al-Hilal, and killed him. The French
colonial administrators, Chevalier and Vandame, are equally victims of politically oriented violence.

There is yet another form of violence which, though physical,
does not seek to achieve any definite political end or even any
objective at all. The rape of Tambira by Dougouli, Wampoulo and
Kratonga, and her ultimate death in a 'latrine built for Saif's serfs',
the sexual torture of Awa by Chevalier, the tragic end of Anne
Kadidia caused by 'a sadistic customer' who had concealed a razor
blade in her washing soap, the unabashed killing of Awa by San-
kolo – all these are wanton acts of cruelty which one must shudder
to see in the novel. They are 'gratuitous' and smack of the English
horror novels of the nineteenth century and the French existentialist literature, not to mention the tradition of Le Marquis de
Sade, all of which Ouologuem must have read with some delight.

It may be thought that Ouologuem presents these horrible acts of
violence to give a barbarous past to the black man but this would be
wrong. The truth is that the author is not saying that violence is the
black man's heritage. What he is trying to do is to present another
aspect of man's nature, that of a human beast; his observation
transcends time and space and involves the whole of humanity.

As for the economic aspect of violence, the author shows it
through the depopulation of the Nakem Empire by local and
foreign slave dealers, by forced labour, hunger, and disease associated with the incessant raids and inter-provincial wars in Nakem.
We are told that at a time, 'under the lash of necessity a father sold
his son, a brother his brother', that 'no villainy was too great if food
might be procured by it' (p. 14). The economic strangulation of the
people, far from being historically inevitable, is merely a device
for maintaining dictatorial power by forcing everyone to have
'no other recourse but to throw themselves on the mercy of Saif...'
(p. 14).

Political domination, torture, and economic exploitation can
succeed in keeping a people in a state of suffering and subjugation

only for some time. The most disastrous and lasting violence is cultural, since it is capable of alienating the oppressed completely from his tradition and environment. Islam and Christianity, in complicity with the Saifs and the notables, are presented in the novel as having done great violence to the cultural personality of the 'niggertrash', and Ouologuem makes a mockery of these religions:

> The religious gymnastics of the five daily prayers of Islam were maintained as safety valve; the poor in mind and spirit were kept busy searching and striving for Allah's Eternal Kingdom. Religion, whose soul had been vomited by the clergy of Nakem, became a deliberately confused mumbling about human dignity, a learned mystification; losing its mystical contents, it became a means of action, a political weapon ... (p. 23)

In much the same way, when the white missionaries came to evangelize the Nakem Empire, Saif forced the slaves and their children to embrace Christianity, and this with a view to placating the colonizers and continuing the cultural 'bastardization' of the serfs:

> After that Saif decided that only the sons of the servant class would be constrained to undergo French education, the masses of the missionaries, and the baptism of the White Fathers, to adopt French dress and shave their heads, while their parents would be obliged to make amends and swear secrecy ... (p. 46)

Cultural violence is again manifest in the profanation of African art, not only by Saif and the notables, but also by Shrobenius and other Western tourists who defy the magico-religious intention of this art and make it an object of international gangsterism and commercialization. It is no wonder then that Ouologuem should take Shrobenius and his like to task:

> This salesman and manufacturer of ideology [Shrobenius] assumed the manner of a sphinx to impose his riddles, to satisfy his caprices and past turnabouts. And shrewd anthropologist that he was, he sold more than thirteen hundred pieces, deriving from the collection he had purchased from Saif and the carloads his disciples had obtained in Nakem free of charge, to the following purveyors of funds: The Musée de l'Homme in Paris, the museums of London, Basel, Munich, Hamburg, and New York ... (p. 95)

Although the name Shrobenius looks like a facile play on the word Frobenius, the famous German ethnographer whose works have in no small measure inspired many Africanists to study and write on African cultures and traditions, one cannot say that Ouologuem is trying to deny the contribution of Western scholarship to the knowledge of African peoples and their civilization. He is rather whipping some of the early European Africanists with whom 'negro art found its patent of nobility in the folklore of mercantile intellectualism' (p. 94), and who coined sensational stories about African life simply to appear as great scholars in the Western world and be raised to 'a lofty sorbonnical chair'.

Another striking feature of *Bound to Violence* is its generally pessimistic vision of the world. Ouologuem contests the notion of Africa as 'the womb of the world and the cradle of civilization'; he runs down the black man's past glories, making his present objectionable and his future rather bleak. We are overjoyed to see Raymond Spartacus Kassoumi receive the modern education necessary for the accomplishment of great things; we see him as the forerunner of a generation of young revolutionaries who would fight to end feudal oppression and free the Nakem Empire and its people from the violence to which they have been bound. But alas! Ouologuem disappoints us and dashes our hopes to pieces when he finally makes the modern educated Raymond a pawn in the hands of Saif and a 'peace-offering' to the colonial power – an attitude which makes a mockery of education and its importance in politicizing the oppressed masses and fortifying them against the dictatorship of feudal overlords.

Although one would have liked to see Saif nailed to the cross and finally buried and forgotten at the end of the story, Ouologuem makes him our contemporary (if not our eventual successor!), and the atrocities of his regime a recurrent phenomenon of African political history. We are appalled to learn that 'projected into the world, one cannot help recalling that Saif, mourned three million times, is for ever reborn to history beneath the hot ashes of more than thirty African republics (pp. 181–2).

Lofty ideals like African unity are to Ouologuem a dream that can never be made a reality; the holy water of Mecca not only has a bad taste, it cannot cure the sick, contrary to the belief of Moslems; God is made a tacit collaborator of the tyrannical leaders of the Nakem Empire, since he watches with silent applause and benediction the hangman deal his fatal blows on the 'niggertrash'. We are told that 'man is in history, and history is politics. Politics is cleavage. No solidarity is possible. Nor purity (p. 175)'.

Ouologuem takes delight in making the characters of his novel suffer; he treats them with disrespect and verbal violence suggestive of a sadist. Apart from Saif Ben Isaac al-Heit, hero of the novel, and the good priest Henry who becomes bishop at the end of the story, all the rest of the characters find themselves invariably sunk in cruel situations where the author offers them no ray of light nor any hope of salvation; a wicked and implacable destiny seems to have ordained in advance the sufferings of the personages. There is hardly any character who does not fall under Ouologuem's crushing wheels: Tambira is raped and killed without ever seeing the fruits of her labour; her daughter, Anne, after losing her parents, is forced to become a prostitute at Pigalle where she tragically ends what has been a life of unmitigated misfortune; the French governors, Chevalier and Vandame, are massacred in cold blood, and their hopes of establishing colonial administration are frustrated.

At one time the author tells us that 'the golden age when all the swine [the tyrants] will die is just around the corner' (p. 174), but it is in vain that we await that golden age, since his Saif – the big swine – though disarmed by the mystic personality of Bishop Henry, remains immortal. In fact all is bad in the society which serves as the landscape of the author's literary creation. However, there is room to wonder whether this pessimism cannot be explained by the fact that he is presenting a world where human misery and oppression abound. What looks like pessimism could then be seen as an exaggerated exteriorization of Ouologuem's internal distress in the face of an endless record of man's injustice to man.

Ouologuem does not present a flattering image of man and society in his novel. Violence and oppression reign supreme and stem from the inordinate ambition of the ruling classes to relegate God to the background and perpetuate their rule of terror over their subjects. His book is not aimed at the glorification of the black man's past, nor at the dismantling of the foundations of his people's civilization. To fully understand him, one has to insert his novel into the context of the general feeling of disillusionment which, as Wole Soyinka, the famous Nigerian playwright and critic, remarked at the conference of African writers in Stockholm (1967), characterizes the present stage of African life. In this regard, it can be said that Ouologuem is not less 'committed' than his predecessors (Mongo Beti, Ferdinand Oyono, Bernard Dadie, etc.) who have unequivocally denounced colonial oppression. But the difference is that his own commitment is more internally oriented, and therefore more critical of the African himself than of the white man who has hitherto appeared in the African novel as the black man's permanent oppressor. Indeed, the use he has made of 'The Legend of the Saifs' in the first chapter of his novel is to establish a background of horrors and dictatorships against which one can understand the dynamics of power in contemporary Africa. He may have sinned by exaggeration and distortion of facts noticeable here and there in his book, but his thesis cannot be treated as outright fallacy, especially when one takes a dispassionate account of dictatorships and militarisms decimating the population and qualified manpower of some present-day African countries.

NOTES

1. This novel has been translated into English. For the purpose of this article the citations and page references are drawn from *Bound to Violence*, translated from the French by Ralph Mannheim and published in London by Heinemann (AWS 99), 1971. New York, Humanities, 1976.
2. Hubert de Leusse, *Afrique et occident. Heurs et malheurs d'une rencontre. Les romanciers du pays noir*, Paris, Orante, 1971, p. 88.
3. Yves Benot, 'Le Devoir de Violence de Yambo Ouologuem, est-il un chef-d'oeuvre ou une mystification?', *La Pénsee. Revue du racialisme moderne*, Paris, 149, 1970, 128.
4. Gerald Moore, 'The Debate on Existence in African Literature', *Présence Africaine*, 81, 1972, 25.
5. E. N. Obiechina, 'Bound to Violence' (review), *Okike. An African Journal of New Writing*, I, 3, 1972, 53.
6. Cf. Philippe Decraene's review of Le Devoir de Violence in *Le Monde*, 12 October 1968, 1.
7. Cf. *West Africa*, 2689, 14 December 1968, 1474–5.

Madness in the African Novel: Awoonor's *This Earth, My Brother* ...

Femi Ojo-Ade

Introduction

Alienation is a recurring theme in African writing. This state of man's incompatibility with his milieu, this polarization between man and nature, this disintegration of man's dreams of bliss by realities of pressure, oppression, and destruction, is easily noticeable in a colonized society. The master–slave relationship that exists in such a society, a relationship that has been adopted and carried forward into the neo-colonialist structure of the independent society, provides a classical setting for the dissipation of sanity and its replacement by dementia.

The African novel, in dealing with the question of alienation, has depicted two types of alienated heros: the one who has managed, in spite of the overwhelming pressures of his situation, to stay on what could be termed 'the right side of the fence'; that is, he does not belong to the mainstream of the social order, he is a 'stranger', albeit a 'sane' stranger.[1] On the other hand, there is the hero who goes overboard, so to speak. Finding it totally impossible to adjust to the inhuman situation existing in his society, not satisfied with mere utterances of protest or with a fairly 'sane' life on the fringe of society, he pushes himself mentally to the limit, and even beyond it, and finally reaches a point where society ostracizes him and deems it fit to put him away in a madhouse. It is with this second type of hero that our study is concerned.

The questions posed are innumerable: why does a man run mad? Why are there so many madmen in the African novel? Is the madman any less sane that the sane society that condemns him? A pertinent remark is that sanity does not constitute a theme of mere artistic interest to the African novelist who, we should remember, belongs to a society where art is a function of life. The proliferation of works dealing with this peculiar theme can only indicate its presence and great impact within the societal structure.

Examples of the Mad Hero

Chinua Achebe's Ezeulu,[2] chief priest of the god Ulu for the six villages of Umuaro, runs mad because he is unable, or rather unwilling, to submit himself to the power of collective wisdom and because he tries to overemphasize his individual role as priest. In the complex web of relationships between god, community, and individual, the last is the least important. The god sides with the community. 'Their god had taken sides with them against his headstrong and ambitious priest and thus upheld the wisdom of their ancestors.'[3]

That is the villagers' honest analysis of the situation. We must, however, take into consideration a further detail: the role of the colonial power strongly represented by Winterbottom.

The colonial contribution to the psychological disintegration of the African is also exemplified in Ngugi's *A Grain of Wheat*.[4] The setting is the Mau Mau era of the struggle for independence; the hero is Mugo, a detention camp veteran who betrays the national cause to save his own neck. Voices – of guilt, of retribution, of innocent beings mired deeper in suffering through the individual's selfish disposition – pursue the hero until something in him snaps.

Colonialism is not the only 'purveyor for psychiatric hospitals'.[5] Mental disorder results also from racism, apartheid, neo-colonialism in all its forms and other dehumanizing ideologies and practices that, rather than stand in exclusivity or in opposition to each other, are attended by an undeniable complementarity. What colonialism and these other postures have in common is a basic debasement of humanity, a certain enslavement of the mind by a group surfeited by the aggrandizing elements of its own false superiority. The victim of racism and apartheid is, of course, the black man or woman. It is Bessie Head's Elizabeth, heroine of *A Question of Power*,[6] a 'Masarwa',[7] a half-breed exiled from South Africa into Botswana, a stranger in her homeland, and still a stranger in the place she would like to call a new home. A low breed. A bastard. Daughter of a madwoman. Her non-identity, statelessness, chronic loneliness, and life on the verge of her terrestrial hell, added to her inherited mental anguish, all make her a logical guest of the madhouse. She remains a victim to the very end.

An eternal victim, also, is the hero of Ayi Kwei Armah's *Fragments*:[8] Baako, an excellent Ghanaian student in America, the land of money, honey, and racism, runs amok living there as a black number – that is, a non-existing figure – among so many threatening snow-white numbers. He perseveres and manages to complete his journalistic training, only to return home to face a more astonishing and traumatic form of prejudice, that emanating from the brotherly minds of his compatriots. Baako is one of those few genuinely committed Africans described in another of Armah's novels:[9] 'The few who try sincerely to create in life those new spaces they have found in their minds, this life destroys them so easily.'

Such devoted and honest sons of Africa refuse the crumbs offered by the former masters, resent being lackeys of a sham civilization preached by African stooges of white mentors lying in dark shadows, reaffirm the need to truly free the shackled nation from its chains. Alienation within one's society. Alienation from a society ruled by foreign masters. Common to the works here glossed over is an indictment, mild or trenchant, of the society that gives birth to the madman or woman. Victims of their own brothers, Baako and Elizabeth join the white man's victims, Mugo and Ezeulu, in a land removed from the reach of the common mind. Some wallow in this twilight zone fraught with shadows, voices and footsteps, while others die. Kofi Awoonor's hero, Amamu,[10] is one of those who disappear.

Awoonor's *This Earth, My Brother* ...

The Setting

Awoonor's novel constitutes one of the landmarks of African fiction. It is a work filled with complex symbols and hidden meanings. It is pregnant with ideas. Ideas about the pressing realities of today's Africa and an insight into the future of the continent. The setting is present-day Ghana, which is a microcosm of black Africa. The Africa of corruption, graft, stagnation. The Africa of imported practices and notions. The Africa of empty intellectuals and shallow intellectuals and shallower rulers. The Africa where mad people call others mad.

In *This Earth, My Brother* ..., the complementarity between milieu and man is excellently displayed. One moulds the other, explains him. Man feeds his milieu, modifies it. They both evolve together, sometimes in harmony, sometimes in antagonistic fashion. When harmonious evolution exists, man is at peace with his world; he moves along life's path in what might be called anonymity, absorbs the elements of nature, and dies, naturally. However, with harmonious evolution might come apathy, moral and psychological stagnation, an inability to influence the continuity of life and nature. Society's vast majority is made up of those in this first group: nameless faces, anonymous personalities, peaceful minds at one with the universe. Law-abiding citizens, they are usually called. On the other side of the spectrum are camped those 'unfortunate'[11] few who find it impossible to evolve docilely with the milieu. The few are perspicacious, impatient, honest, uncompromising. Or, if they are blind, patient, dishonest, compromising, they are so unwillingly. To them, man cannot, man should not, drift along with life's tide; he must do something to influence his surroundings and his destiny, and change it. They are called revolutionaries, or rebels, or madmen. The fact is, only a perfect society can breed, without any form of pretence, children who live in it without any conflict. Such a society is non-existent in today's Africa, or world. It would therefore follow that only lack of consciousness of social realities, or rather a prevalent bad conscience, could explain the harmony under discussion here.

Awoonor brilliantly portrays this far-from-perfect society, a society that can easily contribute to the mental disintegration of a man concerned with true moral uprightness, human dignity, and progress. The country is the quintessence of underdevelopment. Of a lorry-road, the novelist writes: 'It was mainly built, if it was built at all, of mud, and gravel collected by women from the gravel pits beneath the Aka River. When it rained, it was closed to traffic' (p. 7).

When the rains come, almost everything in Deme comes to a stop. Indeed, the road is a symbol of the country as a whole. 'The road winds through tomorrows, for there are no yesterdays, and tomorrows they are wiped away by tears in the eyes of orphans, in the eyes of widowed women in the eyes of husbands who lost their wives in childbirth in the convent where white sisters in long gowns administer ether and cut open wombs with a pair of sewing scissors' (p. 48).

Stagnation. Pitfalls. Accidents. Despair. Death. Roads built by yesterday's white colonialists and inherited by today's black neocolonialists, a word synonymous with nationalists. Roads leading to nowhere but death. Roads winding through the dunghills of disease-infested communities, through the corrupted, decaying bodies of prostituted bastards. The road of Africa, with its cornucopia of malpractices; ill-planned, grandiose constructions; shady acts complemented by shady attitudes. The road is essential for movement and communication, but it hardly meets the needs of the people.

The People

Like the road, there are the self-righteous, all-important souls leading the nation to nowhere. Awoonor, with quick, masterful strokes, assembles these representatives of modernism.

Alex, the principal secretary in the Ministry of Agriculture. Age: forty-five. Short, rotund, twenty-five years' experience in the Civil Service. 'Through sheer doggedness he had pushed his way to the top' (p. 21). Self-confident, impatient with college-trained, harebrained snobs.

Bob, a failed scientist turned banker. Capacity for tomfoolery. Trying hard not to grow old. A comedian with expertise in joking about female genitals.

Row, police officer in plain clothes. Always drunk. Long devotion to colonial service, now zealous devotion to the nationalists, or to any regime that fate might put in power.

The faceless dentist whose hobby is sleeping with his female patients.

The agriculturists at the Public Works Department, 'planning the nation's agronomical salvation from moth-eaten desks filthy with old tattered files' (p. 19).

Old executive officers and senior executive officers, 'with failing eyes, and a nagging and discomforting anxiety about how much their pensions and gratuities were going to amount to when they retired from the service' (ibid.).

The state secretary of the colonial era. A powerful African, 'he talks even with white men' (p. 43).

The new black 'masas'[12] sweating profusely in sweaters and leather jackets under the scorching sun of the tropics.

Lebanese moneybags, now naturalized citizens of black Africa, 'chattering animatedly in Arabic and Pidgin from huge American cars purchased with loans from the national banks of free and independent Africa' (p. 113).

The director of standardization, trained in a well-known American university, born of Ghanaian prostitute and a Syrian father, swaggering all over the place with his important office worn proudly on his lapel, and no notion of his real responsibilities.

London 'been-to's' reminiscing about the good old days in Her Majesty's capital city.

The editor of a daily newspaper with the reputation of an ass but with the belief that he knows everything about everything, that is, nothing.

The snobbish, empty-headed army colonel, 'impatient with "civilians" and obsequious to his superiors', and his new language that is neither English nor his native tongue.

So the portraits go on and on. The *civilians*, contemptible figures all, are headed by the president of the nation. The Benevolent One. 'Follow my laws, my children, follow my laws for I am the one who brought you from the dust of degradation' (p. 28).

And he cast the people, his people, back into degradation. The president, well protected in his bullet-proof limousine. The president's castle, with 'lights blazing from it as if it were on fire'. Guards with rifles. Tunnel leading out to sea, an improvement on that used for the slaves transported to the diaspora.

The president is overthrown, naturally: 'All of it is Nkrumah's fault – the rogue' (p. 93). The army, upright, faithful to the national aspirations and goals, disciplined to the very bones of their well-sinewed bodies, must take over at once. The army.

Immense appropriations are made to increase the striking force of the army of a starving, naked and diseased nation to march and wear its boots newly received from England under certificates of urgency ... New epaulettes, new strings, new crowns, for newly appointed generals and brigadiers, and uniforms for latrine carriers. Fear death by guns. (p. 30)

New names, new titles, new faces. Old tricks, old ideas, old ways. Graft. Corruption. Personal gain. Old Africa. The army keeps everyone in check, except itself, naturally. The new leaders of the nation, the new messiahs, naturally disciplined, need no limitations. They know where and when to stop, which is nowhere and never. And the madness of the departed civilian leader did not arouse as much fear in the minds of the vast number of have-nots as does the unbridled discipline of the men with the guns. While the civilian could only harm you in your pocket – you, the tax-payer – or in your everyday life – you, the consumer, father, mother, children – the uniformed master is more dangerous. Fear death by guns.

If the leadership has changed hands from kente-clad, pot-bellied, Very Important Personalities to frightful colossi in well-ironed uniforms and hard-soled, shining boots, life at the bottom of the pile has not changed one bit. The poor, 'their emaciated bodies [have been] starved of food and joy for ages ... There is no deep sleep even for the poor' (p. 19). These 'squatters on the dunghill of modern Africa' (p. 150) have no home. Men in transit. Men in disarray. Men of the slum. The name of the slum is Nima, 'a city within a city'.

> It was intended, in the minds of its inhabitants, to be a temporary dwelling place. They hoped to move when their fortunes changed for the better. But the war was over. The sojourners never moved. It always needs a Moses to move any captive race of squatters. Nima never had one. (p. 151)

The 'smell of suburban shit' forever fills the air in Nima. The squatters have no morals, no decency, nothing: *civilized* opinion of the elevated empty barrels living in the gilded castles left by their white masters. And the new 'masas', black bodies harbouring white souls, treat the poor with opprobrium. Masters and underlings know the right attitude to life: 'Chop some make I chop some' (p. 22). If you are caught doing what society calls wrong, and if you have to explain, simply invent some reason. And you know, as a matter of expediency, you have to be a good liar, a born black teller of white lies.

Indeed, those who 'sabe book'[13] can easily extricate themselves from any thorny situation. Book. Education. Privileges. Possibilities. The poor have no possibilities so they scurry away from the law.

> The law is an enemy to these captive people. It means blows administered by angry representatives. It means fines, handcuffs, tears and blood. It means cells with pans for taking a shit in. It means long waits for trial. It means loss of work, hunger for those left at home. (p. 158)

In this land where to be reasonable is to be unreasonable, where wisdom is being able to exhibit foolishness cunningly, where the most nationalistic man is he who most expeditiously and generously steals from the coffers of the nation without foundation, in this land of madmen pretending to be sane, the lawyer is a god. 'He is the one who gets you out of trouble; he is the one who gets you into trouble' (p. 159). The lawyer puts you on the right side of a law without a right side. Lies. Pretence. Corruption. False respect.

Amamu

Amamu, the hero of *This Earth* ..., is a lawyer; London-trained; talented; respected and admired; flooded with clients. He enjoys all the trappings of his profession and position; for, the very word, 'lawyer', is a passport to success in anything he does.

A traffic policeman stops Amamu and scolds him for breaking a traffic law. The poor chap quickly does an about-face and begs for forgiveness when he realizes that the man is a lawyer.

At a nightclub, the lawyer is given the best service. At the airport, a customs official helps him find his wife's misplaced luggage, mainly because he is a lawyer.

Amamu is aloof and proud. He is very assertive and often brutally distant. A been-to, and a been-to with genius. He is one of those 'brilliant children of our soil who has wrenched from the white man the magic of his wisdom' (p. 16), and on his face is 'a grey look of satisfaction' (ibid.). All indications point to the fact that he is an integral part of the social structure and he does nothing, at least nothing that one can pinpoint, to really change the system. Then he runs mad. Why?

The fact is, the man has enjoyed his privileges half-heartedly from the first, and the brutality with which he sometimes treats the poor is caused by his sense of guilt and failure, his inability to do something concrete and symbolic to save these captives of African modernism. He seems to wish to flee from reality. He gets drunk or tipsy most of the time. His notebook tells of the dilemma of a man who, considered a god in his milieu, knows deep down that things must change, that he and those like him, parasites sucking dry the blood of the poor, must be destroyed. In his notes, he becomes an observer of his own life and that of his compatriots. Cynicism. Pessimism. Perspicacity. 'The self-illumination that comes of the losing of senses' (p. 29). And the man has never found it easy to communicate with his colleagues in the privileged class. They call him 'a queer man [because of] his habit of sudden withdrawal' and his propensity for discussing such strange subjects as philosophy and theosophy. His friends whisper to themselves: 'the man is mad' ...

> He would go on and on. Suddenly he would realize that no one said anything, no one interrupted. So he would become silent, withdrawal was his immediate refuge. Then he would gaze away to sea, his mind wandering away. After a while, his friends would pick up their conversation which had been interrupted. The voices would float around

him. Suddenly he would call Richard and ask for his bill. And without a
word to his comrades, he would descend the creaky stairway and drive
away into the evening. They would all say he was mad. But very
learned.[14]

Too much knowledge, they say, leads to madness, and men with
a touch of genius in them have always been considered mad.

Other Forms of Madness

More of Amamu later. For madness in this nation of decay is not the
exclusive territory of the learned. Madness and the violence of war.
The white man's war. Abotsi, the Burma veteran.

> Some came home mad. Among them was Abotsi . . . He was gentle. He
> wasn't actually mad. He was eccentric. He would salvage from the
> dunghill dead goats and fowls. He would come and sit quietly under the
> coconut tree on the compound. And tell stories of his days in Burma. He
> was a magazine carrier. He said, the Japanese are good fighters . . . He
> would ramble on and on about rations, Japanese, ghosts, guns, deaths,
> wounds, everything. (pp. 68–9)

Abotsi steals drinks at dances organized by the privileged classes
of society. The man has been civilized – almost, one might be
tempted to intone – by the white man's war: he even steals into the
hall to hear a cantata show put up by a choir from Lome. Memories
of dead bodies stalked by vultures. Memories of long days without
food. Voices in the dark. Voices of a dying enemy soldier, a human
being, pleading for mercy. Voice of the platoon leader barking out
orders that he himself has never taken, will never take. Voices of
innocent children being bombed. And here back home, peace at
last. As if there has never been a war. As if people like Abotsi have
not sacrified their life and their sanity so that the rich may become
richer, and the poor poorer. So Abotsi 'at intervals, would let out a
grunt and say, "People don't know" ' (p. 69). They don't know, they
don't want to know, they never want to know . . . the truth.

> They said when he came from Burma, he did not perform the purifi-
> cation ceremony which was required. So the ghosts of the Japanese he
> killed followed him. And made him mad. He did not perform the
> ceremony because he did not have money. It was expensive. Anything
> he saved he spent on his food . . . He was either hungry or angry or both.
> (p. 70)

The fat rich men in Europe and their black cousins in revolutionary Africa are stuffing their attaché-cases with new bills. The

moralist politicians are performing their oratorical ballet on the podium and drinking their ice-cold beer in hotels in independent Africa where most of the black faces are servants or stooges, where there is only one telephone that does not work, and where the air-conditioning became faulty the day it was installed. The career civil servants, forever patriotic and devoted to their duty, are sticking their noses in the torn pages of the British General Orders while their multi-coloured girlfriends are sitting on their laps and already thinking of the night out at their second profession called prostitution. And Abotsi has no money to perform a simple sacrifice that might have saved his sanity. But people don't know.

Abotsi's friend, Tailor, knows. Tailor used to be rich, smuggling *akpeteshie*.[15] Unfortunately for him, he was caught and imprisoned. His family abandoned him. 'The hands that have eaten with chiefs' are now empty. Alone, broke, and broken, he went back to his old trade of making clothes. A loser has no friends. Tailor has no customers. Bitterness sets in. One day, the catechist comes in to ask for church dues. Tailor chases him off with a matchet. Christians are 'thieves and liars'.

Tailor's friendship with Abotsi is one of equals. Tailor is the only one who understands him. When Abotsi falls gravely ill, it is Tailor who is called to take care of him. But hospitals, symbols of the nation's good health – which means bad health – are not meant for madmen and paupers. They have to stay in line and they will forever remain victims to the whims and caprices of pompous doctors, while the VIPs are cared for immediately. Abotsi is refused treatment although the nurse realizes that he may be dying. The paupers and madmen have to wait until tomorrow, only tomorrow never comes.

- Could the doctor come and see him?
- Doctor! What! You don't mean we should phone doctor because Abotsi is ill? What!
- Please, we beg you, please.
  He looked up briefly and rolled toward the telephone.
  He was fat and exuded extra food snatched from patients too ill to eat.
- Is that doctor? ... Yes sir: no sir; I know him. No he is not exactly mad. No sir. All right, sir. Tomorrow then, sir. A nurse came ... muttering something about people who smelled like he-goats being brought into hospitals. (p. 73)

Abotsi dies before his tomorrow comes. The poor, eternal sufferers on earth continue to suffer in after-life. Christian lies about judgement day 'Our Father who art in heaven – and on earth –

do as You please.' Catechism is the most important subject in the primary school. Learn about God's work or learn to take those stinging lashes from the teacher's cane. Attend God's ceremony or the headmaster will attend to your backside. There is Paku, a schoolboy older than his mates. He is absent from Palm Service because he has to check animal traps that will provide for his empty stomach. The authorities want to give him the big stick on the buttocks and the young man says no. He is expelled. Months later, back he comes in his new army uniform. The headmaster, quick to forgive and smart enough to realize nationalist talent when he sees one, gives a moving speech in Paku's honour. 'Everyone must brighten the corner where he is.' Paku, the rejected stone, has become the head of his corner. The last shall be the first but, right now, the first remains where he is and the last must remain the last, except he has a gun. And Abotsi is refused burial in the Christian cemetery. He is finally laid to rest in a pagan cemetery. May his pagan soul rest in pagan peace.

Like Abotsi, Dzesan is a Burma veteran. He says the government has cheated him out of his money, so he takes his gun and opens fire on everyone in sight. Sule is also a veteran.

> He put himself in uniform, made one for his five-year-old son, and marched with the infant from dawn till noon every market day on the main road singing 'Kayiwawa beturi', the theme song of his Burmese days. He screamed orders at his platoon – i.e. his five-year-old son – who responded in little jerks, sweat streaming down his comely little face. His Father's eyes would be red as he screamed. (p. 78)

Our Father who art on earth, please lead us to the land of promise. Dzesan asks for his money and they drag him away. He wants to kill more Japanese – after all, they are the enemies of our great colonial masters – and they drag him away. He knows colonialism is not over, anyway. Once a slave, always a slave. The empire shall never die, says the great colonial officer. Long live our gracious queen. Sule knows, too. His son must be taught how to be strong, how to fight the white man's war. For the white man is now the black man. Only the skin tone has changed. Talk of effects of the scorching sun of Africa ...

Madness in the church. Repeat the Lord's Prayer a million times, especially the part asking not to be led into temptation. Rev. Paul Dumenyo starts with great credentials: excellent student, fervent disciple of the Almighty, a perfect respecter of the Holy Word. Then, he has an affair with a student who becomes pregnant. Meanwhile, Paul's mother has chosen a bride for him in their village. On the wedding day, in God's house, in the presence of the whole pious congregation, the pregnant girl rushes in crying and telling of her inflated state. So the holy Paul, bent upon paying the penalty for his sin and upon changing the evil ways of the world, becomes a pilgrim. He takes to the streets in his clerical clothes, keeps walking and singing, his face lifted to the sky. He says he is going to heaven and vows that he is not mad. 'Some say that I am mad. I am not. It is only that I have seen the evil ways of the world' (p. 95). The evil ways of the world include human love and harmony, so say Paul's teachers, and they are excellent Christian soldiers.

Amamu's Madness

People just don't know. But Amamu does, he has known from the time he was a little boy running around with his mates throwing stones at madmen. The adults of the community, wise men all, incessantly tell the children never to be friendly with madmen. They are the enemies of society, outcasts fit to be thrown to the dogs, to be exorcized like the evil spirits that they are. Offspring of wise parents, these children will naturally grow up to be wise men in their turn, eternal sleepwalkers in a land of sweet filth and blissful corruption. They will never know. But Amamu has always known. He is the little boy that stands out among the group of youngsters following Abotsi to his final resting place.

> The children from the house followed at a distance. Their mother had forbidden them to come. But they knew him. Especially the wild-eyed strapping lad of twelve. He was his friend. He gave him snail tops and trimmed them for him ... The wild-eyed lad slept fitfully that night. He saw him in his dreams, sitting propped against the coconut tree staring at the well, telling long tales of Burma and Japanese and rations, and of magic over guns. (p. 74).

Little Amamu knows. While his fellow urchins are zealously taking aim at Rev. Dumenyo,

> ... he alone did not cast a stone. He stood, trapped like an animal. He could hear the shout of his comrades, as they chased their enemy into the Presbyterian Mission Compound. (p. 96)

The grown-up Amamu, learned lawyer that he is, remembers the incident vividly until the day he dies.

> The boys rushed shouting, He is here, he is here: I cast down my stone and went home to my mother's house with the coconut tree and the

salt-water well. Then I heard the long anguished ululation of the funeral procession from the Holy Trinity Cathedral where the choir was rehearsing the Messiah winding towards Osu cemetery. The General is dead. The General is dead, and the nation is weeping. (p. 105)

Weep for the dead general. Another saviour is gone. The best. The most patriotic. The one and only messiah. He is gone for ever, never to be replaced by anyone else. Tomorrow brings another messiah, however, exactly like the departed general, even better than he ever was. Adulation. Praise-songs. Hero-worship. In dark Africa, upper-class thieves, and high-up nonentities are the greatest heroes. Throw stones at the madman but shed hot tears for the moralist general whose girlfriend rides in the nation's limousine while his wife, armed with the marriage licence, is hidden away in the closet.

Amamu knows, he has always known. Before going overseas in search of the golden fleece, he works as a reporter with a socialist newspaper. He is sent to report on an incident in a village where the traditional durbar has been suspended by the colonial authorities. The ancestral stools are seized by government officials, the riot squad is called in, three people are killed, and the village is razed to the ground. Police loot houses and snatch several women as a reward for the execution of their patriotic duties. Amamu's article is shelved by his editor. The latter does not want to step on any toes. Propriety dictates silence. Mutual guilt dictates compromise. A man who lives in a glass house does not throw stones. Socialism must give way to nationalism.

Amamu knows. Nationalism means you should 'chop make I chop some'. If you do not want it, then let others have it. The worst you can do is to complain of nationalistic corruption and graft and patriotic thievery. The best you can do, must do, to survive is to be an integral part of the wise majority. Close your eyes, pretend not to see. Hold your peace and play dumb. But Amamu finds it impossible to do that. Perverse morality instead of heavenly immorality. Stupid honesty in place of prudent dishonesty. When the man – 'too much book only turns a man's head' – starts to discuss these weird subjects, eyes glare at him with spite; some glance at him in wonderment. The man has got to be mad.

We have all been taught the golden lesson from the very beginning: never pay attention to the raving of a madman. He does not know what he is saying. Anyone speaking the language of the minority must have his head examined. They should send him to the asylum. Of all the interesting things happening in our revolutionary Africa, how come the man can only talk of these crazy things? The fool! The fact that he wants nothing, asks for nothing from us, makes us hate him even more.[16] After all, we Africans are the most hospitable people on earth, the most kind-hearted, the most willing to help the needy. If you are not among the needy, then we have no use for you. You see, we have to look down upon somebody, benevolently. That is why Amamu has to stay on the outside; he is learned; he is superior; he is genuinely concerned about the decay of our beautiful motherland. He has to be mad.

It all dates back to many years ago, at Amamu's birth. Son of Jonathan, the postmaster, and Dzenawo, the child resembled his grandfather, 'a tree on which they all leaned and under whose shade they all took shelter' (p. 12). There was something different, special, about the child and that never changed. Unfortunately, the grown man refuses to provide shade for a race of corrupt, apathetic parasites and slaves who are ready to wallow in their non-identity for ever.

Later in life, the strapping boy went to live on the coast where he found his almond tree and, more important, his 'woman of the sea'. 'I told her my story of the nature and the bitterness of the birth-water that nurtured me. Of the womb that carried me. Of the pangs that delivered me' (p. 4).

Images of mammy-water. Images of sorrow, and pain, and sad-ness, temporarily. Images of joy, and happiness, and hope, per-manently. The innocence of the child. The ecstasy of ideal love. In all his adventures at home and abroad, Amamu always remembers his woman of the sea. In a dream beyond the trite reality of this world, the youth disappears, walking hand in hand with his woman, exploring and appreciating nature, living life in innocent happiness. But that is not life as it is lived every day. Soon comes a series of eye-openers for the growing child. The disappointment of failure. The civilizing corruption of society. The joyful apathy and defeatism of the vast majority of sleepwalkers. The prostitution of traditions. The inhumanity of messiahs. The constant shadow of death. A man aspires to great heights, and the greatness lies in the 'fat books' of the 'wise colonialists'. He devours them and soon obtains the diploma. He has been away, so he returns home ready to contribute to the advancement of his nation. Only he does not know the first rule of the patriotic game: never you attempt to change or criticize anything. Who do you think you are, anyway?

The man begins to suffer inside, begins to die ever such a little. It has been established that he is set apart from the rest. There can be no change. The woman of the sea is not here among mere mortals; maybe only she – and he is convinced that only she – can help him to survive the physical and moral holocaust threatening to consume a whole race. 'Let us return to the magic of our birth for which we mourn' (p. 29). But the magic hour is lost for ever. It never happens more than once and it is impossible to hold down. The wise ones will tell you not to be naïve; a child's world is unreal, the child must grow up into adulthood, he must meet his responsibilities and enjoy the 'good things' of life. Good education. Marriage and a wife. Home. 'Home is my desolation, home is my anguish, home is my drink of hysop and tears. Where is home? (p. 29).'

Home is where Alice lives. A cultivated been-to, a solid bourgeoise, daughter of a retired judge. Artificial teeth. Artificial hair. Artificial life. Amamu finally has nothing to say to her. He finds real love in an unexpected corner, in the run-down hole inhabited by a prostitute he once defended, Adisa. Now, everyone knows the man is mad. 'Prostitute-lover.'

Temporary peace. Love imprisoned in a dead-end situation. Alice knows about Adisa. She threatens divorce, tortures the lover of a street woman. Death strikes close to home: Amamu loses his brother. His headaches become more constant than ever before. Alice does not care about those headaches. Let the bastard suffer. She breaks a china plate on his head. He offers no resistance, just keeps staring. He knows that love, true love, does not distinguish between social classes.

People just don't know. Amamu does. He sees the suffering of the squatters in Nima, he witnesses the moral torture of his own servant, Yaro, whose brother, caught stealing, is beaten to death by the zealous representatives of the law.

Amamu's Vision

The headaches become worse. They say the man is mad and they refuse to see that his vision is clear, precise, about the approaching destruction of a people that do not seem to want a better destiny.

> We need flowers, gay as those in my butterfly fields to make garlands for our leaders plus our natural rulers ... Then they will perform the dance of death for us to the music of electric guitars and drums studded with skulls outdoored from old ancestral shrines ... The banquet hall shall be flooded in light and flowers, a little girl shall take a bow before the chief leader, who will be trying deperately to suppress a fart. He is seriously concerned about the moral decay of the nation. (pp. 115–16)

The leaders must not fart in public, but they have no qualms about stealing in public from the public. We have always loved to celebrate, so our leaders drag their overweight bodies into the national hall, wash their hands with champagne, and dance to African music played with the latest foreign instruments.

And the madman's vision continues: 'And with illuminating logic, solutions shall be produced in Constituent Assemblies where the honourable member of Manso west will plead with tears that the use of contraceptives be spelled out and entrenched in the constitution' (p. 117).

Naturally, our leaders and their girlfriends have to be fully protected against any eventuality. They are very wary not to flood the nation with illegitimate children. One should also remember that family planning, the pill, zero population growth, are all 'civilized' notions and practices, preached to us by those wanting us to jet-propel our beloved nation into the twentieth century.

Still another prediction by the crazy man: 'In the age of bombs and the perfection of political stratagems, a host shall flee their homeland, and lap up the paradise of exile lands. Old men shall die in transit between little arguments produced by trained soldiers from Sandhurst' (p. 133).

The predictions are already being borne out by present actions and events. The madman's vision has become reality. Think of the innumerable Africans in exile. Language forgotten. Family abandoned. Civilization of the suit and tie. Civilization of money and material. Mutual spite between leaders and rebels. And Africa continues to move backwards. Think of the meaningless internecine wars. Military and undisciplined discipline. Uniforms quickly exchanged for mufti. Corruption both civilian and military. Temporary presidency turned into personalized inheritance. And Africa has jet-propelled herself into the twenty-first century.

Death, the Ultimate Answer

Amamu becomes more and more depressed. As he finds out, if you cannot cope with the decay, if you cannot hope against hope, death is the ultimate answer. 'There is only one possibility: Despair and die' (p. 116). His despair stems from the decay seen all over the unconcerned nation. Others refuse to see the decay and, a most depressing fact, he, like other intellectuals, 'the best of nature's freaks' (p. 134), keeps talking of change without doing anything concrete to bring it about. Talk. Big, empty talk. While children are dying and are seeing their parents die. While many are starving. While the leaders are feasting and taking summer vacations in their European villas. The revolution is not for today, not for tomorrow, maybe not for ever.

> And this earth, my brother, shall claim me for her own. Tonight there is a deep silence in the land. Joe says it is the hush hour of the holocaust: it is the silence of death. (p. 116)

The 'funny man' is thus resigned to his death. He knows he cannot escape now. It is too late. He sees his passing as a sacrifice; at least that will give a meaning to his existence: 'One should die so that the rest shall be saved' (p. 143). Sacrifice in the African mould. The gods do understand, but only when the sacrifice is properly performed, only when the people understand the purpose of the symbolic act. Unfortunately, these people do not understand. They do not know. Amamu's sacrifice is in vain.

One day his headaches become totally unbearable. He can no longer live without his maiden of the sea. The search has to begin at once. He steps out of his house, shoeless, with only a singlet on his back. He walks, runs, walks, tirelessly towards the sea. The strength of a madman. The fear instilled in every living being by a strange man. People run from him. Dogs bark as he passes by. But he sees no one, he hears no one. His maiden of the sea and his almond tree are waiting on the coast, and he must hurry. There, at last. The maiden rises from the sea. Peace. No more pain, no more sorrow. Bliss. It is 'the hour of his salvation'.

Sacrifice for the ills of a nation that deliberately wallows in the mud. A nation that does not know. Amamu would have done best to remain for ever on 'his island of solitude and joy'. Impossible. People will seek you out, offer you a helping hand that will only drag you farther into the pit. Besides, you are part of the community and must not enjoy your island of bliss alone. And you must not refuse to help, *or to be helped*. They come for Amamu after the third day. He is there gazing at the sea, under his almond tree. His father and mother are with them. They take him away to the mental hospital. There, he dies.

The kind doctor in charge intones: 'Most of the time we cannot understand' (p. 183). Amamu's father adds a word: 'Only God knows.' God, always God. Memories of the catechism class, the teacher's cane lashing at the wetted bare buttocks, hitting hard with Christian piety and vengeance. Memories of Christian education in an independent colony. Honour thy father and thy mother, and let thyself be honoured by all those that must remain inferior to thee. Memories of Christian mission in Africa. Seize the land from the heathens and give them the Holy Bible.

We cannot understand. We refuse to understand. Poor, blind people. Like the professional beggar feigning blindness by day, making his pile of money, and retiring to his mansion by night. Like the moralist leader extolling the nation to great heights and uprightness while he himself has a million skeletons in his closet. Like all of us refusing to see the decay closing in and destroying a society that has always prided itself on its unparalleled quality. Tranquillizers for the mad. Sedatives. Pills. Let him cool off. He needs a rest, that is all. They will never stop doing what they are not supposed to do, the idiots! Put him in the small room, and if he makes any trouble, hit him hard; they need to be brutalized, sometime ... We do not understand; we do not know.

Baako knows. So does Elizabeth. And Mugo. And Sekoni.[17] They know that in Africa, 'there will be authentic disalienation only when things, in the most materialistic sense, will have recovered their place'.[18] They know that in the society that gives birth to their madness lies the basic cause of the problems preying on their minds. They know that they are saner than others, many of whom see the rationale behind their actions and attitudes but are themselves too scared or cowardly to join them in their lonely, condemned world. Significantly, the artistic creators of these madmen are mostly in agreement with their point of view. The tragedy is that the lonely voice of the madman is overwhelmed by the silence of the 'wise' majority in the wasteland. Awoonor knows, but he still insists that that voice must be brought out loud to shame the silent saints. He knows that the end of it all is death, and there is no turning back.

Amamu knows, and he is dead.

NOTES

1. Into this category would fall many of the heroes of African novels dealing with the colonial experience.
2. Chinua Achebe, *Arrow of God*, London, Heinemann (AWS 16), 1965. New York, Doubleday, 1969.

3. ibid., p. 230.

4. Ngugi, *A Grain of Wheat*, London, Heinemann (AWS 36), 1968. New York, Humanities, 1968.

5. Frantz Fanon, *The Wretched of the Earth*, New York, Grove Press, 1968, p. 249. In this excellent analysis of the colonial experience, Fanon specifically examines cases of mental disorder among Algerians fighting the war of liberation.

6. Bessie Head, *A Question of Power*, London, Heinemann (AWS 149), 1973. New York, Humanities, 1977.

7. *Masarwa*, 'the equivalent of "nigger"', a term of contempt which means, obliquely, low, filthy'. See Bessie Head, *Maru*, London, Heinemann (AWS 101), 1972, p. 12.

8. Ayi Kwei Armah, *Fragments*, London, Heinemann (AWS 1974). Boston, Houghton Mifflin, 1970.

9. Armah, *Why Are We So Blest?*, London, Heinemann (AWS 1974). New York, Doubleday/Anchor, 1972, p. 84.

10. Kofi Awoonor, *This Earth, My Brother* ..., London, Heinemann (AWS 108), 1972. When quotations are used from this text, I have simply inserted their page number after the quotations. Where quotations have been placed among the notes, I have of course cited the title of the text.

11. Term used naturally from the viewpoint of the vast majority of 'law-abiding citizens'.

12. *Masa*, the africanized form of 'master', used by servants for their colonial employers; later transferred to their replacements, the African masters.

13. *This Earth, My Brother* ..., p. 158; 'sabe book' = knows book, i.e. educated.

14. ibid., pp. 25–6.

15. *Akpeteshie*, a very strong local wine, called various names in African countries. It has been banned in favour of imported liquor whose effect on the body has hardly been proved to be any less destructive than that of the local product.

16. See p. 1. In his notebook, Amamu discusses his relationship with others.

17. Sekoni, one of the main protagonists of Wole Soyinka's *The Interpreters*, is a foreign-trained engineer who, upon returning home, works hard to produce an experimentral power station only to see it rejected by the ignorant establishment. The trauma and frustration of life at home make him insane.

18. Frantz Fanon, *Peau noire masques blancs*, Paris, Seuil, 1952, p. 11. Translated from the French by the present author.

Ngugi's *Petals of Blood*

Eustace Palmer

Ngugi wa Thiong'o's latest novel, *Petals of Blood*, is easily his most representative. It incorporates all the major preoccupations of his career as a novelist. Indeed, it is not too much of an exaggeration to say that this most ambitious and comprehensive work incorporates all the major preoccupations of the African novel from its beginnings to the present day. The African novel, generally speaking, is a reaction to the consequences of imperialist occupation and exploitation, a historical process which comprised three phases. First, there was the phase of imperialist conquest with consequent erosion of African values and disruption of traditional society; this was followed by the phase of anti-imperialist rebellion; finally there was the period of post-independence, largely one of readjustment in an attempt to rediscover lost values. Ngugi's first novel, *The River Between*, was concerned with the first phase, since it portrayed the disruption caused within traditional society by an alien educational and religious system; the second and third, *Weep Not, Child* and *A Grain of Wheat*, deal with the second phase, the Mau Mau struggle for liberation. *Petals of Blood* deals not only with these two phases, but also gives an extended treatment of the third. Of all African novels it probably presents the most comprehensive analysis so far of the evils perpetrated in independent African society by black imperialists. It subsumes several other aspects of Ngugi's earlier novels – the widespread and effective use of symbols and images, the concern with education and religion, the resourceful and morally courageous women and the indecisive young men who are called upon to play a major role in society, but are unable to do so successfully because they are plagued by a sense of insecurity or guilt. Even the narrative technique seems to be a conglomerate of the methods of *A Grain of Wheat* on the one hand, and *The River Between* and *Weep Not, Child* on the other. The novel is constructed on grand epic proportions, but it is an epic, not just of the

East African struggle, but of the entire African struggle. No wonder it has been described as the most ambitious novel yet realized by the pen of an African.[1]

The narrative technique of *Petals of Blood* is not as complex or subtle as that of *A Grain of Wheat*. Most of it is told in the form of reminiscences rather than flashbacks. The story starts in the present with the four main characters – Wanja, Karega, Abdulla and Munira – in jail on suspicion of being implicated in the murder of the three African directors of the theng'eta brewery. It really takes the form of Munira's recollections as he sits down in his cell writing copious notes in order to clear his own mind about the significance of the events and satisfy the demands of the probing police inspector. Thus from the present the story goes back twelve years to Munira's recollections of his first arrival in Ilmorog. It periodically returns to the present and Munira in his cell, and on one or two occasions goes even further back in time to his experiences while at school at Siriana in the 1940s and the Mau Mau uprising of the 1950s. Otherwise the novel moves progressively forward from Munira's first arrival to the present, and to the resolution of the murder riddle. It would be inaccurate to say that *Petals of Blood* makes use of shifting chronology. The narrative method consists for the most part of reminiscences which nevertheless progress sequentially.

The novel's title, *Petals of Blood*, points to the centrality of the symbolism in the elucidation of the meaning. One dominant symbol cluster relates to flowers and other forms of vegetation. At times these suggest regeneration, fecundity, and luxuriance; but more often, as in the poem by Derek Walcott with which Ngugi prefixes the novel, they suggest destruction, corruption, evil, the unnatural, and death. It might seem from this poem that the petals of blood of the title are connected with the 'potent ginger lily', one of the destructive and repulsive plants which give a normally natural and beautiful scene an eerie, unnatural, and evil aura. The imagery therefore suggests the distortion of things from the normal and natural to the abnormal and evil, and the introduction of chaos and destruction where there should be beauty and order. But in the body of the novel itself we discover that the flower with the petals of blood belongs to a plant that grows wild in the plains and, unlike the flower in the prefix, is itself the victim of evil. Its innocence, like that of Blake's sick rose, has been destroyed by the agents of corruption. The flower thus becomes a symbol of the entire society Ngugi is concerned with – potentially healthy, beautiful, and productive, but its potential unrealized and itself destroyed by the agents of corruption and death.

The plant with the petals of blood is actually the theng'eta plant which grows wild on the plains that are associated with luxuriance, vitality and vigour. It is also a plant that is associated with Ilmorog's pristine traditional splendour, for it was used in making the drink which inspired the old seers, poets, and players. It also symbolizes truth and purity, for the flower with the four red petals was used to purify the drink and the drink itself had the remarkable quality of forcing people to confront the truth about themselves: 'Only you must take it with faith and purity in your hearts.' Therefore, when the people of Ilmorog, under the leadership of Nyakinyua, that staunch upholder of traditional values, decide to re-engage in the production of theng'eta, it symbolizes a decision to return to the purity of their traditional values, and the transformation of theng'eta into a debased modern spirit by the capitalists suggests the erosion of traditional values and the destruction of traditional innocence by the corrupt and depraved agents of modernism.

The drought is another pervasive symbol in the novel. Here Ngugi has used an actual historical and ecological fact – the recent disastrous drought in most of Africa – for symbolic purposes with telling effect. The drought symbolism is often juxtaposed with rain symbolism suggesting the fecundity and luxuriance which the region, under normal circumstances, ought to enjoy. The telling descriptions of the people's suffering, the poverty of the harvest, the scarcity of food, and the death of the animals ought to convince us that the drought is an actual physical fact. Yet there is no denying its symbolic significance as well. The drought is also political, spiritual, economic and emotional, as with Wanja who, yearning after a release from barrenness, becomes restless and moody in proportion to the aridity of the environment. The drought generally refers to the people's deprivation of all those things which should make life meaningful.

Then there is the symbol of maiming which also relates to the people's spiritual condition. The one-legged but very resourceful Abdulla is the most concrete symbol in the novel of man's inhumanity to man. But the physical maiming, which the Ilmorogians almost extend to his donkey on one occasion, also relates to a spiritual condition, for the people all carry maimed souls. Abdulla's lame leg is therefore merely the physical manifestation of a general spiritual fact.

The scene of most of the events of the novel is the community of Ilmorog which grows from a small traditional village into a modern capitalist complex. But Ilmorog could easily have been any other Kenyan village. It is a microcosm of Kenyan society as a whole and its experiences are a paradigm of what happened to a number of similar Kenyan communities. Ngugi's very compelling historical presentation gives us glimpses of the glory of Ilmorog's past. It was a purely traditional society untouched by Western values, where the dignified courageous peasants reckoned their wealth in land, cows, and goats. At the start of Part Two, in a most impressive chapter called 'The Journey', Ngugi, making use of legend and oral lore, celebrates the valour of the first heroes of this community, showing the gradual change from a largely nomadic to an agrarian civilization, and presenting their prosperity, contentment and sense of community. The imperialist intrusion which soon followed and the inhumanities perpetrated were the first blow to Ilmorog's pride, and the consequent disruption heralded the beginning of Ilmorog's decline.

So that even before the period of the start of the novel we see that the once thriving community of Ilmorog has fallen on evil times. And at the start it appears as a desolate unprogressive place from which the young are only too happy to get away. It is significant that the only young people who come to Ilmorog and stay there have all been spiritually maimed in one way or another. And for the first part of the novel Ilmorog is blighted by the drought and her suffering enhanced by the neglect of the political authorities, in particular its Member of Parliament, Nderi, who having got the people's votes stays away in the city, concentrating instead on his capitalist enterprises. Eventually Karega, the bright young teacher in the community, puts forward the daring plan that they should march to the city, confront their Member of Parliament with their problems and force him to acknowledge his responsibilities. With the march the people of Ilmorog rediscover that pristine Ilmorog spirit when their warriors went in pursuit of hostile nations who had stolen their cattle and goats and would not return until they had recovered their stolen wealth. The march reminds the reader of a similar exercise in Ousmane's *God's Bits of Wood*, and like that one it is an ordeal which tests the people's capacity for endurance and brings out the best in the leaders like Wanja, Karega and Abdulla. The success of the march in alerting the people of Kenya as a whole to the plight of the people of Ilmorog is the turning point in the latters' fortunes.

Ilmorog is now earmarked for rapid development and there are visible signs of a revival in the small community. The revival is suggested by means of rain symbolism, the rain which falls immediately after the march being, in the elders' opinion, God's response to their sacrifice. Ngugi also uses images of fecundity and fertilization to suggest the earth's response to the rain: 'This waiting earth: its readiness powered Wanja's wings of expectation and numerous desires. Feverishly she looked out for tomorrow, waiting like the other women, for earth to crack, earth to be thrust open by the naked shoots of life.' Some of the images are taken from the oral tradition:

> The older folk told stories of how Rain, Sun and Wind went a-wooing Earth, Sister of Moon, and it was rain who carried the day, and that was why Earth grew a swollen belly after being touched by Rain. Others said no, the raindrops were really the sperms of God and that even human beings sprang from the womb on Mother Earth soon after the original passionate downpour, torrential waters of the beginning.

And the spirit of rebirth finds a counterpart in the erstwhile arid souls of individuals: 'Wanja was possessed of the rain-spirit. She walked through it, clothes drenched, skirt-hem tight against her thighs, revelling in the waters from heaven.' In Ngugi's novels walking in the rain is always a good sign.

But the luxuriance which now pervades Ilmorog is different from earlier ones, since it is punctuated by doubts. The people, with memories of their experiences in the city fresh in their minds, are uncomfortably aware of a more troubled world 'which could, any time, descend upon them, breaking asunder their rain-filled sun-warmed calm'. The new birth is an unknown power bringing uncertainty in its wake and intimations of forces other than droughts threatening the security and tranquillity of their lives.

And the people's doubts are fully justified. As the capitalists move in with their roads, banks, factories, distilleries, and estate agencies, the old traditional Ilmorog is irreparably destroyed. The destruction of the hut of the mysterious spirit Mwathi by a giant bulldozer is the concrete symbol of the annihilation of a once proud society by the forces of modernism. The reader watches with profound sympathy as the bewildered and deceived peasants, unable to match the business acumen and financial standing of the big men from the city, inevitably lose their lands and all their possessions and helplessly degenerate into labourers or worse. The courageous Nyakinyua, who is obviously the embodiment of all the traditional values, is given real tragic stature when she decides, single-handed, to put up a determined fight against all those forces that have deprived her of her heritage. Her resolution constitutes the last flagging attempt of a once dignified and secure society to resist the encroachments of the new men. But it is doomed to failure, and the reluctance of others to support her suggests the demoralization that now pervades. Ilmorog is soon transformed into a capitalist complex with all the attendant problems of prostitution, social inequalities, and inadequate housing. It has been twice exploited and destroyed; once by the white imperialists, and now by their successors, the black imperialists.

The hero of the novel is Munira, the teacher who decides to settle in Ilmorog. Devotees of Ngugi cannot fail to recognize in him reminiscences of Ngugi's three earlier heroes – Njoroge in Weep Not, Child who pins his faith on education and refuses to face the world of adult responsibility, Waiyaki who in spite of his admirable qualities fails to attain the stature of a manly hero through his indecision, and Mugo who is tortured by a sense of guilt and insecurity. In fact Munira is an anti-hero, an ultra-sensitive young man whose life is a failure. Unlike Mugo, his sense of insecurity degenerates into an inferiority complex, a conviction of his irretrievable mediocrity. During his student days at Siriana he had been involved in a strike resulting in his expulsion, but where the other leaders, like Chui, were able to reorganize their lives by sheer determination and resilience, Munira, lacking the capacity to engage in the world of adult endeavour and experience, can only drift from one failure to another. He is a passive spectator, hovering on the fringes of important actions, and withdrawing from involvement, like Mugo. But where Mugo wished to be left alone as an act of deliberate policy in order to guarantee success, Munira's desire for non-involvement is a concomitant of his character and personality. He recalls not just Ngugi's own Njoroge who dreads the world of adult competition and struggle and is basically immature, but also Dostoyevsky's insecure introspective heroes.

Ngugi's presentation of Munira unwittingly lends credibility to the adage 'He who can does; he who can't teaches.' His passionate desire being for a safe place in which to hide and do some work, Munira withdraws to the remote village of Ilmorog and settles down to the career of a teacher. There, safe from the competitive adult world, away from the glare of publicity, the intellectually timid Munira can create his own empire and at last be a leader and a success. He is therefore at his best in the classroom.

Ngugi uses significant images to define his character. First of all there is the image of the closed space – like the classroom. While the people of Ilmorog as a whole are associated with open spaces – the fields and the plains – Munira is always associated with the four walls of a room: 'And they were all busy putting seeds in the soil, and he watched them from the safety of his classroom or of Abdulla's shop.' This recalls Mugo's symbolic bolting of himself inside his hut in order to guarantee security against the encroachments of the outside world. Then there are images of shadows and twilight. Munira relishes twilight because it is the prelude to the 'awesome shadow', the darkness into which he can lose himself, merge with everything, and achieve anonymity.

Ngugi demonstrates sure psychological insight in the presentation of his hero. We have not only his thoughts and actions, but the forces which have conditioned him. His shrinking introspective personality is an unconscious reaction partly to his overbearing, contemptuous, and superbly successful proprietor-father, and partly to his materialistic and no less successful brothers and sisters who have been able to carve niches for themselves in the highly competitive capitalist Kenyan society. But although Munira possesses a certain measure of idealism, it would be a mistake to suppose that his withdrawal from involvement is due to an idealistic revulsion against his corrupt society; it is due more to cowardice than to idealism.

Like Waiyaki in The River Between, Munira succeeds in becoming accepted and idolized by the people as a teacher. He thus achieves a sense of fulfilment at last and his love for Wanja also draws him into involvement. The sexual prowess he demonstrates in his love-making helps give him that sense of mastery and masculinity that he has completely failed to manifest in the world of adult affairs. But it is the association with Wanja which reveals the cracks in his personality and eventually leads to his disintegration. For when the young Karega arrives on the scene he deals the final blow to Munira's self-respect by winning Wanja's love. The section of the novel in which Ngugi analyses the rivalry between the two men for Wanja's love is most compelling. His presentation of Munira the basically insecure man, tortured by sexual jealousy, is very realistic. Munira takes every opportunity to find fault with Karega's work and finally engineers his dismissal on a most flimsy pretext. He thus becomes a hypocrite, liar and destroyer who is no different from the other forces that have plagued and degraded the idealistic Karega. By his squalid manoeuvres he alienates whatever sympathy the reader might initially have been tempted to accord him.

Munira's transformation into a religious fanatic at the end is one of this novel's major weaknesses. A violent death seems to be a logical and well-deserved conclusion to the fortunes of the three African directors of the theng'eta brewery, but that it should be brought about by a fire started in a moment of inspiration by a religious fanatic seems a melodramatic contrivance which takes a remarkably serious work back to the level of the detective thriller. Munira's plunge into religious fanaticism at the moment when he sees his evangelistic one-time sweetheart is much too sudden to carry conviction. The art here seems much cruder than that we have come to associate with Ngugi. His decision to set fire to Wanja's brothel 'which mocked God's work on earth' and save Karega from the clutches of a woman whom he now sees as Jezebel is no more convincing. Karega hardly seems to be in need of this kind of salvation, both because Wanja's possessive hold over him is not demonstrated and because he seems perfectly capable of taking care of himself. Munira's decision can only be accepted as a sign of mental derangement: but the process of derangement is not demonstrated.

Wanja, the source of Munira's disintegration, is the most important woman in the novel. Unlike Munira who is associated with closed spaces, Wanja's dynamism and vitality are suggested by her association with the fields and the plains. She belongs to that remarkable breed of Ngugi women – Mwihaki, Nyambura, Muthoni, Mumbi, Wambuku – all of them brave, resilient, resourceful and determined. There is an element of masculinity in all of Ngugi's major women, just as there is an element of femininity in all of his major men. They probably have to be masculine to make up for their menfolk's indecision and lack of resolution. But there is no denying that it is the more masculine qualities of Wanja's character that are stressed. In spite of the assertions and references to her beauty, Ngugi does not succeed in creating a sense of her physical appeal to the same extent that Ouologuem does with Tambira in Bound to Violence or Ekwensi with Jagua in Jagua Nana. Apart from comments about her make-up, hair-do, and dress, there are hardly any detailed references to her physical features. Nor does Ngugi succeed in presenting the kind of mesmerizing hold a woman can exert over a man which Soyinka enacts so brilliantly with Simi in The Interpreters. Far from wishing to enslave men, Wanja's ruling passion throughout is the need to preserve her independence, and it is the enegery, drive, courage, and resourcefulness she brings to this task that impress us most. It is her energy, initiative, and inventiveness that begin the transformation and revival of Ilmorog.

Wanja is central to Ngugi's development of his theme of social disintegration. Her story represents the most thorough demonstration in African literature of the causes of prostitution in modern African societies. As a drop-out from school, Wanja is forced to play the tough city game in order to survive in that jungle and even after her regeneration in Ilmorog, when she had discovered a new sense of purpose in helping to engineer that society's revival, she is thrown back into high-class prostitution by the schemes of the new black imperialists. Wanja can be creative and imaginative, but she is also a practical realist who recognizes that in order to survive in this new society one must be prepared to use its weapons. Mere idealism will never do. Like Karega, we may not agree with her methods, but we can certainly appreciate her reasons. She is associated throughout the novel with fire symbolism, being involved in at least four fires: the first gruesome one in which her aunt is killed and which breeds in her a neurotic dread of fires; another which occurs during her life of prostitution in the city and in which she is almost destroyed; one accidentally started by Munira soon after Wanja's arrival in Ilmorog; and the final murderous conflagration deliberately engineered by Munira. The fire is significant on several levels. First, it is literally an agent of destruction, a threat to Wanja's existence; in this sense all the various occurrences of fire are a prefiguration of Munira's destructive act at the end. But on another level the fire represents a ritual of baptism. Wanja undergoes an ordeal by fire in which she is exposed to the horrors of existence; her character is tested, and she emerges slightly tarnished, perhaps, but toughened. On a third level the fire is a purifying agent, representing a kind of cleansing for Wanja. It reminds her of the fire of the beginning and the fire of the second coming which, like water, cleanses and brings purity to our earth of human cruelty and loneliness. Ironically, this is what Munira's arson at the end unwittingly does for her. After it she feels the stirrings of a new person who had been baptized by fire.

To a large extent *Petals of Blood* concentrates on the post-independence disillusionment which had only been hinted at at the end of *A Grain of Wheat*. It gives a most comprehensive picture of what the author sees as the evils pervasive in Kenya under black rule. The Member of Parliament whose corrupt activities were barely suggested in *A Grain of Wheat* appears as a real life-size character demonstrating his incompetence, corruption, and indifference to the people's suffering in a number of telling scenes. He has become one of the country's wealthiest capitalists, a fitting illustration of a common phenomenon in Africa – the use of politics as a stepping-stone to material aggrandizement. The party in power also comes in for the most scathing denunciation because of its corruption, thuggery, sectionalism, and indifference to the people's plight. In a grotesque parody of the anti-imperialist Mau Mau oath, the party forces people to swear an oath intended to perpetuate the complete dominance of a particular tribe. And all the time it blinds itself to the real problems of the country which are poverty, starvation, and inadequate housing and educational provision. Ngugi also shows tremendous concern about the clash between the old traditional values and the decadent values of a modern capitalist society. In particular, he exposes the tendency of the modern capitalists to debase those values, as when they convert the time-honoured songs of the initiation ritual into obscene entertainment at their parties, or pervert the oath-taking custom for the most sordid ends.

Ironically, it is those who almost sacrificed their lives during the Mau Mau struggle for liberation that are the most degraded and exploited in this independent Kenya. It is one of Abdulla's roles to emphasize this. Abdulla, who is potentially the most interesting character in the novel, ought to have been much further developed by Ngugi. He emerges as the most convincing moral spokesman. Originally a divided self because of his ambiguous racial origins, he is transformed into a man by the great liberation struggle which he had entered in the hope of bringing about a better day. His reminiscences give us as powerful glimpses of the suffering during the emergency as any to be found in the pages of *A Grain of Wheat*. His being maimed in the struggle is a concrete symbol of the sacrifice that had to be made. In this sense he is rather like his donkey with which he is closely associated. The donkey has always been a symbol of sacrifice – a scapegoat that takes the beatings on behalf of society. It is significant that Abdulla always refers to his donkey as his other leg, and when the people, in a desperate bid to propitiate the gods and end the drought, propose to use the donkey as a sacrificial victim and maim it, Abdulla correctly sees it as a maiming of his other leg. But after independence his disillusionment is, of course, total. During the march to the city, Abdulla, like Ousmane's Maimouna, becomes the rallying force, sustaining the others, in spite of his disability, by sheer resource-fulness. But in the midst of the ensuing prosperity he is degraded, ending up as the most abject peasant who is forced to sell skins and oranges for a living.

On the other hand it is the traitors of the people – Kimeria, Mzigo, Chui and Nderi – who prosper after independence. It is they who now ride the sleek Mercedes Benzes, own housing estates and resort to golf clubs once frequented by the white imperialists. Ngugi spares no pains in exposing the cynicism and hypocrisy of it all, just as he forcefully registers his concern at the exploitation of the toiling masses. He also stresses the fact that the nature of the system results in under-utilization or destruction of potential. Wanja and Karega, both of them highly intelligent and resourceful young people who could have made a most significant con-tribution to their nation's life, are forced to drop out of school. And because of his integrity and idealism Karega is persecuted by this society and forced to drift from menial job to menial job. There could be no more powerful symbol of the destruction of potential than Karega in a drunken stupor in Munira's room, after having been rescued from a bar-brawl.

Karega and the lawyer are the embodiments of Ngugi's moral and social positives in this novel. They are the spokesmen for his socialistic solutions. But while the lawyer, like Armah's teacher, is an idealized symbol of perfection and purity, a mere voice who gives his views in lengthy speeches, Karega is realistically evoked. Like Wanja he is a dynamic, vital individual associated with the plains, and he brings to his vocation as a teacher a drive and intellectual power which puts Munira's in the shade. Together he and Wanja act as forces of regeneration in Ilmorog. It is Karega who confirms the impression that Ngugi has been gradually leaning over to socialism as the solution to Africa's problems. But through this spokesman Karega, he also seems to imply that socialism was a natural way of life in traditional African society. Appalled by the capitalism and materialism he sees around him with its consequent injustice and inequalities, Karega comes to the conclusion that for a proper and equitable reorganization of our society we must go back to our African origins and learn lessons from the way in which the African peoples produced and organized their wealth before col-onialism. Such a study, Karega feels, would reveal systems which were fair and equitable, in which wealth was owned by those who produced it and where there was virtually no unemployment. In a bid to bring about this kind of socialist society in modern Kenya,

Karega becomes a trade union agitator, tirelessly mobilizing the workers and the masses until a world would be created in which 'the inherited inventive genius of man in culture and science from all ages and climes would be not the monopoly of a few, but for the use of all'. There can be little doubt that Ngugi endorses Karega's socialist analysis and solution – solidarity of the workers and the masses – as the hope for the future. But intelligent and idealistic though Karega is, his analysis involves oversimplifications and confusions. His view of the organization of African society in the past and his implication that it was colonialism that introduced injustice and inequalities will probably not stand up to scrutiny. It is doubtful whether his creator has thought out the solutions to these problems more clearly than Karega has.

The confusions are even more blatant when one considers Ngugi's treatment of the theme of education, which has assumed a special importance in all his works. In this novel, as in the earlier ones, education is seen by the people as the hope for the future and Karega and Munira, like the teachers in the other novels, are lionized and treated as cultural and political heroes. But the treatment of the theme is taken one stage further. The purpose and content of imperialist education is thoroughly scrutinized and its relevance to the African situation questioned. It is presented as an oppressive, irrelevant, and racialist system geared towards the perpetuation of white domination and instilling into the pupils a respect for British institutions and attitudes. When Karega and his revolutionary school contemporaries organize strikes, first against the white Cambridge Fraudsham and then against the black Chui, they demand an African content to the education they have been receiving. They object to a system which teaches them about the European environment and demand one which will make them know themselves and their own environment better. Most reasonable readers would endorse these demands. But when they go on to call for the abolition of the prefectorial system and the 'knightly order of masters and menials', cry up black power, demand to elect their own leaders, call themselves African populists and object to being taught world history and world literature, they surely reveal themselves as immature adolescents who are incapable of making discriminations of value. They would throw out the baby with the bath water. The lawyer is right in asking Karega 'What did you really want?' And not surprisingly, Karega does not seem to know. But Ngugi ought to know. However, he has given no clear indication whether he endorses Karega's stand on education.

Organized religion also comes in for some very savage satire in this novel. Christianity, which in earlier novels was shown to exercise a firm hold over the lives of the people, is presented here as oppressive, unsympathetic, and hypocritical. Munira's father, who is a patriarch of the church as well as a pillar of the state, is actually a capitalist and black slaver of the most rabid sort. This determined opportunist who in his younger days had turned his back on traditional society, now wholeheartedly participates in the sordid exploitation of the masses. Like Joshua's in *The River Between*, his religion is a life-denying force which has stifled the life in Munira's wife and children. Essentially he is an irreligious and godless man who cannot see that his Christianity ought to preclude the taking of an oath geared towards the consolidation of tribalism. The behaviour of the Revs Kamau and Jerrod reinforces this impression of religious bankruptcy. The latter would rather read a sermon to starving itinerants about the need for industry than succour their wants and help a sick boy receive medical attention. And when Ilmorog attains prosperity he becomes a society clergyman, the vicar of the most fashionable church in the neighbourhood. The church is, in fact, a great proprietor, its priests being little different from the other black capitalists and imperialists.

Ngugi has often been accused of not doing enough to impart an African flavour to the language of his novels. This charge could certainly not be laid against *Petals of Blood*, where Ngugi makes extensive use of proverbs and songs, rendering them directly, at times, in the indigenous language. In fact the extensive use of the oral tradition in this novel reinforces one's sense of a society that used to be cohesive and dignified, and in most cases the relevance of the songs and legends can be demonstrated.

Petals of Blood has been described by one reviewer as a rambling novel.[2] This is unjust. Nevertheless, on putting down the novel the reader has an uneasy feeling that Ngugi has been too ambitious, that he has attempted to do too much within the compass of a single novel. There are both thematic and stylistic reminiscences here, not just of Ngugi's own earlier novels, but of Ousmane, Armah, Ouologuem, Achebe, Soyinka, and others. Such a work is bound to be uneven in quality. There are brilliant scenes, superbly realized, alternating at times with rather more tedious ones. This is partly due to the fact that Ngugi's chosen method of narration – the use of reminiscences – involves much more telling than showing. There seems to be a preponderance of narration and assertion over detailed scenic demonstration. We hear people talking about their past experiences rather than see them enacted before our eyes. How much more effective it would have been to have seen Karega's trade union activities enacted than to be told about them by himself! It is also a pity that Ngugi decided to place at the centre of events a hero like Munira who is not only spineless, but succeeds eventually in totally alienating the reader's sympathy. Mugo, in spite of his self-confessed treachery towards Kihika, never loses the reader's sympathy, because of his basic courage and honesty. There seems to be a certain uncertainty about Ngugi's attitude towards his hero. At the start he gives him a certain measure of idealism, but then suggests that his non-involvement is due not to idealism but to cowardice, and at the end he makes him a villain. This element of mistiness surrounding the hero seriously impairs the novel's impact on the reader. Nevertheless, no one can fail to acknowledge its importance and relevance. It is indeed a major publication.

Notes

1. Angus Calder, in a review in The Scotsman.
2. Homi Bhabha, TLS, 12 August 1977, p. 89.

Ngugi's Christian Vision: Theme and Pattern in *A Grain of Wheat*

Govind Narain Sharma

N gugi wa Thiong'o's *A Grain of Wheat* has generally been looked upon as a political novel, depicting the ups and downs of Kenya's struggle for freedom. As an ardent patriot Ngugi is thrilled by the courage and heroism displayed in the struggle, but as an enlightened and progressive thinker he is disturbed at the way the principles of that struggle have been betrayed by the new rulers. So there has been betrayal, not only during the struggle, by men such as Karanja, but also after it, by the new brand of politician. Betrayal and disillusionment are thus the main themes.[1]

To interpret Ngugi's novel in this way is to miss its extraordinary richness and complexity, and can even lead to complaints like Kofi Awoonor's that it is lacking in 'a degree of depth'.[2] I wish to argue, on the contrary, that it is precisely the possession of this depth and subtlety which constitutes the singular distinction of Ngugi's novel. For its real theme, I believe, is not betrayal or disillusionment but rebirth and regeneration, the end of brokenness and alienation and the restoration to wholeness and community. In giving concrete embodiment to this theme Ngugi makes a creative and imaginative use of the Christian myth and offers his own interpretation of Christianity.

At the simplest level *A Grain of Wheat* is not so much a novel of protest as of vindication. Ngugi sets out to dispel the myth sedulously fostered by the colonial rulers that the Mau Mau was 'something purely and simply evil, atavistic and completely unrelated to the mainstream of African nationalism or any decent political sentiments'. 'To most Africans, Mau Mau, in fact,' he boldly asserts, 'was a heroic and glorious aspect of that mainstream. The basic objectives of Mau Mau revolutionaries were to drive out the Europeans, seize the government, and give back to the Kenya peasants their stolen lands and property'.[3] *A Grain* is thus a political novel of vindication, portraying and justifying Kenya's struggle for independence and the Mau Mau movement as the core of that struggle.[4] All those who took part in that struggle are the heroes – good people – as contrasted with those who tried to frustrate it, either directly, through tyranny and oppression endeavouring to break the spirit of the people; or indirectly, through collaboration with the colonial rulers. It is perhaps correct to say, as Peter Nazareth does, that at this level 'the novel has no protagonist but has several important characters'. It is, however, difficult to go along with him when, in his anxiety to emphasize that the novel has only one plot, he states that no character is 'more important than the others in the structure of the novel and [that] all are interlinked'.[5] For the central role of Kihika is obvious even at this level, though Ngugi is more inclined to assign to the party itself the role of protagonist. And the party for Ngugi does not mean only the great leaders from Harry Thuku to 'the Burning Spear'; its backbone is those ordinary men and women whose little, nameless, unremembered acts of self-denial and sacrifice are essential to sustain any movement of national liberation or reconstruction.[6] Thus it is the small men and women – Kihika, Mugo, Gikonyo, Mumbi, Warui, Wambui and Njeri – who are the heroes and heroines of the novel. But Kihika stands pre-eminent among them: he is the young hero who sees the vision of an independent Kenya, is 'moved by the story of Moses and the children of Israel',[7] and like the great prophet hopes to lead his people to the promised land. His eloquence makes the people aware of their servitude, and inspires them to plunge into the struggle for freedom; it is his martyrdom which 'waters the tree of freedom' and keeps the struggle alive by infusing new life into the party (p. 21), which finally leads to freedom.

The search itself and the intensity with which it is pursued are, however, indicative of a deeper malaise in Gikuyu society. 'The Emergency destroyed us' (p. 6) says the lame buffoon Gitogo who has invented a colourful tale of his own exploits during the Emergency; and a considerable portion of Ngugi's novel is devoted to a portrayal of the violence that was done not merely to the body – the land, homes and hearths of the Gikuyu people – but also to their soul, in the form of the spiritual suffering and agony inflicted on them by the white man. This suffering and agony were extremely painful and demoralizing but they had a regenerating effect too on the sensitive, intelligent, and morally aware. The moral and spiritual ferment which the Emergency created in their souls

initiated a process which involved great soul-searching, and ultimately led to a spiritual rebirth. This theme of regeneration
through suffering is suggested in the quotation from the Bible
which Ngugi uses as the epigraph for his work.[8]

The use of biblical text and typology reveals a curious and baffl-
ing ambivalence in Ngugi's attitude towards Christianity. 'I am not
a man of the Church. I am not even a Christian,' Ngugi declared
categorically in his speech before the Fifth General Assembly of the
Presbyterian Church of East Africa at Nairobi on 12 March 1970.[9]
Seven years before this declaration he was speaking with a touch of
irony of Njoroge's 'Christian progress' in *Weep Not, Child*;[10] and
the portraits of Christians and references to Christianity are anything but complimentary in *A Grain*. The ardent Christians in the
novel – the Rev. Jackson Kigondu and teacher Muniu – are, with the
sole exception of the Rev. Morris Kingeri, canting hypocrites and
conniving traitors who act as police informers and whose elimination by the freedom fighters does not call for the shedding of a
single tear. It is reasonable to assume that Kihika is speaking for the
author himself when he recounts the missionaries' shameful role as
the agents of imperialism who connived in the stealing of the black
man's patrimony when, at their behest, he meditated with eyes
closed.

In spite of all this it seems impossible to read and interpret *A
Grain of Wheat* without taking into account the Christian myth,
which not only constitutes the basic framework of the story and
incorporates the author's message but also dominates his use of
image and symbol.[11] All the leading characters of the novel –
Kihika, Mugo, Gikonyo, Mumbi – make use of Christian concepts to
express their dreams and aspirations, their lapses and fears. And
the central message of the novel is profoundly Christian – the duty
of each man and each society to work out its own salvation, the only
way to the attainment of this salvation being through suffering and
sacrifice. The biblical text which proclaims this message and
which is used as epigraph for the novel forms part of the answer to a
rhetorical question posed by St Paul in his First Letter to the
Corinthians: 'But you may ask, how are the dead raised? In what
kind of body? How foolish! The seed you sow does not come to life
unless it has first died; and what you sow is not the body that shall
be, but a naked grain, perhaps of wheat, or of some other kind . . .' (I
Corinthians 15:35–6). The message is reiterated through the words
of St John, a verse underlined in black in Kihika's Bible.[12] Kihika is
the seed which, by dying first, comes to life; the 'corn of wheat'

which by falling into the ground and dying 'bringeth forth much fruit'.

A serious objection, however, remains: how could a Mau Mau soldier, a man who accepted the use of violence as a legitimate mode of political action, embody the Christian message? Ngugi was prepared for the objection and is ready with the answer. Christianity does not condemn the use of violence unequivocally. Violence is criminal only when it is used 'to protect an unjust, oppressive order. Violence in order to change an intolerable, unjust social order is not savagery: it purifies man.'[13] The essence of Christianity is contained not in the idea of eschewing violence at all costs but in that of redemption through suffering and sacrifice. Jesus became the Christ by the act of crucifixion, by his willingness to sacrifice himself for the good of others. By saying that 'if Christ had lived in Kenya in 1952 ... he would have been crucified as a Mau Mau terrorist',[14] Ngugi leaves little doubt about his belief that Kihika is a true Christ who, through sacrifice, not only justifies himself but also brings about a revolution in the lives of his friends and followers by showing them the way to spiritual regeneration, to the true life of the spirit which, as St Paul told the Corinthians in his Letter, can be gained only by dying in the flesh. The recognition of Kihika as a true Christ is made in the novel itself in Mugo's painful questioning as to why Judas, 'a stone from the hands of a power more than man', should be blamed for Kihika's crucifixion, for he as Christ would have died on the cross anyway (p. 199).

The concept of regeneration is applicable to the individual as well as to society. Personal salvation is visualized as the end of alienation and return to community through self-discovery, which involves acceptance of responsibility as a human being and a willingness to be honest with oneself. Mugo's decision to purge the guilt in his own soul by confessing to his betrayal of Kihika indicates his growth to a man's state and symbolizes the end of his alienation; so also does Gikonyo's reconciliation with Mumbi, after the memory of the vision of Mount Kerinyaga with 'its snow-capped tops just touching the sky' has 'softened' him to appreciate Mugo's courage in facing his guilt at the risk of losing everything. He now begins to see himself as the father of Mumbi's children and, as a token of his love for her, resolves to present a wedding gift consisting of a woman's figure big with child (p. 280). Social salvation – what Nadine Gordimer calls the 'let my people go' theme, the words underlined in red in Kihika's Bible (p. 37) – is projected in the journey of the Israelites (the Gikuyu people) from Egypt (the state of servitude) to Canaan (the state of freedom).

Kihika and Karanja provide the moral polarities in the novel. 'But a few shall die that the many shall live. That's what crucifixion means today' is Kihika's modern version of Christianity (p. 217). 'As for carrying a gun for the whiteman,' Karanja observes, explaining his conduct to the young and idealistic Mumbi, 'well, a time will come when you too will know that every man in the world is alone, and fights alone, to live' (pp. 165–6). These formulations of the philosophies of alienness and community dominate Ngugi's depiction of the spiritual evolution of his characters.

The drama of spiritual struggle is enacted in its most graphic form in the development of Mugo, a highly complex character, sensitive, thoughtful, and imaginative, but also a nervous and restless soul, personifying the tensions and agonies of a troubled land. One side of his nature urges him to a complete withdrawal into himself, left free to lead his own life; another leads him to think of himself as a prophet and saviour. He is alone, like Carlyle's Teufelsdrock the archetypal orphan, symbolizing in his person the African's alienation which had made him a stranger in his own land. But this aloneness itself had a meaning, for 'Moses too was alone keeping the flock of Jethro, his father-in-law' (p. 143). Mugo has a compelling sense of his own election: 'In his miraculous escape from death [in the beating that took place at Rira camp in which eleven men died], he now saw the guiding hands of fate. Surely he must have been spared in order that he might save people like Githua from poverty and misery. He, an only son, was born to save' (p. 153). From an orphan, tended by a distant aunt, a drunken woman who derided his efforts and whom it was his one desire to kill, he has evolved by 1955 to the state where he considers himself the instrument of the Lord 'to save the children of the needy, and . . . break in pieces the oppressor' (p. 142), the 'chief who would lead his people across the desert to the new Jerusalem' (p. 153). This was the climax of his life; the slide from this high point was quite sudden, 'for a week later D.O. Robson was shot dead, and Kihika came into his life' (p. 143). The appearance of Kihika brings to light his self-deception, the inconsistency of his position: he would be a saviour but when the opportunity offers itself he takes the road of retreat and betrayal, choosing to be a Judas rather than a Moses. Henceforth he is a tortured soul, in the anomalous position of being a hero in the eyes of other people but a traitor in his own. His feeling of alienation is oppressive till the day he confesses his guilt and completes his self-discovery. This second birth, denoting his restoration to wholeness and community, is suggested by his return to Githua's mother to whom he appears as a reincarnation of her dead son.

The dialectic of aloneness and community dominates the spiritual evolution of Gikonyo too, the gradient of his life resembling in many ways that of Mugo's. From a modest beginning he becomes a talented carpenter, an admired man who succeeds in winning the love of the sweetly beautiful Mumbi. Unlike Mugo, who is thrown into the freedom struggle against his will, Gikonyo deliberately responds to the call of the nation. But the suicide of Gatu in the concentration camp at Yala plunges him into gloom and depression, depriving him of all hope in the future of Kenya and leading him to confession of the oath to secure his release. The 'terrible revelation' that comes to Gikonyo when he knows of Mumbi's having been unfaithful to him with Karanja is that 'nothing could grow between two people. One lived alone, and like Gatu, went into the grave alone ... To live and die alone was the ultimate truth' (p. 135). In this mood of cynicism and frustration he childishly lays hands on Mumbi, provoking his mother's angry rebuke: 'But you are a man, now. Read your own heart, and know yourself' (p. 201). Though Gikonyo is now fairly well-to-do and has a new house, in the depth of his spiritual malaise he stands alone. But he is a thoughtful and sensitive man and when he goes to meet Warui, the veteran freedom fighter who had taken part in the 1923 procession, who 'placed his faith in the God of the nation and ... the spirit of the black people', he asks himself about the secret of Warui's happy and contented life: 'Was it because he had lived his own personal life fully as a man, a husband and a father, or was it because he had lived his life for his people?' (p. 192). This self-examination finally brings him, while laid up with a broken arm in Timoro hospital, a realization of his own shortcomings. Through this and admiration for the courage of Mugo in facing his guilt like a man, he is ready to take a more tolerant view of Mumbi's lapse. The return of love implies a restoration to fellowship and community.

Like Mugo and Gikonyo, Mumbi too has her troubles, though she is the only major character in the novel who does not suffer a real fall from grace despite her succumbing to Karanja in a weak moment when she is overcome with emotion at the news of her husband's impending release. The sight of her people's huts being burnt down by the home guards and the pain and suffering it caused her parents was a harrowing experience for her. 'Something gave way in my heart,' as she later tells Mugo, 'something in me cracked when I saw our home fall' (p. 159). These lapses and sorrows, however, only make her more human, for she is otherwise an angelic figure, the only one besides Kihika who keeps her vision intact, never losing her warm humanity, her good sense and nobility. Peter Nazareth sees her as 'the archetypal woman ... woman as romantic, faithful lover and mother'.[15] Perhaps it would be more correct to describe her as the spirit of Kenya; its beautiful and bountiful earth, ancient yet ever young; dark, deep and mysterious; patient and long-suffering, which, in spite of being ill-used by unscrupulous adventurers, has retained its goodness, fecundity, and warmth. She exercises a wholesome influence on the other characters, arousing them to a better knowledge of themselves. The open honesty with which she told her own story to Mugo made him ashamed of his morbid secretiveness, 'cracked open his dulled inside and released impassioned thoughts and feelings' (p. 195). When at the last critical moment he is tempted not to confess his crime and let Karanja bear the blame for Kihika's death, it is the thought of Mumbi's reaction that keeps him on the straight path (p. 267). When Mugo is scurrying at the bottom of the pool – his own guilt – the sight of Mumbi, 'the earth; life, struggle, even amidst pain and blood and poverty' (p. 171), seems beautiful to him, but the vision is beyond his reach. His error lies in his fear that if he confessed his crime he would lose for ever the possibility of turning this vision into a reality. He fails to realize that the confessing of his crime, dying in the flesh, would instead of alienating him from Mumbi bring him closer to her, thus restoring him to earth, life, and community. For she is generous, forgiving, and compassionate, an embodiment of Ngugi's humane vision which, while recognizing the potential of heroism in man, is more conscious of his frailty and fallibility. How can ordinary men like Mugo and Gikonyo be harshly judged, when even 'heroes' have been found wanting: 'Long ago, Young Harry had also been detained, and sentenced to live alone on an island in the Indian ocean for seven years. He had come back a broken man, who promised eternal co-operation with his oppressors, denouncing the Party he had helped to build. What happened yesterday could happen today. The same thing over and over again, through history' (p. 122). Mumbi thus represents another aspect of Ngugi's vision, the softer and more humane: she is Ruth; as compared to the more virile Christianity of Kihika, 'her idea of glory was something nearer the agony of Christ at the garden of Gethsemane' (p. 102).

In the same speech in which he had disclaimed being a Christian, Ngugi had suggested that he was a 'religious writer', because he was interested in people's 'hidden lives; their fears and hopes, their loves and hates'.[16] He is a religious writer, and A Grain of Wheat is not merely a religious novel but also a Christian one, for his vision, as we have seen, is essentially Christian. More than political freedom, Ngugi's interest is in moral and spiritual freedom, without which the former can have no real meaning. The attainment of spiritual freedom alone – the persistent use of the metaphor of rebirth is quite significant – can bring about the end of the Gikuyu people's alienation and can restore them to a perfect community of fellowship and love, the promised land of Canaan. Personal and social salvation are interdependent: Gikonyo was not mistaken in his belief that 'His reunion with Mumbi would see the birth of a new Kenya': it happens to be the simple truth. The use of the word 'reunion' suggests that Kenya had enjoyed, in the past before the advent of the white man, the bliss of an organic, happy community. The transcendent moment of his union with Mumbi in Kinenie Forest stands for Gikonyo as 'a ritual myth of a forgotten land, long, ago' (p. 114). Mumbi's tea parties at which she entertained everyone, and the frolicsome festivities in the forest in the lap of Kenya's blissful earth, provide glimpses of a lost paradise which sustain the freedom fighters during the long night of the Emergency. They are symbols of hope telling them that they would be born again, be reconciled to their Mumbis and have opportunities of presenting to them long-deferred wedding gifts depicting women big with children.

NOTES

1. See P. O. Ojero, 'Of Tares and Broken Handles, Ngugi Preaches: Themes of Betrayal in A Grain of Wheat', in Standpoints on African Literature, ed. Chris Wanjala, Nairobi, East African Literature Bureau, 1973, pp. 72–85; Douglas Killam, 'Kenya', in Literatures of the World in English, ed. Bruce King, London and Boston, Routledge & Kegan Paul, 1974, p. 125; Kofi Awoonor, The Breast of the Earth, New York, Anchor/Doubleday, 1975, p. 291.
2. Breast of the Earth, p. 292.

3. See Ngugi wa Thiong'o, 'Mau Mau, Violence, and Culture', in
   *Homecoming: Essays on African and Caribbean Literature, Culture
   and Politics*, London, Heinemann, 1972, p. 28. Westport, CT, Lawrence
   Hill, 1973.
4. Note Ngugi's own statement that his novels are 'in the same vein' as
   autobiographies like Muga Gacaru's *Land of Sunshine*, Mugo
   Gatheru's *A Child of Two Worlds*, J. M. Kariuki's *Mau Mau Detainee*,
   Waruhiu Itote's *Mau Mau General*, and Grace Waciuma's *Daughter of
   Mumbi*. See *Homecoming*, pp. 70–1. Peter Nazareth also observes that
   Ngugi's novel 'provides a rationale for Mau Mau in intellectual terms
   ...'. See his *Literature and Society in Modern Africa*, Kampala, East
   African Literature Bureau, 1972, p. 148.
5. See his review of Kofi Awoonor's *Breast of the Earth* in *Research in
   African Literatures*, 6 (Fall 1975), 274.
6. Ngugi's radical Marxist outlook is best reflected in his critical attitude
   to the work of Soyinka and his warm approval of the stories of Leonard
   Kibera and Samuel Kahiga: 'Soyinka's good man is the uncorrupted
   individual: his liberal humanism leads him to admire an individual's
   lone act of courage, and thus often he ignores the creative struggle of
   the masses. The ordinary people, workers and peasants in his plays
   remain passive watchers on the shore or pitiful comedians on the road.'
   Kibera and Kahiga, on the contrary, in their 'tough' collection *Potent
   Ash*, 'write about the small man: they show the dignity of the poor and
   wretched of the earth, despite the violence of body and feeling around
   them'. See *Homecoming*, pp. 65, 71.
7. *A Grain of Wheat*, London, Heinemann (AWS 36), 1968, p. 99. All
   further references, which are incorporated into the text, are to this
   edition. New York, Humanities, 1968 (2nd edn.).
8. Biblical texts are used as epigraphs four times in the novel – at the
   beginning of the novel; then at the beginning of Chapters 4, 9, and 14;
   see pp. 1, 37, 147, 229.
9. *Homecoming*, p. 31.
10. *Weep Not, Child*, London, Heinemann (AWS 7), 1964, p. 151. New
    York, Collier Books, 1969.
11. Peter Nazareth, in his excellent essay, refers to the 'central irony in *A
    Grain of Wheat* [that] while the colonial government, the servants of
    the colonial government and many Africans condemn the Mau Mau
    movement as evil and senselessly murderous, Kihika receives his
    inspiration from the Bible'. The irony can be explained to some extent
    if we understand Ngugi's attitude to violence. Moreover, it is not just
    that Kihika's 'moral inspiration' came from the Bible: *A Grain* is really
    a religious novel in which the whole concept of sin and salvation is
    derived from Christianity. For Nazareth see his *Literature and Society*,
    p. 144.
12. See *A Grain*, p. 229. In the interest of clarity I have used the text in The
    New English Bible. I have not been able to understand the significance

of the different colours – red and black – used by Kihika while under-
lining the texts in his own Bible.

13. Homecoming, p. 28.
14. ibid., p. 34.
15. Literature and Society, p. 138.
16. Homecoming, p. 31.

Popular Literature in East Africa

Elizabeth Knight

To term any literature in East Africa popular is something of an overstatement given the nature and size of the reading public. Kivuto Ndeti[1] estimates that in Kenya there is 45 per cent literacy in the rural areas and 90 per cent in the urban sector, but the latter comprises only 10 per cent of the country's 12 million population. Even among students with the keenest interest in literature, those reading African literature are very few according to Angus Calder speaking at the 1971 Colloquium at Nairobi University. Futhermore the sales figures for Spear Books – Heinemann's contribution to the popular market – show only an average of 3,000 copies sold of each title. Charles Mangua's *Son of Woman*, however, sold 10,000 copies in six months and the follow-up, *A Tail in the Mouth*, sold 15,000 copies in two months. These figures compare unfavourably with those for sales of popular fiction in Ghana.[2] The term 'popular literature', then, needs some clarification.

Taban lo Liyong's and Onyango-Ogutu's collections of oral literature, the songs of Daudi Kabaka and E. Nandwa, and the poetry of Shaaban Robert are all deserving of the title 'popular literature' in that they are works of the people reflecting their values and enjoyed by the greater part of the population. However, the literature I deal with in this paper is neither so popularly based nor so widely enjoyed. It is a literature produced largely for the recently literate urban reader and is defined by Victor E. Neuburg as 'what the unsophisticated reader has chosen for pleasure'.[3] I intend to focus on the fiction produced by the major publishing houses in East Africa, and innovators like Comb Books, to exploit this expanding non-academic market. Heinemann has produced Spear Books and Oxford University Press has New Fiction from Africa. Then there are Foundation Books's African Leisure Library, Longman's Crime Series, Afromances, and a whole tribe of Comb books while East African Publishing House and Literature Bureau continue to cater also for the ordinary reader.

The language of these books is a quite distinctive form of English. Richard Hoggart's description of the attitude of writers of fantasy to their language is appropriate here. It is:

> ... not the attitude to language of the creative writer, trying to mould words into a shape which will bear the peculiar quality of his experience; but a fluency, a 'gift of the gab' and facility with thousands of stock phrases which will set the figures moving on the highly conventionalized stage of their readers' imaginations. They put into words and intensify the daydreams of their readers.[4]

The characters of writers like Charles Mangua, D. G. Maillu, and Murangi Ruheni talk this same colloquial, confident language which is so different from that of the early Ghanaian popular writer J. Benibengor Blay, or the beautifully mannered Shona of Patrick Chakaipa.[5] Often it resembles the journalese of *Drum* magazine and indeed *Bless the Wicked* by its editor reads like a series of articles from *Drum* although nowhere is this acknowledged to be the case.

The style is usually conversational and intimate, ranging from Maillu's direct address to his bottle, brother, wife, through Samuel Kahiga's first-person narrative in *The Girl from Abroad*, Mangua's constant appeal to his long-suffering reader, to Mwangi Ruheni's somewhat confused persona in *The Future Leaders*. In all cases the relationship with the reader is a very direct one with none – or few – of the distancing techniques of more serious writers. Another manifestation of this is the amount and frequency of dialogue, or monologue in the case of D. G. Maillu. Capitalizing on the song school, Maillu has produced a very uneven series of works using the dramatic monologue technique, be it in the form of a letter as in *Dear Daughter* or verse as in his three-decker *The Kommon Man*. His protégé, Maina Allan, has also taken up this form in *One by One*.

These dramatic monologues are far removed from the work of Okot p'Bitek. In this stanza from *After 4.30* a husband justifies his conduct to his wife:

> Woman, I've utterly exhausted myself
> always trying to please you
> yet you follow me up
> with your chronic nagging
> and insistence!
> I conduct my home in such a way that
> when diplomacy has failed to do for me
> what I think is right
> I don't hesitate to employ violence
> and I ...   (p. 194)

This is not really poetry but prose sentences dissected and arranged in short lines on the page. The language of poetry may not differ from that of prose but its form and basic unit of the image surely do. Simply putting prose sentences arbitrarily into lines makes nonsense of poetry. The rhythm and cadence of a prose sentence either over-rides its enforced poetic form or the division into lines forces a different stress on to the sentence and so obscures, if not obliterates, sense. I cannot help wondering if this style, like that of the popular writers in England of the 1840s, is designed to fill up the maximum number of pages with the minimum of effort and so provide an easy living. Indeed for all their appeal to the 'common man', not even Comb mini-novels are cheap. These works are by no means the short, inexpensive pamphlets of Onitsha or Shona popular literature.

D. G. Maillu's strength lies not in poetry but, like so many popular writers, in his use of language. Talking of jestbooks, V. E. Neuburg writes:

> ... if these little books performed a social function it was to provide an instant culture. Anecdotes and witticisms could be quoted from them, and their contents plundered to make conversation – and probably even sermons – sparkle with borrowed wit. (pp. 91–2)

Phrases from Maillu such as 'unfit for human consumption' from the book of the same name and 'marriage is but a slip knot' (*The Kommon Man, Part 1,* p. 69), Malimoto's witty anecdotes, and much of the 'urbane' dialogue in *Son of Woman* and *Sky Is the Limit* fall into this pattern. This urbane dialogue is a particularly distinctive feature of the genre, being an amalgam of predominantly American with some British slang with the occasional archaism – an indication of the literary diet of these authors. To take a random sample, Kahiga includes 'hobbledehoys', 'buddy', 'rubbers', 'the heck of it'; Mangua has 'blinking', 'tumble', 'blighter', 'cooler', 'By Jingo'; and Maillu uses 'I beseech you', 'man', 'bitch', 'hoodwink', 'alas', and a whole range of synonyms for the sex act.

As the language is uneven so, too, the register is apt to change abruptly. The novels therefore tend to have a greater range of tone than more serious works, particularly in the comic vein. The irony of an Ngugi or Okot is replaced by a rather heavy-handed sarcasm as in *The Kommon Man's* address to his wife,

> Keep on repeating to them that
> I'm cruel to their mother.

It's good that they should know
you're perfect
and I, though a human being, am but
a mad wild pig.
All poor men are mad wild pigs
and their children should know it (Part 2, p. 128)

but also by a delight and facility in word play. A nice example of this is the poem in *Son of Woman* (p. 56), an extended riddle in rhyming couplets in which Dodge's beer bottle addresses him. There are moments of sheer farce when Eriya, the revivalist, tries to climb to heaven in Godfrey Kalimugogo's short story 'The Vanished Village' (p. 160), or when Jonathan Kinama's village wife and screaming children descend on him in his office in *Unfit for Human Consumption* (p. 62). At other times there is simple joy as in the budding romance between Maiko and Delila in *Troubles*, absurd fantasy such as Dodge's plans to escape from the police station (p. 113), and tragi-comedy like the Indian ticket inspector's dogged adherence to duty in the face of a non-paying passenger/terrorist in *A Tail in the Mouth* (p. 61). This frequent change in mood means the books are always in danger of bathos, sentimentality, and melodrama. So Naito's tearful song for Maria is followed by details of his supper (p. 23), D. G. Maillu frequently resorts to a tear-jerking song of an impoverished mother to her child, appealing to sentiment rather than social conscience, and the hurried climax of *The Experience* with the characters stranded in a swamp, without a gun and with the roars of lions all around them, is crudely sensational.

Characters in these novels tend to be stereotypes. There is the graduate, sex-loving, beer-drinking, frequently broke, civil-servant hero like Reuben Ruoro (*The Future Leaders*), Matthew Mbathia (*The Girl From Abroad*), William Mwangi (*Sky Is the Limit*) – save his shyness – and Dodge Kiunyu (*Son of Woman*). These figures are indistinguishable, although Kiunyu's language is slightly racier than the rest. Other types that recur are the hypocritical Christian such as Father Burrow (*A Tail in the Mouth*), the prostitute secretary (*After 4.30*), and the racist white man like Jones (*Son of Woman*) and Slater (*The Future Leaders*).

There are certain characters, though, who undoubtedly stand out from the rest, largely because as minor characters they do not have to fulfil an already formed picture in the urban, twentieth-century reader's mind of the modern hero, or anti-hero. Marjorie Oludhe-Macgoye's Vera is a case in point. Ms Oludhe-Macgoye's own background in Nyanza helps her to create not only a convincing portrait of this white teacher but also of her relationship with Africa and Africans. The scene in the train (p. 16) when Vera is escorting her pupils to the town is beautifully observed. Vera's attempts at friendship cause her students much anxiety and disgust at the thought that she did not have an inside toilet at home and that she approves of educated mothers doing menial tasks at home. Another telling vignette is Samuel Kahiga's depiction of Mumtaz, Matthew's Asian secretary, where he feelingly describes the pressures placed on her by her community and does not come up with the glib answer of rebellion.

Frequently the best protraits are taken from traditional village life, itself a rare feature in East African popular literature. This is true of Murangi's cantankerous, wife-beating father Ngaradu in *Sky Is the Limit*, Bernard Chahilu's Mahiukili, a Baluhyia farmer fighting to retain his traditional status against the onslaught of his wife's Christianity, his daughter's education, and his son's delinquency in *The Herdsman's Daughter*, and Elizabeth Nanjala's minor character Wesonga, a pathetic cook on the lower rungs of society in a small town who marries the heroine in *The Boyfriend*.

The last two books are very similar in that they both deal with the education of a Baluhyia girl in a transitional society. They have the same strengths and weaknesses that extend to most popular literature in East Africa. The traditional settings are very well evoked, in Chahilu's book in particular, being firmly rooted in everyday details. With the introduction of a plot – the deflowering of the heroine as part of the headmaster's political manoeuvrings – characterization and descriptive detail go by the board and the novel ends like a Victorian melodrama. In Ms Oludhe-Macgoye's excellent thriller the factual details of the plot at the end over-ride all other literary and social concerns evinced earlier in the book. In Edward Hinga's *Sincerity Divorced* the husband–wife debate develops into a tedious annotation of the wife's exploits and not 'a morality play of universal import and concerned with timeless matters'.[6]

Of *A Tail in the Mouth* Angus Calder wrote:

> ... the novel takes an immensely wide sweep through a vast range of politically and historically significant incidents and settings, as if Oyono's *Houseboy* had been tacked on to Ngugi's *A Grain of Wheat* with one of Ekwensi's urban melodrama's thrown in for good measure.[7]

The novel becomes all plot. Calder also notes the mechanical use of flashbacks and this attempted sophistication in the telling of a straightforward adventure story becomes as repetitive as the linear, multiple climax narrations of *The Future Leaders* and *One by One*. Maillu's monologues similarly meander from statement to statement with no logical progression or structure.

Totally disregarding form, he talks to the reader directly; matter becomes all-important. The values he portrays are common to most of these novels. Their market is largely urban and so, too, is their setting, with all the attendant social attitudes brought about by rapid urbanization along a Western pattern – rootlessness, cynicism, materialism and escapism. The parallels with nineteenth-century Britain are striking. Of the general process Louis James has written that 'the essentially rural lower-class culture which expressed itself in ballads, broad-sheets, and chapbooks, was fragmented when the worker moved into the towns'.[8] While Maillu's works can in no way be termed traditional they do contain fragments of that tradition in his fondness for aphorisms like 'the chameleon can change its colours but it cannot change its behaviour' (*My Dear Bottle*, p. 112) and 'when two bulls fight, it is the grass that suffers most' (*The Kommon Man, Part 1*, p. 57). Edward Hinga still recalls the traditional fine for sleeping with an unmarried woman (p. 20) but is embarrassed by elders judging his affairs (p. 105). Mwaura's *Sky Is the Limit* juxtaposes traditional and modern worlds as do *The Boyfriend* and *The Herdsman's Daughter* but like Kalimugogo's 'the Vanished Village' they show the village 'black and boneless, for its sap was steadily draining into the big town'.[9]

When Miti in *The Experience* pushes his father over he rejects village values (p. 36). Sam in *A Tail in the Mouth* dislikes the countryside (p. 22) – at the beginning of the novel for this character is not consistently drawn – and the obligations of the extended family (p. 24). The same is true of Maiko Matolo in *Troubles* (p. 18) and June in *The Girl from Abroad* (p. 84). Dodge is totally sceptical of traditional belief (p. 28), disgusted by the smells of the market place (p. 39), and hates the idea of working in the countryside (p. 64). Matthew in *The Girl from Abroad* is circumcised in hospital as is Antoni in *One by One*. In *The Kommon Man, Part 3* praise songs have been replaced by satire (p. 254). However there is still an occasional sense of loss as witnessed in Kahiga's nice observation of the inelegance of June and Matthew's love-making compared with the natural grace of the animals into whose environment they have trespassed (p. 60). Then there is the secretary's lament in *After 4.30*,

> The countryside is our only hope
> for bringing up
> better people
> morally stronger   (p. 104)

but this is weakened by her inconsistent attitude and the notion is not developed.

Like so many of the protagonists she is deeply cynical, the first law in her urban world, and that of popular writers in general, being 'don't ask why' (p. 204). These characters are not upright and fired with moral convictions, as are Chakaipa's creations, but are cynical or superficial anti-heroes. Adrian Roscoe calls *Son of Woman* 'the escapist frivolity of an amoral literature'[10] and Dodge is not the only character in this mould. There is also his literary successor, Sam. It would be difficult to find a less committed character, for he rapidly changes from being against the freedom fighters, to becoming a member of Mau Mau, then a homeguard, and finally a freedom fighter himself. The wife in *Sincerity Divorced* is similarly uncommitted on moral issues, at one moment planning the death of her future husband and at the next stating it to be a sin. Washington Ndawa (*No*), Jonathan Kinama, (*Unfit for Human Consumption*) and Watetu (*One by One*) all seek their own pleasure, no matter what the effect on others may be, as do the people the Kommon Man observes.

In this hedonistic society portrayed in the popular literature, drinking, having sex, and accumulating wealth are the major pre-occupations. At the 1971 Colloquium Andrew Gurr postulated that writing about sex might be East Africa's answer to the Absurd and that 'if there's nothing meaningful between birth and death, copulation does serve to pass the time away'.[11] However while literally being a space-filler in those novels, the sex act is often a desired end in itself and not an expression of the purposelessness of human existence. The heroes in these works are aggressively masculine; their virility is judged by a high sperm count (*The Girl from Abroad*, p. 57), a large penis (*One by One*, p. 82), and the number of women they can lay and how often (*Son of Woman*, p. 8)

Few of the novels are in fact pornographic. Charles Mangua, for instance, never details Dodge's 'tumblings'. Sola Oyadiran is rather harsh in talking of the 'heap of pornographic books being unleashed on East African readers by David G. Maillu of Comb Books in Nairobi'.[12] This certainly applies to *One by One* with its reduction of the sex act to a number of athletic positions and with no reference to human relationships or emotions. But many of the books are curiously moral although not so pointedly moralistic or didactic as Ghanaian or Shona popular fiction. Watetu's promiscuity leads to a crude justice as does Washington Ndawa's infidelity (*No*, p. 95). With reference to eighteenth-century literature Leo Lowenthal writes of:

> ... the sensational novelists who loaded their works with sex and sadism, inserting, as a kind of afterthought, a warning line or two, pointing out to the reader that his, or more frequently her, fate will be a ghastly one if he or she slips from the path of virtue. Under the guise of 'satiric indignation', revelations of vice and licentiousness in high and low places were exploited in novels.[13]

This is an apt description of these Comb novels.

There are gratuitous, graphic descriptions of sexual intercourse in Maillu's work as when Maiko has sex with his secretary, Ema, to ensure her promotion (*Troubles*, p. 113), but this is followed by a short poem decrying the practice (p. 118). Again the Kommon Man vividly imagines his wife's affair with Makoka (*Part 2*, p. 92) but the whole trilogy is a condemnation of her materialist-inspired actions. The sexual content in these novels is certainly ambiguous. Maillu, for example, has many serious points to make about the state of society and, in part, *The Kommon Man* is intellectually demanding. Is the sexual content then the carrot to entice the ordinary reader to serious thought on the problems of urban life or is the philosophy a rather lengthy afterthought and conscience-salver? Maillu's stand is not unequivocal.

While the heroes are asserting their manhood the heroines, from June (*The Girl from Abroad*), Tonia (*Son of Woman*), Pauline (*The Future Leaders*), and Ng'endo (*Sky Is the Limit*), to Watetu (*One by One*) are thankfully not passive, submissive creatures. Yet there are some elements of a Western-style romance literature of the women's magazine type. Simply because these writers are East African – like those of the soft porn previously mentioned – does not alter the fact that they are agents of a kind of cultural imperialism. They are putting forward a way of life, a concept of beauty and of love that is essentially Western. Obiechina in his study of popular literature in West Africa has remarked that 'in pre-colonial Africa, romantic love, whether as an autonomous experience or as a stepping-stone to marriage, was played down and subordinated to familial and community interests'.[14] In many of these works romantic love becomes the dominant feature to the extent that Kalimugogo even transports it back to the traditional, village background. Writing of Musa's illiterate father who has never strayed far from the village, he states: 'the old man was in love. It was the month of July, or it had just ended and its influence still lurked behind. And Mbete was in love' (p. 74).

The Kommon Man acknowledges kissing to be an alien habit (*Part 3*, p. 121) but he indulges in the equally Western practice of writing love letters (p. 128) and those of Richard (*The Herdsman's Daughter*, p. 158) read like an exercise in literary English. Romantic love dominates in the life of Nekesa, too (*The Boyfriend*), reaching a climax in the Dr Kildare romance that develops between her and Jeff over the deathbed of a young patient (p. 116). Matthew falls prey to such sentiment when he has a phone call from June, 'magically tuning the strings of my soul and playing a song' (p. 22), even though she is, in effect, a total stranger. In *Troubles* D. G. Maillu pulls out all the romantic clichés in the description of the relationship between Maiko and Delila. He is attracted to her by a mysterious force (p. 52) and 'by degrees he was becoming involved in her personality' (p. 69), 'but being a woman, she was too weak for a determined man' (p. 78) and so after he has made a woman of her 'Delila lay there and her's was a new world' (p. 81).

The urban ethos as presented in the popular literature is highly Westernized and individualistic. This individualism frequently takes the form of introspection that generates pseudo-intellectual discussions such as that which Maiko has with himself on the meaning of life (*Troubles*, p. 22) or popularized psychology as when Edward Hinga attempts to explain his wife's character (*Sincerity Divorced*, p. 7). When the Kommon Man sees man as a lonely creature (*Part 1*, p. 160) he is describing most of the main characters of popular fiction. Although often gregarious they are isolated individuals for the best part of their lives, never developing permanent relationships with another human being. When Musa in *Dare to Die* threatens to return to the countryside, the unnamed protagonist kills his friend for fear of the loneliness of the city (p. 10). Ms Oludhe-Macgoye offers an important and credible alternative to this view in her description of Majengo with its new intertribal neighbourliness but even here the victim of a mugger is isolated 'for in the city no door would open on such a scene' (p. 45). June in *The Girl from Abroad* has fully adopted Western thought and relishes the idea of independence and no obligations to others (pp. 83,4).

Romantic love vies with sexual attraction on a person-to-person level; the family is not involved. The successful characters follow

Western fashion – Delila is a notable exception – be it the pointed
shoes of the early sixties (*The Girl from Abroad*, p. 5), straightened
hair (*The Kommon Man, Part 2*, p. 24), a white wedding (*After 4.30*,
p. 121), speaking English (*Dare to die*, p. 26), or a Western education. The persona of *Dare to Die* arrives in Nairobi proud of his
education and convinced he will get a job (p. 26) and Embenzi
becomes melodramatically ill when she is not allowed to continue
her education (*The Herdsman's Daughter*, p. 135). The prostitute-
secretary of *After 4.30* still places all her hopes for the future in her
son's schooling (p. 61) and Nelima recognizes education as a
passport up the social ladder for Jack for 'he was part of the educated minority. She could never win him' (p. 39). Samuel Kahiga
neatly expresses the status afforded the educated man who 'went
abroad to come home a victorious warrior armed to the teeth with
degrees' (p. 31).

Of this educated urban élite Ndeti writes:

> ... they are Westernized in thinking, style of life and general sense of
> values; they have a high degree of political and economic con-
> sciousness; greatly appreciate achievement; and are fairly materialistic
> in outlook. (p. 52)

Matthew, Obonyo (*Murder in Majengo*), Reuben (*The Future
Leaders*), Mwangi (*Sky Is the Limit*) all belong to this materialist
clan, the Wabenzi, with their conspicuous consumption. Those
who have not achieved such heights aspire to them, as is also the
case with Onitsha market literature (p. 22). The most extreme
example is Serumaga's heart seller, in the book of the same name,
who literally sells his heart to a rich southern American for a
million dollars. June is depressed by the materialism in Nairobi (p.
24) but she is just as much one of the élite with her education and
reference to the restaurant she and Matthew eat at as 'deliciously
civilised' (p. 65). Even the rural Watetu refuses Amos because of his
poor salary (p. 53).

The passport to such a life is seen not so much in hard work – in
fact Maiko is one of the few characters who is actually seen working
(*Troubles*, p. 56) – as in bribery. Watetu is advised to sleep with the
manager to get a job in Nairobi (p. 49), Matthew accepts that bribery
is necessary to pass a driving test (p. 13), Dodge puts his lack of
promotion down to not bribing his superiors (p. 9) and because the
lawyer lent Lois her school fees she knows that afterwards 'naturally she could not expect to go straight to the station' (*Murder in
Majengo*, p. 10).

Bribery and petty crimes, from pilfering office typewriters (*Unfit for Human Consumption*, p. 16) to using a government vehicle on private visits (*Son of Woman*, p. 85), are an accepted way of life and the corruption of high officials is stated often enough to become cliché. Ms Oludhe-Macgoye weaves into her thriller details of the political manoeuvrings of Wasere and Rapar of the banned opposition party who turn out to be as committed only to their self-aggrandizement as those in power. The latter are exemplified by the headman Thuo (*A Tail in the Mouth*, p. 218) who has spent the Party money and the Honourable Somboloya whose 'laurels grow on the manure of people's blood' (*The Kommon Man, Part 1*, p. 30). Post-independence life is one of disillusionment for Sam, having returned from the forest:

> To hell with nation building and your big talk. When I haven't got clothes, food, house, land, employment, etcetera, and my starting place is worse than where I left off, then I don't want to hear any high and mighty talk about brotherhood and nation building. I have to build my house before I can build a nation. (p. 212).

The same poverty faces the common people in *The Kommon Man*. All undesirables are chased away by the police, countrywomen have to go hungry all day in order to welcome the president, and bad conditions are covered up (*Part 3*, p. 251).

The popular writers themselves cover up many social and political ills in that they do not look into their causes or dwell on their results. Maillu and Kahiga mention the realities of the Asian community. Kahiga notes that Mumtaz's work permit is about to expire and she will have to leave Kenya (p. 17) and Maiko's boss, Mr Patel, is away in Britain (p. 155), but neither writer probes the reasons behind this exodus. Similarly, unemployment, police brutality, and poor housing conditions are mentioned in most of the novels but only as the background from which the protagonists seek to escape, except in the case of the Kommon Man (*Part 1*, p. 150). As Ime Ikiddeh has said of Ghanaian popular fiction, it does not 'exploit political and other topical issues of the day except very remotely' (p. 106).

In the country which was the first to introduce a free, nationwide family planning service, the attitude to contraceptives is amazingly casual. Ms Oludhe-Macgoye attacks the ignorance about contraception despite publicity campaigns (p. 14), and the protagonist in *My Dear Bottle* complains of his wife's lack of persistence in birth control (p. 151). Despite the odd reference to 'rubbers' the onus is always on the woman, resulting in the exile of the girl in

Dear Daughter and the frequent recourse to abortions (*After 4.30*, p.
178; *The Boyfriend*, p. 111; *The Future Leaders*, p. 112). The predominantly male writers of popular literature fail to take a stand on
this issue and venereal disease is regarded very much as an occu-
pational hazard (*Troubles*, p. 8) in the pursuit of happiness.
It is this pursuit of happiness that is the over-riding theme and
purpose of popular literature. Much is done simply for 'the heck of
it' (*The Girl from Abroad*, p. 34). Of Onitsha literature, Obiechina
has written:

> The economic attitudes of the Onitsha pamphleteers mark them out as
> materialists. They desire change and the innovations which change
> brings, including the new consumer durables. In this respect, they
> contrast sharply with the West African intellectual authors, most of
> whom tend to relate most of the ills of contemporary West African
> society to economic individualism and the corrupting of materialism.
>
> (p. 24)

The same is true of East Africa although the materialism is often
tinged with a high degree of cynicism. This trait is never, however,
traced to its source or allowed to interfere with the protagonists'
advancement. So after his portentous dream Mwangi, having been
told 'You will not find happiness by isolation, move out to the
people. Find out what you can do for them' (*Sky Is the Limit*,
p. 179), reaches the conclusion that 'he had to help himself before
he could help others' (p. 245). His own material well-being and
comfort comes first and helping others is reduced to charity in the
same way as Charles Mangua's characters ease their consciences
by donating, or thinking of donating, money to the blind school
at Thika.
Primarily these books are for relaxation and enjoyment. It is
perhaps harsh to condemn popular literature for being uncommitted – politically, socially, morally – but that is its essential
characteristic. Individual achievement is its theme and it is
expressed in a fluency in a peculiar type of colloquial English,
material wealth, and sexual prowess, and almost invariably in an
urban setting. However, if the ordinary reader turns to D. G.
Maillu's *The Kommon Man*, combing through the trivia, soft porn,
trite moralizing, and cynicism, he may find the hymn of the common man (p. 181) which speaks as clearly of social injustice as does
Okot p'Bitek's *Song of Lawino*, but with less anger and more cynicism. Speaking of chapbooks, V. E. Neuburg wrote:

> Their unsophisticated contents had laid hold upon the popular imagi-
> nation for a long time; they provided the means by which unlettered

members of a pre-industrial society could move into an urban industrial society increasingly dominated by print. (p. 121)

So perhaps these books, enjoyable in their own limited right, will also serve as in introduction to more serious African literature.

NOTES

1. Kiviuto Ndeti, *Cutural Policy in Kenya*, Paris, UNESCO, 1975, p. 52. New York, Unipub., 1975.
2. Ime Ikiddeh, 'The Character of Popular Fiction in Ghana', in C. Heywood (ed.), *Perspectives on African Literature*, London, Heinemann, 1971, pp. 106–16. New York, Africana Publishing Corporation, 1972.
3. Victor E. Neuburg, *Popular Literature. A History and Guide*, Harmondsworth, Penguin, 1977, p. 12. New York, Penguin, 1977.
4. Richard Hoggart, *The Uses of Literacy*, Harmondsworth, Penguin, 1957, p. 209. New York, OUP, 1970.
5. George P. Kahari, *The Novels of Patrick Chakaipa*, Salisbury, Longman, 1972, p. 45.
6. Arthur Kemoli, foreword to E. Hinga, *Sincerity Divorced*, Nairobi, East African Literature Bureau, 1970.
7. Angus Calder, review of *A Tail in the Mouth* by Charles Mangua, *Joliso*, I, 2, 1973, 68–78 (68).
8. Louis James, *Fiction for the Working Man. 1830–1850*, London, OUP, 1963, p. 28.
9. Godfrey Kalimugogo, 'The Vanished Village', in *Dare to Die*, Nairobi: East African Literature Bureau, 1972, pp. 151–77 (p. 170).
10. Adrian Roscoe, *Uhuru's Fire. African Literature East to South*, Cambridge, CUP, 1977, p. 175. New York, CUP, 1977.
11. Andrew Gurr, *'Literature and Institutions'*, in Andrew Gurr and Angus Calder (eds), *Writers in East Africa*, Nairobi, East African Literature Bureau, 1947, pp. 115–21 (p. 119).
12. Sola Oyadiran, review of *No; Dear Monika; Dear Daughter*, by David G. Maillu and *The Act*, by Andrew M. Mwiwawi, *The African Book Publishing Record*, III, 3, 1977, p 149.
13. Leo Lowenthal, *Literature, Popular Culture and Society*, California, Pacific Books, 1961, p. 71.
14. Emmanuel Obiechina, *An African Popular Literature*, Cambridge, CUP, 1973, p. 34. New York, CUP, 1973.

BIBLIOGRAPHY

Maina Allan, *One by One*, Nairobi, Comb Books, 1975.

Bernard Chahilu, *The Herdsman's Daughter*, Nairobi, East African Literature Bureau, 1970.

Edward Hinga. *Sincerity Divorced*, Nairobi, East African Literature Bureau, 1970.

Samuel Kahiga, *The Girl from Abroad*, London, Heinemann (AWS 158), 1974. New York, Humanities, 1974.

Godfrey Kalimugogo, *Dare to Die*, Nairobi, East African Literature Bureau, 1972.

D. G. Maillu, *The Kommon Man, Part 1*, Nairobi, Comb Books, 1975.

D. G. Maillu, *The Kommon Man, Part 2*, Nairobi, Comb Books, 1975.

D. G. Maillu, *The Kommon Man, Part 3*, Nairobi, Comb Books, 1976.

D. G. Maillu, *After 4.30*, Nairobi, Comb Books, 1974.

D. G. Maillu, *My Dear Bottle*, Nairobi, Comb Books, 1973.

D. G. Maillu, *Unfit for Human Consumption*, Nairobi, Comb Books, 1973.

D. G. Maillu, *Troubles*, Nairobi, Comb Books, 1974.

D. G. Maillu, *No!* Nairobi, Comb Books, 1976.

D. G. Maillu, *Dear Daughter*, Nairobi, Comb Books, 1976.

P. G. Malimoto, *Bless the Wicked*, Nairobi, Foundation Books, 1973.

Charles Mangua, *Son of Woman* Nairobi, East African Publishing House, 1972.

Charles Mangua, *A Tail in the Mouth*, Nairobi, East African Publishing House, 1972.

Joshua N. Mwaura, *Sky Is the Limit*, Nairobi, East African Literature Bureau, 1974.

Elizabeth Nanjala, *The Boyfriend*, Nairobi, Comb Books, 1976.

Marjorie Oludhe-Macgoye, *Murder in Majengo*, London, OUP, 1972.

Mwangi Ruheni, *The Future Leaders*, London, Heinemann (AWS 139), 1973. New York, Humanities, 1974.

Eneriko Seruma, *The Heart Seller*, Nairobi, East African Publishing House, 1971.

Eneriko Seruma, *The Experience*, Nairobi, East African Publishing House, 1970.

South African History, Politics and Literature: Mphahlele's *Down Second Avenue*, and Rive's *Emergency*

Okpure O. Obuke

There is a strong temptation to assume that autobiographies are simply historical records of the lives of their authors. To some extent this may be true. But usually the main purpose for writing an autobiography is the major determinant in the selection of incidents. This conscious selection of incidents to reflect a purpose may be discerned in Ezekiel Mphahlele's autobiography, *Down Second Avenue*. Mphahlele in September 1970 had explained the main motive for writing his autobiography in 1969. According to him, apart from the personal satisfaction of having his autobiography published, the work was intended to serve as a source of fortitude to his people and also to present the horrors in South Africa to the world.[1]

In order to fulfil such a purpose, the work must be placed firmly in the South African context of apartheid. The use of 'factual' history will therefore give historical validity to his work as protest against apartheid. In such circumstances, the work ceases to be merely the factual records of Mphahlele's South African history as it affected his life. Admittedly, the work is 'history', but it also makes a 'political' statement through a literary art form.

On the other hand, Rive, who approaches the same apartheid situation in South Africa through what is ostensibly fiction, has as his background the same 'factual' history of South Africa. Thus, both Ezekiel Mphahlele's *Down Second Avenue* and Richard Rive's *Emergency* have much in common; first, both writers use the factual history of South Africa as background for their works; secondly, both works are almost biographies of their heroes – Ezekiel Mphahlele's *Down Second Avenue* is certainly his own autobiography, while Rive's *Emergency* is essentially a record of three dramatic days in the life of Andrew Dreyer. The use of a series of flashbacks to Andrew Dreyer's past life gives us a nearly complete biography of Andrew.

The main factual history of South Africa which forms the background of Rive's *Emergency* is the Sharpville shootings of Monday 21 March 1960. On that fateful Monday the PAC (Pan-Africanist Congress) had called on Africans to leave their passes at home and surrender themselves for arrest. This decision was intended to be a peaceful reaction against the notorious and repressive 'Press Act' which requires Africans to carry passes with them wherever they go. Failure to carry passes means immediate arrest and subsequently a fine or imprisonment. The PAC decreed that if they were arrested, they would refuse bail, defence, and fines. It was hoped that such a protest would force the apartheid regime to repeal the Pass Law.

On that Monday, at about 6 a.m., Sobukwe with other leaders including Ndziba, Ngendane, Nyoase, and sixty followers marched to Orlando Police Station, surrendered themselves, and were arrested. At the Sharpville Police Station, over ten thousand Africans congregated and surrendered themselves for arrest for not having passes. The police barred the gates and some of the crowd began to throw stones. The police then opened fire. Sixty-seven people including eight women and ten children were killed. One hundred and eighty-six were wounded, including thirty-one women and nineteen children.[2] Three policemen had slight injuries.

At Langa Location, Africans had responded to the PAC call for a meeting in contravention of the Riotous Assemblies Act. Here also police opened fire on the crowd and the crowd also stoned the police. Only three Africans, however, were killed at Langa Location. In comparison to the Sharpville incident, the Langa Location shootings were less serious. The week that followed these shootings was one of chaos and the breakdown of law and order. Africans sought revenge by acts of arson and the police responded by arrests of political leaders and suspects. There was mounting tension, Africans boycotted work, and on Wednesday 30 March 1960, a state of emergency was declared.

The Sharpville incident and its immediate aftermath form the background of Rive's *Emergency*. The main action of the novel takes place in Cape Town and focuses on the days 28 March to 30 March 1960. Structurally, the novel is divided into three parts. Each part is headed by a day of that three-day period, and each section describes roughly the events of that day in Andrew

Dreyer's life. Thus, the narrative moves in a linear progression over a three-day period. But the novel is not completely chronological. There are a series of flashbacks which reconstruct Dreyer's early life.

Emergency is not, of course, history; it is fiction. Rive's problem is therefore how to reconcile history with fiction in a work of fiction and yet retain historical credibility. The method he adopts is to treat each day in a separate section, narrate historical events, mention names of historical places and organizations. But he also treats the events imaginatively, introduces fictional characters, and goes beyond the mere narration of the historical events into the hearts and feelings of both the blacks and whites who live in South Africa. However, this attempt to give imaginative treatment to historical events has not been wholly successful.

One of the problems with the novel is the structure. The novel is rather episodic; incidents are developed somewhat erratically, and events are only loosely tied together. It may be argued that Rive is dealing with a historical situation and a disjointed series of events. This argument is not satisfactory because Rive devotes long passages to narrating the past history of Andrew Dreyer that do not advance the action of the novel or really do anything to improve our understanding of the hero. It is not even a question of one section's not being properly connected to succeeding or preceding sections; simply that within each section events are not sufficiently coherently developed. The flashback technique, instead of serving as a source of illumination, becomes more or less a digression.

In Section One, for example, the novel opens by being placed firmly within a historical context. There is reference to the historical events of 28 March 1960 in South Africa, and we are also reminded of the previous shootings at Langa. This is 'factual' history. But from the time Andrew goes home to Mrs Carollissen, runs to Ruth, meets Abe and Justin Bailey, recalls the death of his mother, his days at school, his experiences in District Six, gives brief portraits of his friends, and escapes to his sister's house, the whole structural movement becomes unsteady. These detailed descriptions of Dreyer's early life, his experiences, family, friends, and sister are imaginatively re-created and are part of the fictional elements in the novel. The purpose is to give us the background of the hero's early life and to comment on the miseries of District Six. Even in his own family, Andrew is an outsider because of his 'extra-blackness'. His miseries are miseries arising from the race consciousness that is the bane of South African society. Richard

Rive's problem is how to blend artistically the historical realities and the imaginative element in a work of fiction. There is constant switching from the 'fictional' to the 'historical', and from the 'historical' to the 'fictional'. Part Two, for example, begins with Andrew's escape to his sister's house, and the next ten chapters are devoted to the recollection of Andrew's days at school and the years spent in teaching. Even in these chapters the political problems of Andrew have a historical basis. In South Africa, for an African to be involved in politics is to court the wrath of the apartheid regime.[3] These chapters are also intended to show the development of Andrew's political awareness. By Chapter 11 there is a return to the historical events of 29 March 1960. This is the strike of the Africans which nearly paralysed the essential services in various parts of South Africa.

In addition to this strike which is 'factual' history, the political polemics engaged in by Abe and Justin have a historical basis. The period of the late 1950s was one of great ideological ferment in South Africa. The split between the PAC and the ANC in 1959 and the birth of the Unity Movement show to what extent there were conflicts among the blacks and coloureds in their approaches to the race problems. One of the most serious problems that faced the movements was how to handle the question of race separation. Abe does not accept the PAC ideology, nor that of the ANC.

I don't agree with either. Quite apart from their Africanist orientation which is as bad as white racialism, they haven't even begun to consider fundamental problems such as the kind of society they envisage.[4]

Thus, through fictional characters and fictional situations, Rive presents a critique of the 'factual' political situation of South Africa in the late fifties and early sixties.

The love affair between Andrew and Ruth is an example of the mixture of 'fiction' and 'factual' history. The 'Mixed Marriage Act' of 1949, and the amended 'Immorality Act' of 1950 prohibit marriage between whites and non-whites and also sexual relationship between whites and non-whites. The effect of this law is vividly dramatized in the predicaments of the two lovers as a result of police harassment:

'Ruth?'
'Yes, Andy?'
'We've done a non-European thing.'
'I read that somewhere.'
'Yes, me and a white lady did a non-European thing.'
'I still love you.'

'I love you also.'
'I don't care about the police, or my family, or what people think, I only want to be with you.'
'This is South Africa, dear.'
'I don't care.'[5]

There is no doubt that Rive is in this conversation between the two lovers making comments on the 'historical realities' of South Africa.

In Chapter 8 of Part Two there is a series of references to historical facts: the general election of April 1953 in which only whites were allowed to vote, the exception being that coloured males were allowed to vote in Cape Province; the Public Safety Bill by which the governor-general is empowered to declare a state of emergency in any one part of the country or in the whole Union; the Separate Amenities Act (1953), the Criminal Law Amendment Act, the Bantu Education Act (1953), and the Separate University Education Bill (proposed 1957, held over),[6] all these references in this chapter are to the 'factual' history of South Africa. The 'fictional' incident in the ticket-box at the station[7] is a reference to the existing racial laws in South Africa imaginatively re-created in 'fictional' form. Even the incident at the petrol station between Andrew and the white attendant is a commentary on the economic position of Africans in South Africa.[8] Richard Rive, through careful manipulation of his characters and use of commentary, presents the 'factual' history of South Africa and his protest against apartheid is implied in the very comments and actions of his characters.

This manipulation of events and characters hardly allows his characters to exist as 'free' human beings; neither are they allowed to develop freely. The result is that we know very little about the characters in the book besides their involvement in an apartheid situation.[9] Rive's talents do not seem to lie in the development of character and the coherent construction of a long novel. He seems to be more successful in presenting short, vivid scenes and creating dramatic tension that captures the tense atmosphere that pervaded South Africa after the Sharpville shootings. Rive certainly is a master of short sentences, and he makes use of them to a great advantage in describing the outbursts of violence. Even in calmer scenes, they are used effectively. For example, in the description of Andrew's visit to Ruth's room in Part One of the novel, Rive combines a few long sentences with short sentences very effectively:

Andrew poured himself a brandy and mixed it with soda. There was an unread *Argus* on the couch, but he felt in no mood to read. Music. That was it. Her record cabinet was at the side of the player. Smetana. He knew the work backwards. *Moldan* from *Ma Vlast*. My country. Patriotic music, the stirring of rational consciousness. A firm favourite of his. He opened wide the french doors and a light breeze smelling of pine blew in. He put the record in position, started the player, and switched off all the lights.[10]

Rive, however, does not allow his hero to indulge in personal reflection for long. Andrew's mind goes back to the 'historical' events of the day and the Langa funeral. Even the final abdication of Abe, and his preference for exile instead of remaining in South Africa, has 'historical' implication. It could be seen as a comment on the hard choice South Africans face from time to time; whether to escape into exile or remain. Like the political polemics between Abe and Justin, Rive is wary of passing any judgements. Rive makes his hero remain, but he does not condemn Abe, both Abe and Andrew say a warm 'Goodbye', and part.

However, this constant insistence on the apartheid situation and the manipulation of incidents and characters for the sole purpose of protest is the main weakness in *Emergency*. 'Factual' history and the 'facts' of apartheid seem to be too conspicuously displayed without being effectively transmitted into a well-organized artistic work. Lewis Nkosi's remarks about South African literature could not have been more applicable than to *Emergency*:

> To read a novel like Richard Rive's *Emergency* is to gain a minute glimpse into a literary situation which seems to me quite desperate. It may even be wondered whether it might not be more prudent to 'renounce literature temporarily', as some have advised, and solve the political problem first rather than continue to grind out hackneyed third-rate novels of which *Emergency* is a leading example.
>
> What we do get from South Africa therefore – and what we get most frequently – is the journalistic fact parading outrageously as imaginative literature. We find here a type of fiction which exploits the ready made plots of racial violence, social apartheid, inter-racial love affairs which are doomed from the beginning, without any attempt to transcend or transmute these given 'social facts' into artistically persuasive works of fiction.[11]

Although Ezekiel Mphahlele's *Down Second Avenue* is a work of protest, as is Rive's *Emergency*, and although both make use of 'factual' history and present the 'facts' of apartheid, the final product of their work is significantly different. Mphahlele's *Down Second Avenue* achieves a measure of success which *Emergency* does not. Part of the reason for this difference may be due to the fact that while Rive almost rests content with protest, Ezekiel

Mphahlele aims at something more than protest. In the 'Epilogue', he says that it is 'something of a higher order, which is the ironic meeting between protest and acceptance in their widest terms'.[12]

Mphahlele uses the 'factual' history of South Africa and the facts of his life not simply as vehicles of protest but also as means to create an artistic work. Structurally, *Down Second Avenue* appears to be episodic. On a superficial reading, one may have the impression that each chapter of the book is separate and that there is no underlying connection between chapters and between chapters and the whole. Often, a chapter or a section is no more than a portrait of some members of his family, his friends, or his neighbours. Each chapter generally concentrates on a single incident – sometimes simply a description of an incident or a place. For example, Chapter 1 is headed 'The Tribe', and it is a description of his family – the grandmother, his mother, brother, and sister. Chapter 2 is simply the 'Leehona Sands'; Chapter 4 is a description of an incident at a water tap. In Chapter 9, he gives a portrait of the hawker's daughter, and in Chapter 10 the portrait is of Ma Lebona, and so on almost throughout the book.

Despite this episodic appearance, the book has a structure that gives it coherence. The use of 'interludes' is one of the devices to tie the various parts of the novel together. There are five 'interlude' sections which roughly divide the book into six parts.[13] These 'interludes' not only connect one part of the novel with another, and therefore serve as a means of giving coherence to the novel structurally, but they provide commentaries both on what has gone before and what is to follow, and also on the South African situation. In this way, the author attempts to combine protest with art. For example, the interlude on page 33–5, the first of the interludes,[14] begins with comments on the preceding section, 'Saturday Night'. The interlude begins: 'Saturday night. Darkness. Sounds of snorting from my uncle at the corner.[15] After brief comments on Saturday night, the author introduces the theme of protest and talks of police raids. He describes how his grandmother used to hide tins of beer under the floor 'behind the stack'. But the interlude looks forward to the succeeding section and at the same time Mphahlele talks of how on Saturday night he thinks of school and his classmates. He talks of his feeling of inferiority, his weakness, ignorance, and self-consciousness. Finally, he makes reference to 'tomorrow' when the 'Militia' will be 'marching through', and 'the women's societies marching through in bright uniforms led by a beautiful and loud brass band'. Immediately after the interlude, the next section deals with his school experiences, headed 'Backward Child'. Thus the interlude not only links the two sections but offers comment on the apartheid situation. This technique is applied with some regularity throughout whenever the interludes occur.[16] The interlude on pages 145–7 provides another example. The preceding section ends with the 'going away' of Grandmother to Pretoria to live with his 'mother and sister'. The interlude then begins with 'Marabaetad' that has gone, gone with the going away of Grandmother. It then gives a picture of Second Avenue, and looks forward to the wedding of Ma Lebona.

Moreover, Mphahlele uses 'Second Avenue' as a symbol not only of the effects of apartheid but also structurally to connect one section of the novel to the other. There is constant return to 'Second Avenue' as the narration progresses from one section to the other. Even in the interludes, there is this constant 'come-back' to Second Avenue. The reflections of poetic experiences are often connected with Second Avenue:

> There are many more second avenues with dirty water and flies and children with traces of urine running down the legs and chickens pecking at children's stool. I have been moving up and down Second Avenue since I was born and never dreamt I should ever jump out of the nightmare.[17]

'Second Avenue' as used in this book is not simply the place where the writer lived, but also the mark of apartheid – what he calls 'the nightmare'. In the chapter headed 'Into the Slums' there are vivid descriptions of the life at Second Avenue. In Second Avenue lived the maternal grandmother, Aunt Dora, and three uncles. In these slums Ezekiel Mphahlele was to spend a great part of his early life. Here he was exposed to stark poverty, the poverty that is the lot of Africans in apartheid South Africa. The constant quarrels between mother and father depicted in the book arise from poverty. The problems in Second Avenue are complex: there is the general poverty, the insufficient accommodation, the unhealthy surrounding, and the lack of modern amenities. In the interlude on pages 189–95, Mphahlele describes these problems vividly. He recollects how they had to 'contemplate the beauty of distant electric lights', how in the 'hot nights' there was no sleep, and how he had to wait until 'the family has gone to bed' before he could find a place to do his studies. This is Mphahlele's protest; this is the use of 'factual' history as it affected his life.

In addition, structurally and thematically, *Down Second Avenue* is held together by the story of the life of Ezekiel Mphahlele. Even in sections dealing with incidents and people which do not have much to do with the author, we never forget that we are dealing with his experiences. Incidents are presented as Ezekiel experienced them, and people as he saw them. Essentially, *Down Second Avenue* is a record of Ezekiel Mphahlele's life until he was thirty-seven in 1957, when he managed to leave South Africa for Nigeria.

In so far as Mphahlele's intention is to present the 'factual' history of South Africa and the 'facts' of his own life in a work of art, the 'horrors' of the apartheid system are not overdrawn. He does not attempt to hide the ugly facts about his own family, never idealizes the African. He does not seek to apportion blame on apartheid for everything done by Africans; rather he attempts to present life in South Africa 'simply' as he experienced it. His father is always drunk and his vicious habits are not hidden. In the section 'Into the Slums', there is this portrait of his father who neglects his responsibilities to his family yet at the same time wants to do something for his children. 'He, on the other hand continued to bully, grouse, roar and fume. Mother did a brisk business in selling home-brewed beer. He drank elsewhere and came to her to ask or demand money.'[18] Then follows a description of an open quarrel between father and mother. Even in his drunken state, the father still remembers to bring home some sweets for the children. In the same way, the author, in spite of his hatred for his father, manages to express both this as mixed with feelings of pity, fear and desire for the love of a father. There is no doubt about the son's love for his mother, but what we have is the emotionally disturbing picture of a child faced with domestic troubles beyond his control. In the same way, there is the portrait of the grandmother, religious but at the same time superstitious; Aunt Dora is both kind and a fighter; the Africans are both ignorant and superstitious, and the fear of witchcraft and darkness plays a great part in their lives.

Similarly, Ezekiel Mphahlele devotes much time to his education and problems of employment. He does not hide the fact that his teachers declared him 'backward', but in his sufferings we are constantly reminded of apartheid legislations: the Bantu Education Act, Separate University Education Bill, Group Areas Act, Native Laws Amendment Act and a series of other Acts that made it extremely difficult for Africans to express their opinions, move freely, and get 'good' employment.[19] Chapters 17 to 20 are devoted to these experiences. But they are described simply as 'facts' of his life. His hatred of apartheid is clearly discernible, but occasionally there is an element of humour in these descriptions. For example, in the chapter 'Troubled with Whites', he says:

> I had my share of troubles with whites and their superior airs. It was 'yes, John', here; 'yes, Jim', there; 'What do you want boy?' here. I answered rudely whenever I was sure someone would hear me. A few times I had white lads chasing me in order to beat me up for 'rudeness' and 'put the kaffir in his place'. Luckily they never caught me.[20]

In this way, Ezekiel Mphahlele uses 'factual' history of South Africa and the 'facts' of his life to serve a purpose beyond protest.

If purpose is the major determinant of selectivity of materials for a work of art, as has been argued in this paper, Mphahlele's *Down Second Avenue* is no less a confirmation of this view. Like Richard Rive's *Emergency*, the 'factual' history of South Africa provides the background against which 'facts' of Mphahlele's life and fiction are jostled together and manipulated to produce a work of art. This is the major achievement of Mphahlele in *Down Second Avenue*.

NOTES

1. Ezekiel Mphahlele, *Down Second Avenue*, 'Introduction', New York, Anchor/Doubleday, pp. i–xxvi. Mass., Peter Smith.
2. The figure of people killed is at times put at sixty-nine, and those injured at eighty.
3. For details of apartheid legislation, see Elizabeth S. Landis, 'Apartheid Legislation', *Africa Today*, November/December 1957, 45–8.
4. Richard Rive. *Emergency*, London, Collier, 1964, p. 163. All references in this paper are to this publication. New York, Macmillan, 1970.
5. Richard Rive, *Emergency*, p. 85.
6. Elizabeth S. Landis, op. cit., 45–8.
7. Rive, op. cit., pp. 123–7.
8. Rive, op. cit., pp. 149–51.
9. See B. Lindfors's comments on Rive's characterization; *Journal of the New African Literature and the Arts*, Fall 1966, 10–16.
10. ibid., 34–5.
11. Lewis Nkosi, 'Fiction of Black South Africans', *Black Orpheus*, 19, March 1966.
12. Ezekiel Mphahlele, *Down Second Avenue*, London, Faber, 1965, p. 179.
13. The interlude sections are on pages 33–6, 60–3, 145–7, 173–5, and 189–95, in Ezekiel Mphahlele, *Down Second Avenue*, New York, Anchor/Doubleday, 1971. All future references in this paper, unless otherwise indicated, are to this edition.

14. Ezekiel Mphahlele, op. cit., pp. 33–6.
15. ibid., p. 33.
16. See interludes listed under note 13 above.
17. Ezekiel Mphahlele, op cit., p. 147.
18. ibid., pp. 16–17.
19. Elizabeth S. Landis, op. cit., 45–8.
20. Ezekiel Mphahlele, op. cit., p. 125.

The Free Spirit of Ekwensi's Jagua Nana

Loretta A. Hawkins

All groups have, it appears, embodied within their literature, their own 'free-spirited', uninhibited, almost admirable, fictitious harlot. And so Cyprian Ekwensi, in the manner of Somerset Maugham (Sadie Thompson), Defoe (Moll Flanders), and Mason (Suzie Wong), has created for literary eternity a modern-day Nigerian prostitute with whom the reader, in spite of himself and his own inhibitions, sympathizes. Jagua Nana's adventures in teeming Lagos must not be viewed as a life of degradation due to ill-fated circumstances or exploitation on the part of others. Wilfully, freely, and with abandon, Jagua lives the life she chooses with no regrets.

The novel bearing her name concerns itself primarily with political corruption and 'fast living' in Lagos, and its impact on the lives of some of the people living there. Superimposed on this apparent concern, however, is the dominating presence of Jagua Nana herself, who, although in love with Freddie Namme, a teacher many years her junior, sleeps regularly, unashamedly with other men so that she can 'wear fine cloth'.

One's unconscious search early in the novel for reasons to justify Jagua's nonchalant attitude and behaviour concerning her 'love for sale' role is futile, and upon finding no high-minded external ones such as severe poverty, starvation, or forced services, nor any internal motives, such as trauma, nymphomania, etc., one must accept reasons that are less than noble.

Ezekiel Mphahlele, in The African Image, suggests that Jagua is the feminine counterpart to Lajide in People of the City: defenceless and struggling to survive in the claws of a corrupt society. He asserts that Jagua and her fellow streetwalkers 'have to sink or swim in a life which has little else to offer for a woman to make a career out of'.[1] His assertion might hold true for Jagua's fellows, but there is little evidence in the novel to support this theory and its applicability to Jagua. Over and over it is illustrated that Jagua has the opportunity to divorce herself from Lagos society and over and over it is shown that she wilfully refuses to, with no regrets. In the face of total absence of justifiable motives for her style of living, the reader can only conclude that Jagua does what her 'God-given female talents'² make possible simply because she prefers that life to any other.

One task to be undertaken in the analysis of a character, if an accurate interpretation is to be arrived at, must be the author's intended purpose in the creation of that character. D. R. Dathorne in *The Black Mind: A History of African Literature* observes that 'in an interview ... Ekwensi remarked that he was a "writer for the masses" and "not a literary stylist" and certainly this emerges in *Jagua Nana*'.³ Ekwensi offers few, if any, excuses for Jagua's non-conformity to her traditional Ibo upbringing, and Jagua herself expresses little guilt for her wrongdoings. She either theatrically laments a past action or dismisses it as being of little consequence. One instance where she does express seemingly sincere remorse for a past action is shown where, after having refused to hasten home upon the news of her father's illness (he dies before her arrival, crying out her name), her plea is eloquently simple: 'God forgive me.'⁴ The fact that she does not acknowledge guilt for most of her amoral actions and attitudes suggests that she does not view them as being 'right or wrong'.

The very name of this character, Jagua, is used in the context of the novel as an adjective used frequently by the characters of Lagos to indicate prestige, high fashion, sophistication, and glamour, in the manner of the British car. The fact that Jagua is the *only* name she is called (except by her brother Fonso who uses the name Nana) suggests that she *was*, in essence, jagua: a name epitomizing the spirit of freedom and vivacity of personality with which she was born. This further suggests that she was Jagua *before* leaving her simple village life to become a part of the 'high life' that only Lagos and other cities like it offered.

One might wish to indulge in imagined motives to justify the conduct of Jagua, alluding in the end to the impact of Westernization on her and those in a similar situation. Whatever might have been the motivation of the others is immaterial here: Jagua was a free-spirited, determined individualist, living her life free of codes of ethics, traditional boundaries, or tribal pressures; and it was this spirit of freedom that made Jagua unique.

Examining the adolescent Jagua, we find a young girl who is very much like her later self. Living in a remote village, we find her not as a young girl sharing concerns of other girls in her age-group, but rather as one who is already entranced with her womanly self-image. She is indifferent to custom, for 'to the shock of the villagers she wore jeans and rode a bicycle ... talked loudly and her laughter was throaty ... [and] men drew to her side and wanted her'.[5] Her self-complacent attitude manifested itself in her constant changing of clothes and experimentations with make-up. Even at this early stage, Jagua recognized the power of her great beauty to attract men. 'Every few hours she went down to the waterside and took off her clothes and swam ...'[6] The boys, whom she realized were peeking, amused rather than alarmed Jagua. We clearly see that Jagua's personality and attitudes were established well before she ever ventured to Lagos, or experienced the influence of a corrupting society.

While still in her village of Ogabu we find Jagua involved in an arranged marriage to a man to whom we must at least give credit as being a 'good' husband-provider. Yet, it is from him, and his hum-drum life-style, that Jagua runs away to Lagos initially. She clearly views herself as being Jagua, and he as being 'not Jagua-ful'.[7]

In this act of running away, we see yet another dimension of Jagua's unwillingness to be bound either in body or spirit. For not only does she not give undue concern in her flight to any possible consequences to her husband (this manner of separation does not countenance prescribed custom like the returning of bride-price, etc.), her primary source of irritation is that the train's three-hour journey to Lagos is too slow. We are led to conclude that Jagua's presence in Lagos is not due to any set of unfortunate circumstances, but rather to her own free will.

Once in Lagos, after having met and become the mistress of Freddie, Jagua entertains other men for her major source of income. To Freddie's protestations, she justifies her conduct on the fact that Freddie, as a poor man, cannot provide her with the luxuries with which the other men pamper her. Her attempts to keep secret her numerous 'affairs' are motivated not from guilt or shame, but because of Freddie's disapproval of them.

When Freddie attempts to obtain a passport to England, Jagua's role is crucial, providing a 'dash' that probably involved further use of her God-given talents. We come to the realization that Jagua's body is, primarily, her wealth, and that she uses it accordingly. Beyond that, however, we conclude that she does obtain a certain degree of fulfilment from her frequent sexual encounters. Robert W. July, in his essay *The African Personality in the African Novel*, refers to Jagua Nana as an amateur prostitute, 'not in the sense of lacking skill or eschewing remuneration, but in the sense of loving her work'.[8] That she loved her work is a fact that cannot be denied, but it must also be pointed out that 'a style of living' rather than mere financial stability was Jagua's main concern. This devotion to her career has again been acknowledged by Bernth Lindfors in his critical essay 'Cyprian Ekwensi: An African Popular Novelist', wherein he describes Jagua Nana as 'an ageing Lagos prostitute who is in love with her work'.[9]

Jagua's free spirit emerges from a cognation to animalism, focusing on the spirit of freedom that such wild beings exhibit; and it is not surprising that Ekwensi describes many of her actions in such terms. When she is in jail, she is described as 'standing behind bars, and looking directly at him with an animal muteness not unlike the face he had just visualised ...'[10] At one point Ekwensi even likens her to a jaguar, the animal after whom (through common kinship with the car) she is named. When Freddie tries to break up the fight between Jagua and Nancy, 'he seized her by the wrists but with the enraged strength of a jaguar she wrested free'.[11] Later 'the maddened woman only turned on him and he felt himself torn asunder as by a lioness'.[12] When Freddie tries again to intervene,' she sprang at him, all claws and teeth'.[13] She tears his passport into pieces, throws his suitcase out of the window, proceeds to chop it to pieces with an axe, and to the tenants who have gathered, she warns 'Ah will chop you head if you touch me!'[14] Surely, here is a woman who is not concerned with what others think of her conduct.

After Freddie's departure to England, Jagua visits his home village of Bagana, at a time when Nancy is also visiting his family. A series of events leads to Jagua coming to the rescue of Nancy, again with the aid of her talents, and brings about harmony between fending factions of the Namme Family. The result of these events is an impassioned affair between Jagua and Chief Ofubara, whose wealth allows him to propose marriage to Jagua, providing her with still another opportuniity to become a respectable woman. This opportunity, like others earlier, to escape the seamy life that Lagos offered is rejected by Jagua Nana because she cannot conceive of her existence apart from Lagos and its exciting life. 'The lowest and most degraded standards of living were to her preferable to a quiet and dignified life in her own home where she would not be "free".'[15] To Dennis, a reckless young 'man of the street' who lives dangerously and dies early, believing that one must live as one wills, Jagua feels a deep sympathy. 'Somehow she felt that this young man's philosophy was intricately bound up with hers. He lived for the moment, intensely, desperately.'[16] And so did Jagua Nana.

NOTES

1. Ekekiel Mphahlele, *The African Image*, New York, Praeger, 1974, p. 277. Heinemann (AWS 146) 1975, London.
2. Cyprian Ekwensi, *Jagua Nana*, London, Panther 1963, p. 6.
3. D. R. Dathorn, *The Black Mind: A History of African Literature*, Minneapolis, University of Minnesota Press, 1974, p. 291.
4. Cyprian Ekwensi, op. cit., p. 133.
5. ibid., p. 125.
6. loc. cit.
7. loc cit.
8. Robert W. July, 'The African Personality in the African Novel', *Introduction to African Literature*, Evanston, North-western University Press, 1970, p. 222.
9. Bernth Lindfors, 'Cyprian Ekwensi, An African Popular Novelist', *African Literature Today*, 3, 1969, 8.
10. Cyprian Ekwensi, p. 18.
11. ibid., p. 31.
12. ibid., p. 32.
13. loc. cit.
14. loc. cit.
15. ibid., p. 124.
16. ibid., p. 93.

Dialectic as Form: Pejorism in the Novels of Armah

Charles E. Nnolim

> There was too much of the unnatural in any man who imagined he could escape the inevitable decay of life and not accept the decline into final disintegration. Against the all too natural, such struggles – could they be anything but the perverse attempts of desperate hedonists to perpetuate their youth against the impending rot of age?[1]

To begin with, this study will try to demonstrate that Armah is a writer whose creative vision reveals a delight with scenes of defeat, frustration, disappointment, loss. He is a writer whose philosophic pessimism is undisguised in each work. I shall go further to demonstrate that Armah is a writer of decadence identifiable with the Goncourts, Walter Pater, Paul Verlaine, and Joseph Conrad, *fin de siècle* symbolists whose works revealed their fascination with decay, corruption, and with the smell of charnel houses. As will also be demonstrated, Armah is both a cosmic pessimist (who views the world as inevitably and intrinsically bad and life in it essentially gloomy and futile), and a retrogressive pessimist or *pejorist* (one who views the world as undergoing an inevitable corruption and degeneration). The linguistic cognates of pejorism (Latin: *pejor, pejoris* – worse – implying that things are always moving from a better to a worse state) are: *corruption, decay, rot, decomposition;* which also go with their own cognates: *shrinking, dwindling, emaciation, sickness, death.*

Armah, who seems to be unusually excited by images of decay and corruption, never fails to focus on the wetness that accompanies corruption and decay (to everyone's disgust). Hence the preponderant images of *ooze, clamminess, slime, lubricity, mucus, urine,* with their accompanying offensive smells, often made more disgusting with the images of *retching, farting, vomiting,* and *bad breath.* In the works of Armah which I shall examine in this study, I shall try to highlight several linguistic clues that eventually converge to mean, in a way that structures each work and lends it form. It will also be shown that Armah buttresses and reinforces his centre (eventually pejoristic or pessimistic) through his setting (invariably a corrupt Ghana); his characterization (corrupt men and women); his figurative language (full of irony, anticlimax, bathos, understatement, counterpoint, and reductive imagery). It will also be shown that his characterization is deflationary rather than inflationary, and the repertoire of his rhetoric lacks the imagery of enhancement, hope, progress, augmentation, or increase, but rather we have the imagery of defeat, decay, frustration, disappointment, shrinking, and dwindling – all subsumed under the figurative language called bathos – since in pejorism all movement is anticlimatically pointed.

In this study, I have examined Armah's first three novels: *The Beautyful Ones Are Not Yet Born, Fragments*, and *Why Are We So Blest?* in order to point to a trend that rings so clearly in each one of them – Armah's pessimism which is pointedly marked by pejorism. That Armah is a writer of decadence is clearly seen in the metaphorical matrix of *The Beautyful Ones Are Not Yet Born*. Here, we are informed that Koomson's mouth 'had the rich stench of *rotten* menstrual blood' (p. 161) while 'a wet belch rose from his throat' (p. 163). The driver angrily shouts to the Man: 'your mother's *rotten* cunt' (p. 3); and even the smell of the cedi to the conductor (the cedi, symbol of materialism and corruption) 'was a very old smell, very strong, and so very *rotten*' (p. 3). The conductor was angry when he saw '*spittle* ... *ooze* out steadily onto the seat' from the Man (p. 5), and he 'spat out a *generous gob of mucus*' (p. 1), while the Man later fell down on 'the mess of some traveller's *vomit*' (p. 102); as the reader watches in disgust a mother calmly 'puts her mouth to the *wet congested* nostrils [of her child] and sucks them free' (p. 35, all emphasis mine).

For Armah, the pejorist, who thrives on these scences of ooze, slime, rot, and decay, Ghana is one giant, stinking lavatory: it is there that many Ghanaians take giant leaps up the pail to avoid the ordure on the floor; it is there that the chichidodo which eats the maggots that grow out of the excreta finds itself often, especially in the concluding paragraph of the novel; it is in a converted latrine that the watchman who helps escort Koomson out of Ghana lives; and it is through a latrine that Koomson and the Man escape through the shithole, covering themselves with excreta whose odour follows the Man home.

The often-quoted passage – the description of the banister – is Armah at his pejoristic best. With its emphasis on the images of rot and decay, it offers a clue to the theme and meaning of *The Beautyful Ones Are Not Yet Born*:

The wood underneath would win and win till the end of time. Of that there was no doubt possible, only the pain of hope *perennially doomed to disappointment* ... Of course, it was in the nature of wood to *rot*. But of course in the end it was the *rot* which imprisoned everything in its effortless embrace ... In the natural course of things it would always take the newness of the different kinds of polish and the vaunted cleansing power of the chemicals in them, and it would convert all to *victorious filth* ...

Apart from the wood itself there were, of course, people themselves, just so many hands and fingers bringing help to the wood in its *course toward putrefaction*. Left-hand fingers in their careless journey from a hasty anus sliding all the way up the banister as their owners made the return trip from the lavatory downstairs to the offices above. Right-hand fingers *dripping with the after-piss* and the *stale sweat* from fat crotches. The callused palms of messengers after they had *blown their clogged noses* for a convenient place to leave the *well-rubbed moisture*. Afternoon hands not entirely licked clean of palm soup and remnants of kenkey. The wood would always win. (pp. 12–13, all emphasis mine)

In a perceptive comment by Achebe during a lecture on 'Africa and Her Writers', in 1973, he struck at Armah's philosophical pessimism. He said that Armah is a brilliant writer 'who seems to me to be in grave danger of squandering his enormous talents and energy in pursuit of the *human condition*'; that *The Beautyful Ones Are Not Yet Born* 'is a sick book; sick, not with the sickness of Ghana but with the sickness of the *human condition*'. He continues:

The hero, pale and passive and nameless – a creation in the best manner of existentialist writing, wanders through the story in an anguished half-sleep, neck-deep in despair and human excrement which we rather see a lot in the book ... But his Ghana is unrecognizable. This aura of cosmic sorrow and despair is as foreign and unusable as those monstrous machines Nkrumah was said to have imported from Eastern European countries ... Ayi Kwei Armah imposes so much foreign metaphor on the sickness of Ghana that it ceases to be true.[2]

The novel, as Achebe has commented, is not really set in Ghana but in a no-man's-land in which a few Ghanaian names are used and in which the Osagyefo's overthrow is further used as a camouflage. The novel has no real identifiable locus in Africa. Nigeria would have done. So would Uganda or Togo. The point is that the novel, such as it is, has nothing essentially Ghanaian about it: no specifically Ghanaian mannerisms or special brand of politics, no language in the local idiom of the people (as we have in Achebe's *Things Fall Apart*), and the major events in the novel never take place in any well-known geographical or political centre in Ghana.

The Osagyefo himself and his overthrow could have been substituted for any of those post-independence African dictators who were swept away by a spate of military coups in which the soldiers promised to clean the country of corruption but ended up as corrupt as the politicians they had replaced.

But from this substantial vagueness in setting stems the universal implications of *The Beautyful Ones Are Not Yet Born*, Armah's first novel but one in which his creative vision is most clearly articulated. Symbolically, Armah's Ghana is Dante's *Inferno*, and much of the events take place in the circles of the avaricious, the gluttonous, and the lustful, which contain sinners who are only appeased with dirt and filth and who stink in the mire of their own corruption. There is also a touch of Bunyan's Slough of Despond – all of these lending a touch of allegory to the novel – allegory that is not fully realized because of the ambiguities which help sharpen the edge of the novel: *ambiguities*, not in the sense of obscurity but in the sense of multi-levelled meanings. For example, although Armah's novel is set in the form of a journey, it is not quite a 'Pilgrim's Progress' for, while help comes to Christian, none comes to the Man; and while Christian and Hopeful after issuing from the Prison of Despair were rewarded with two visions of the Delectable Mountains, no such pleasant visions are granted the Man and Koomson. And while Christian and Hopeful did go up the Delectable Mountain and drink and wash themselves and did eat freely of vineyards, the Man and Koomson end up being mired in excrement, the smell of which never leaves them in the end.

If Armah's Ghana is taken for a moment to represent Dante's Hell symbolically (Hell the home of the despairing and the lost) because of his philosophic pessimism, certain parallels come to light. The teacher, the Man, and Rama Krishna would belong in the Vestibule: they are people whose lives merit neither great infamy nor great praise: 'wretches who have never truly lived', and because of whom 'Heaven, to keep its beauty, cast them out, but even Hell itself would not receive them'. These characters are melancholic, guilty of unbelief in the possible goodness in man or in society, and showing neither faith nor lack of faith. Because Koomson thrives on 'eating' bribes, he belongs in Hell with the avaricious and the lustful and the gluttonous – sinners buffeted by the winds of fortune, victims of their own uncontrolled desires and appetites, full of evidence of bestiality, suffering from incontinence.

The police officers and the bus driver and his conductor belong with the fraudulent in Hell, abusing, as they continually do, the persons and the confidence of those they are supposed to serve. Kofi Billy who commits suicide and Slim Tano who murders Egya Akon belong with the Violent in Hell. The narrator says of Kofi Billy's death: 'it is possible that here was a lot of violence, too much of it, turned finally inward to destroy the man who could not bear it' (p. 74). Kofi Billy himself was an ex-soldier.

If Koomson belongs in the Third Circle with the avaricious, the lustful, and the gluttonous, he also belongs in the Eighth Circle of Hell with the Panderers, the Flatterers, and the Seducers who are immersed in excrement from which a terrible stench is emitted. In this circle, too, I place the lawyers, the politicians, and the merchant women. When Koomson and the Man pass through the shithole of the latrine, they are in the second bolgia of the Eighth Circle in Hell. Dante says:

> From a steaming stench below, the banks were coated with a slimy mould that stuck to them like glue, disgusting to behold and worse to smell . . . and from where we stood I saw souls in the ditch plunged into excrement that might well have been flushed from latrines; my eyes were searching hard along the bottom, and I saw somebody's head so smirched with shit you could not tell if he were priest or layman.

Passing through the shithole by Koomson and the Man provides a symbolic moment in *The Beautyful Ones Are Not Yet Born*: the morally corrupt Koomson also wallowing in shit and covering his body with corrupt matter, while the Man (now Bunyan's Mr Pliable) symbolically corrupts his body, because he had earlier, through his wife, shared Koomson's corrupt wealth when he failed to repudiate the boat deal. Armah's description of the moment resembles Dante's:

> He [the Man] could hear Koomson strain like a man excreting, then there was a long sound as if he were vomiting down there. But the man pushed some more, and in a moment a rush of foul air coming up told him the Party man's head was out . . .
>
> His hands encountered small, rolled-up balls of earth that felt like bits of soil thrown up by worms. The smell of cockroaches fought the human stench, and their droppings stuck to the man's elbows as he crawled through the interior of the box seat. Something that had an icy wetness made his right hand slip and entered the space underneath a fingernail, and he remembered the vomiting sound Koomson had made on his way down. (p. 166)

Finally, Maanan, who in the end falls in love with the new ruler of Ghana, resembles in her insanity, Dante's courtesan, Thais, in the Eighth Circle, who was a 'repulsive and dishevelled tramp scratching herself with shitty fingernails, spreading her legs while squatting up and down'.

But having established Hell as the gloomy, symbolic setting of despair for Armah's novel, one must hasten to add that *The Beautyful Ones Are Not Yet Born* is not Dante's *Divine Comedy*. For, while Dante's journey (accompanied by Beatrice who helps him arrive from the state of sin to the state of grace and salvation) is remedial, in Armah, the Man's journey through Nkrumah's Ghana (accompanied, in the main, by his wife Oyo, who actively prevents him attaining *salvation*, i.e. being his moral self and maintaining, without distraction, his integrity) actually leads him from grace and a sensible detachment to active involvement with Koomson whom he knows to be thoroughly corrupt and on behalf of whom he helps offer the watchman a bribe so Koomson can make good his escape.

I have said earlier that Armah is a writer of decadence and a pejorist. Irony and paradox help structure *The Beautyful Ones Are Not Yet Born* in a way that deepens the gloom of the setting. Now, to speak of irony is to speak of anticlimax, and the ironies and paradoxes in the novel are tinged with bathos. In bathos, we have a sudden collapse of high expectation, a letdown, for pejorism subsumes degeneration, decay, corruption, deterioration from the norm. The image of the Manchild is important in this context – very important as a clue to Armah's pejoristic theme:

> The picture Aboliga the Frog showed us was of the manchild in its gray old age, completely old in everything save the smallness of its size, a thing that deepened the element of the grotesque. The manchild looked more irretrievably old, far more thoroughly decayed, than any ordinary old man could ever have looked. But of course, it, too, had a nature of its own, so that only those who have found some solid ground they can call the natural will feel free to call it unnatural. And where is my solid ground nowadays? Let us just say that the cycle from birth to decay has been short. Short, brief. But otherwise not at all unusual. (p. 62)

The above is one of the key images in the novel. It accomplishes with one deft stroke what Armah's novel is all about. It mirrors the sudden rise and fall of Nkrumah, the birth of Ghana as a new nation – new, yet old and thoroughly corrupt: a nation corrupt before it was born; young as a nation, yet irretrievably old with corruption: it never had a chance to grow up like a normal child-nation. Not even a *coup d'état* by soldiers shouting fresh slogans could wash it clean or change affairs to a healthy direction. And this is one of the spots that Armah's pessimism is sharply pointed:

> New men would take into their hands the power to steal the nation's riches and to use it for their own satisfaction. That, of course, was to be expected. New men would use the country's power to get rid of men and women who talked a language that did not flatter them. There would be nothing different in that. That would be a continuation of the Ghanaian way of life ... But for the nation itself there would only be a change of embezzlers and a change of the hunters and the hunted. A pitiful shrinking of the world from those days Teacher still looked back to, when the single mind was filled with hopes of a whole people. A pitiful shrinking, to days when all the powerful could think of was to use power of a people to fill their own paunches. Endless days, same days, stretching into the future with no end anywhere in sight. (p. 160)

The central despair of the novel reveals itself in the above passage, in the most pejoristic mode. The reductive imagery of shrinking is repeated to point to a rhetorical use of bathos that runs throughout the novel.

Another important paradoxical situation in which the rhetorical matrix of corruption-cum-decay is embedded appears early in the novel. We find this in the character of Rama Krishna who is so preoccupied with the fear of corruption and decay that he tried to escape these by taking the name of Krishna in the hope of immortality, in the hope of achieving his soul's reincarnation through yoga: 'He would not corrupt himself by touching any woman but saved his semen every night to rejuvenate his brain by standing on his head a certain number of times every night and every dawn. Everywhere he wore a symbolic evergreen and a faraway look on his face, thinking of the escape from corruption and of immortality' (p. 47). Rama Krishna paradoxically dies young, of consumption, and with an inside so decayed and rotten that maggots packed themselves inside his heart, thus belying his celibacy and making nonsense of his fears:

> It was of consumption that he died so very young, but already his body inside had undergone far more decay than any living body, however old and near death, can expect to see. It was whispered ... that the disease had completely eaten up the frail matter of his lungs, and that where his heart ought to have been there was only a living lot of worms gathered together tightly in the shape of a heart. (p. 48)

Rama Krishna's unsuccessful attempts to escape corruption reminds one of the futility of such efforts in Armah whose pejoristic philosophy is expressed on page 47 of the novel under discussion (I have quoted it at the beginning of this study): There is:

> too much of the unnatural in any man who imagined he could escape the inevitable decay of life and not accept the decline into final disintegration. Against the all too natural, such struggles – could they be anything but the perverse attempts of desperate hedonists to perpetuate their youth against the impending rot of age?

Irony, ambiguity, and paradox – all pejoristically pointed – have now emerged as the novel's rhetorical pattern. Paradox is further revealed in Oyo's description of the Man as a chichidodo: 'The chichidodo hates excrement with all its soul. But the chichidodo only feeds on maggots, and you know the maggots grow best inside the lavatory' (p. 44).

Character delineation in *The Beautyful Ones Are Not Yet Born* is also carried out through irony and paradox in which each character is eventually revealed in a bad light or as having degenerated from the ideal or norm. The protagonist, the Man, bears the burden of this paradoxical representation, and his being likened to a chichidodo is the first case in point. Another important irony surrounding the Man is seen in the fact that what he tries to get away from he ends up being mired in. All his life he has tried to dissociate himself from the corrupt life of Koomson and his ilk, yet through his wife, Oyo, and mother-in-law, he gets involved with Koomson through the boat deal. At a certain point, when Koomson takes shelter in his house, the Man tries not to breathe the foul smell from Koomson's mouth and the nauseous flatulences from his anus, but he ends up trapped in them and taking large gulps of them through his mouth. And in the end, the Man who, throughout, has tried to maintain an untainted moral posture, through his own volition shares, after the military coup, in the final escape of Koomson, by accompanying him through the shithole of the latrine. And the Man, who at the beginning refused to accept bribes, ends up successfully urging the boatman to offer a bribe to the watchman so that Koomson can make good his escape. Moral theologians tell us that evil prospers because good men do nothing. With the Man, evil prospers because supposedly 'good' men take an active part in promoting corruption. Those who insist that the Man is a man in the middle mistake the point. He is worse than a chichidodo. He eats shit!

Those who think that the last is a harsh judgement of the Man will soon be convinced of the contrary. The ending of the novel which shows the Man physically tainted by shit and morally tainted by descent from his previously avowed high moral posture had been foreshadowed all along through several hints by the author. Earlier, we note that the sight of money easily excites him:

> The day before, going into the shops with his new money in his pocket, he had had the uncontrollable feeling of happiness and power, even while knowing somewhere in the back of his mind that the expensive things he was buying would deepen the agony of his next Passion Week ... There was also, inside the man himself, a very strong happiness whenever he found himself able, for no matter how brief a spell, to do the heroic things that were expected all the time, even if in the end it was only himself he was killing. (p. 114)

And in spite of his vaunted purity of character, the Man is by no means a shining example of a moral or decent member of society. His marriage to Oyo was shotgun (Oyo's 'parents had come with their long story of their daughter ruined', p. 116). So he had to marry her. And further, by his own admission, he tells the Teacher: 'How can I look on Oyo and say I hate long shiny cars? How can I come back to the children and despise international schools?' (p. 92). Ambivalence, therefore, is the hallmark of the Man's character. He is a bundle of pejoristic contradictions.

And the Teacher, the Man's mentor, is a bundle of contradictions writ large in his character. The teacher is supposedly morally detached from the corrupt life one finds everywhere in Ghana. But he demolishes his admirer, the Man, when he admits he is by no means pure. When he tells the Man they are all chichidodos, the Man says:

> 'I thought you were a person entirely free of all this' he answers: 'No. I have tried to be free, but I am not free. Perhaps I will never even be.' (p. 54).

We are let down. It seems there is no just man in Ghana. The pessimism of the novel is thus deepened. Then, the despair of the novel is further pinpointed when the Man says to the Teacher:

> 'You're still hoping, aren't you, Teacher?'
> 'Hoping for what?'
> 'Anything. An end to this ... a beginning to something else. Anything.'
> 'No, not hoping any more. Not hope, anyhow. I don't feel any hope in me any more ... When you can see the end of things even in their beginnings, there's no more hope, unless you want to pretend, or forget, or get drunk, or something.' (p. 60)

A host of other characters in the novel are touched with this despair, and degeneration touches them all in the end. There are the World War II veterans – those illiterate African soldiers who were conscripted to fight another man's war in the jungles of Burma and elsewhere. When they came home from their 'victory' they were abandoned and forgotten by those who forced them to leave home and family. Neither farmers now nor artisans, they drifted about and dissipated themselves in directionless despair. Some, Armah tells us, 'went simply mad, like Home Boy, endlessly repeating harsh, unintelligible words of command he had never understood ... Some went very quietly into a silence no one could hope to penetrate, something so deep that it swallowed completely men who have before been strong. They just plunged into the silence and died' (p. 64). 'Plunged' is a significant word in the arsenal of Armah's rhetoric in which bathos plays a crucial role.

Kofi Billy is also such a one. He, after losing a leg in the war, deteriorates and later hangs himself. Then there was Slim Tano who was instrumental in the murder of Egya Akon. He, too, deteriorated and went insane shouting, 'I didn't do it o o o o!' And Maanan, the woman who falls in love with the new ruler of Ghana, in the end predictably deteriorates mentally and goes insane and is seen by the Man as a woman 'being pushed toward destruction and there was nothing she or I could do about it' (p. 71). Koomson, who exits from the novel with a whimper, leaving behind a beautiful house and a beautiful wife for uncertain exile after the bathetic and unflattering way he left the Man's house through the shithole that covers him with excrement, dramatically points to the pejoristic trend in the novel: this deterioration from a man of power and influence to animal-like cowardly exit like a criminal, this degeneration from a man of position who disdains using a smelly latrine to ease himself, to wallowing, head first, into the excrement shows Armah at his pejoristic best. In the end, Koomson, the moral outcast, becomes also the social outcast on the run. And while Koomson bathetically exits from the novel into exile, the Man goes home to face his hungry children and an unsatisfied wife. In the novel, Armah's pessimism is underlined by depicting an unhealthy body politic whose ugly plight is made worse by characters who are morally corrupt and physically unhealthy. To achieve this, Armah avoids any rhetoric which implies increase, augmentation, progress, hope, or amplification. What preponderates and gives form and meaning is rather the rhetoric in which words like rotting, decomposition, sickness, corruption, decaying, shrinking, dwindling, death, are dominant.

Certain tensions in the movement of the novel are maintained by the effective use of contrast and counterpoint. This counterpoint is seen in the characters of Rama Krishna and Maanan: Krishna, outwardly physically robust but inwardly decayed and rotten, is counterpointed against Maanan who is mentally deranged though outwardly all right. Also the Teacher who, while seemingly isolated from the corruption all round him, admits he is by no means untainted, is counterpointed against the Man who never admits moral taint but gets involved with Koomson (indirectly) in the boat deal and, directly, when he persuades the boatman to offer bribes to the watchman in order to enable Koomson to escape.

The use of counterpoint later develops into rhetorical paradoxes, again pejoristically pointed, in imagery that sometimes seems skewed. This is seen first in the imagery of leaping – leaping that predictably ends in self-defeat. For example, just as Rama Krishna's isolation from life so he could remain purified finds him at death more decayed than those who took no such steps, Armah informs us that those who have succeeded in life in Ghana – those who drive instead of walk – are those who have taken bold *leaps* into corruption – the Koomsons, the Yamoas, the Zacharias Lagoses: 'That has always been the way the gleam is approached: in one bold corrupt leap that gives the leaper the power to laugh with contempt at those of us who still plod on the daily round, stupid, honest, dull, poor, despised, afraid. We shall never arrive unless, of course, we too take the jump' (p. 95).

The next imagery of leaping ends pointedly on a bathetic or downward note. It is about people who leap in the lavatory, in an environment so revolting to the senses: 'And in a few incredible places men seemed to have jumped quite high and then to have accomplished a downward stroke' (p. 105).

Other paradoxes help structure the beginning and the end of the novel. The novel opens at dawn with the Man just awake from sleep in a bus, *walking toward* his office and *away* from his home; it ends with the Man, again just awake from sleep outside a bus, *walking towards* his home in the evening, and *away* from his office. Secondly, the novel opens with the bus moving and flashing its light as dawn approaches; it ends with the bus driving toward approaching dusk. Thirdly, the book opens with the Man refusing to accept the little bribe offered him by the bus conductor; it ends with the Man successfully urging the boatman to offer a bribe to the watchman so Koomson could escape. Finally, the book opens with the Man mistaken by the bus conductor for a silent awake watcher *inside* the bus when, in fact, the Man is asleep – for which he is thoroughly abused by both driver and conductor; it ends with the Man fully awake *outside* the bus, this time actually watching the bus driver proffer a bribe to the policeman, and when the driver knows he is seen by the Man, he inexplicably becomes friendly, smiling and waving to the Man.

Finally, when one reads *The Beautyful Ones Are Not Yet Born* as this study has done, through discovering pejorism as the major vehicle of the novel's meaning, one could easily conclude that Armah's novel is a perfect work of art – perfect because it is a novel in which *fable* or content is in perfect fusion with *sujet* or narrative technique. In addition, the novel belongs with modern novels that have the technique of 'openness' of ending: for our experience of the futility and despair in the body-politic of Ghana keeps expanding even after the action of the novel is rounded up. And this is symbolically mirrored for the reader in the smell of shit which clings to the Man even after the cleansing action of the sea, and in the presence of the chichidodo atop a latrine. The concluding words of the novel show this 'openness' of ending and this ever-expansion of experience after the conclusion of the novel: it certainly is not a better life the Man was going back to and it is not a better or greater Ghana that the military coup has ushered in:

> Over the school latrine at the bottom of the hill a bird with a song that was strangely happy dived low and settled on the roof. The man wondered what kind of bird it could be, and what its name was. But then suddenly all his mind was consumed with thoughts of everything he was going back to – Oyo, the eyes of the children after six o'clock, the office and every day, and above all *the never-ending knowledge that this aching emptiness would be all that the remainder of his own life could offer him.* (p. 180, emphasis added)

The title of Armah's first novel makes a statement that involves looking forward to the future for an answer; it says that the beautiful ones are not yet born: from a look into the novel, one is inclined to ask – will they ever be?

If pejorism is the major concern of *The Beautyful Ones Are Not Yet Born*, Armah's next novel, *Fragments*, centres on futility and disillusionment: on pessimism (Latin: *pessimus*, worst). Ghana is the worst possible world which is glimpsed in the sign in Akan: OBRA YE KO, LIFE IS WAR. In *Fragments*, Armah focuses before the reader's eyes characters defeated by this cruel world. Juana is the first character who comes to mind, even though she is a minor character. But she is what we call a *ficelle* (a minor character who throws light on the major character and events). Juana, an expatriate doctor in Ghana who first was struck by the sign OBRA YE KO, says she is in a land where she finds herself trying 'to forget that now the sum of her life was only that she was here in another *defeated and defeating place, to forget all the reminders of futility*' (emphasis mine).[3]

Elsewhere the narrator says of her life in Ghana where she had gone to pick up the pieces of her shattered life in the Caribbean:

> She searched in herself for something that might make sense, but there was *nothing* she could herself believe in, *nothing* that wouldn't just be the high flight of the individual alone, escaping the touch of life around him. That way she knew there was only *annihilation*. Yet here she knew terrible dangers had been lying in wait the other way – other kinds of *annihilation*. How could she find the thing to break down his *despair* [Baako's] when she had never conquered hers? There would be no meaning in offering him a chance to swing from present *hopelessness* to a different flavor of *despair*. (p. 271, emphasis mine)

There is a touch of nihilism which compounds the despair and hopelessness expressed in the above passage. The italicized words point to the use of word-clusters by Armah, which in the end, add together to *mean* and to point to the central theme. The simple story which *Fragments* tells is a pathetic one that is replete with a series of ecstasies that end in agonies, triumphs that end in defeats, the ideal frustrated by the real and the actual, high hopes defeated by unfulfilled existence. Life's frustrations are presented through a series of juxtapositions and contrasts. The story of Baako, a been-to who pathetically ends up in an asylum, is told through a series of contrasting scenes flashed before the reader. His lonely, unnoticed return from overseas is juxtaposed against the exaggeratedly heady and dizzying welcome arranged for Brempong at the airport. Brempong, his own people's hero, is ushered home in a limousine amidst dancing and noise while Baako suffers the ultimate humiliation of having mere taxi drivers refuse him their services because he seems a nobody – all within earshot of the din of Brempong's tumultuous homecoming. Then, there is the anticlimactic but pointed juxtaposition between the triumphant skilful killing of the dog with the pick-axe by the man with the swollen scrotal sac, and the symbolic deflation of his pride when his scrotal sac burst with the exertion: 'a look of terror stopped the man's triumph as first he felt the drip and then looked down to see what it could be' (p. 29).

Then there are other juxtapositions that end in nothing but bathos. Baako's triumphant flight to study overseas (in the asylum his mother said of the flight: 'it must make you so different to have flown, looking at us all crawling down below'), is counterpointed with his lonely homecoming and his more frustrated existence as a been-to who doesn't own a car. Baako's own idealistic hope to revolutionize Ghana through creative journalism at Ghanavision' is counterpointed with the frustrations he experiences at the hands of the highest policy-makers in Ghana's civil service. The principal secretary tells him: 'If you come back thinking you can make things work in any smooth, efficient way, you'll just get a complete waste of your time. It is not worth bothering about' (p. 119). And later: 'You know, Baako, what you are getting there is not a chance to do any useful work. Heaven help you if you go into Civil Service thinking you are going to work' (p. 110).

Frustrations, futility and despair therefore underline Armah's pessimism in *Fragments*: the futility of Baako's mother, Efua, who has a son and not a son; of Juana, who watches her lover, Baako, degenerate into a mental case while at the same time she watches helplessly the deteriorating medical situation in the hospital ('the doctors here know things are a mess', she complains, 'but they accept it. Like some hopeless reality they can't even think of changing ... They told me I was wasting my time talking of a changed approach' (pp. 191–2); of Baako who, when he found he could not influence for the better Ghana's corrupt civil service, burnt his scripts in despair; and of Baako's grandmother, Naana, who, disappointed in her grandson, laments helplessly that 'what remains of my days will be filled with more broken things', and says of her dying soul that it 'gave up the rushing, unending journey and found rest in despair, not trying again to regain the larger meaning' (pp. 280, 281).

Pejorism is inherent in these vignettes. The above skeletalized appraisal of *Fragments* reveals further that Armah's people and establishments nearly always go from bad to worse with no hope of their ever getting better.

In *Why Are We So Blest?* the protagonist, Modin, is a nihilist *par excellence*: he calls himself a revolutionary, and is a student of insurrections who is 'hoping to apply for a highly paid job as a subversive element' (p. 177).[4] He is also a fatalist:

> I am fated to undergo some form of death. There is no sanctuary. I have known periods of spiritual death when I have shut myself up away from the world. There is loneliness that is a kind of death. But the solution available, involvement with these people, is itself a deeper form of death. (p. 159)

For Modin, 'the force for our own death is within us. We have swallowed the wish for our destruction', in a world which is 'a graveyard for my spirit. Not mine alone. Ours' (p. 159). To make matters worse, Modin has a suicidal proclivity to get involved in friendships and situations that lead to nothing but frustrations, physical pain, and even death. And he knows it:

> I see my manic pushes to the point of danger clearly. I have hidden despair from myself, but lived in it. Each push was another point in search for self-annihilation. I have wanted to destroy myself, but so well-hidden has the desire for suicide been, its temptations have always looked like extreme pleasure offered, taken, tasted. (p. 158)

His friendships with women are always tinged with the same suicidal fatalism. He nearly loses his life over his affair with Mrs Jefferson ('Mrs. Jefferson was a long, free slide along slippery paths', p. 158). Mr Jefferson, on discovering their liaison, nearly stabs him to death. He survives this, but he surely suffers a lot of pain. His next affair with Aimée – a girl who calls herself a monster and who suffers from the general cosmic malaise that prevents her from achieving orgasm (orgasm that 'changes everything' and 'reconciles you to the world', p. 96, actually leads to his death at the hands of insurrectionists.

Degeneration is the slippery path to damnation in *Why Are We So Blest?* Modin is a protagonist whose quest all along has not been for the spiritually elevating but for the morally debasing, for the physically enervating. At the very end, the expansive and extroverted Modin ('my periods of dissipation have been a dispersal of myself; some I fling dangerously wide indeed, then after reaching exhaustion, I need to bring the pieces, if I can find them, back together', p. 158), has withdrawn within himself, a victim of paranoia. At this stage Aimée writes of him: 'He just stays in his shell ... He has deteriorated a lot ... He's lost his drive' (p. 283).

For those who love symbol-hunting, the setting of *Why Are We So Blest?* is a good ground. Laccryville has nothing cheerful or mind-elevating about it – with its connotations of mourning, tears, weeping, the lachrymose. That is Armah's gloomy world where, as Solo says of himself:

> Life has lost the sustaining swing; it is a long time since it became one long downward slide. Along the way everything turned ashen, barren, white. There are stops; not to get refreshed – nothing recreative of life survives along this road – but to let the enveloping sterility cover the desperate mind more completely. (p. 84)

In Laccryville the newspapers print nothing but disasters all over the world: 'They don't print any good news . . . Flood hits Thailand. Copper miners strike in Chile, the war in Vietnam' (p. 97).

Characteristically, the pessimism and futility and despair in *Why Are We So Blest?* are tinged with pejorism: the expansive Modin, in the end, has shrunk to his shell. Modin's diary on his last days shocks Solo by the extreme loneliness it reveals: Solo says that 'these lines transmitted one overwhelming message: loneliness' (p. 268). Aimée's experiences in Africa end on a bathetic note. Her ambition, tinged with enthusiasm, to obtain a job with the UPC, so that she and Modin can continue their revolutionary dreams, ends in disillusionment. At the UPC offices she is raped. And when Aimée, who has come to Africa to live and practise the life of a revolutionary, decides to go home to democratic and bourgeois America, her disillusionment and frustration has reached rock bottom. And all of Modin's relationships end on an anticlimactic note: in addition to breaking with the Portuguese girl Sylvia on the night of their engagement, he has broken with his benefactors Professor Jefferson and Mr Oppenhardt. At the very end, he has begun calling Aimée a racist and they have begun to go their separate ways. The worst of all is Modin's death and the way his body is abandoned in the desert – a lone corpse of a student of insurrections.

Finally, what makes *Why Are We So Blest?* such a pessimistic work is that in it Armah extends the frontiers of his pessimism beyond Ghana: he makes despair and futility part of the twentieth-century malaise that crosses national boundaries so that a major theme is the futility of forging friendships among people of different countries and races. They are bound to misunderstand one another. They are bound either to withdraw within their own shell or, failing to change the world, go back where they have come from.

All things considered, Armah is a *dark* writer, in the sense that Milton was a *dark* poet, Rembrandt a *dark* painter and Schopenhauer a *dark* philosopher. Writing in the post-bellum twentieth century (with its cataclysmic wars, economic woes and unimagined psychological tensions), and in post-independence Africa (with painful memories of colonial repression and brutality, political instability in Africa, and the disintegration of age-old values), Armah's philosophic pessimism places him in the ranks of writers we truly call 'representative'. He is one of those writers who articulate in bold language what others are too modest or too nice to put in print. At the same time, one must express revulsion at the insensitivity in Armah's language in which there is a lack of discriminating taste and, one must say, a lack of *class*. Achebe, in *A Man of the People*, accomplished much of what Armah tried to do in *The Beautyful Ones Are Not Yet Born* with respect to the body-politic of their respective countries. Armah did not have to spill vomit on white paper in his first novel in order to depict for us the corruption that has eaten deep into the social fabric of Ghana. But having made this point, one must admit that when it comes to the recurrent and persistent use of word-clusters that provide linguistic clues to an author's artistic device, Armah's consistent use of pessimism and pejorism has become a major vehicle of meaning in his works: it has proved to be a very effective, consistent, and artistic rhetorical device.

NOTES

1. Ayi Kwei Armah, *The Beautyful Ones Are Not Yet Born*. London, Heinemann (AWS 43), 1969. New York, Collier, 1969, p. 47. Further references to this edition will only be indicated by citation of the page number within the text.
2. Chinua Achebe, 'Africa and Her Writers', *Massachusetts Review*, xiv, 1973, 624–5. The emphases are Achebe's.
3. Ayi Kwei Armah, *Fragments*, London, Heinemann (AWS 154), 1974. p. 17. Further citations from this edition will be made by page reference within the text. New York, Collier 1971.
4. Ayi Kwei Armah, *Why Are We So Blest?*, London, Heinemann (AWS 155), 1974. New York, Doubleday/Anchor, 1973. Further citations will be made by page reference within the text.

Nortje: Poet at Work

R. G. Leitch

All hungers pass away ...' is one of the last poems, if not the last poem, composed by the poet Arthur Kenneth Nortje. Although many of his manuscripts are available, these are usually fair copies without drafts, or drafts without fair copies, or simply fragments. Of 'All hungers pass away ...' a draft as well as a fair copy is extant; also, it is published. An analysis of the process of its creation is necessary if we are to gain further insights about the poet's modes of composition.

The draft is written on a poster inviting contributors to submit poems, pictures and stories to Mary Holland. The poster is interesting in that it depicts a kneeling figure, blindfolded and bound, with an executioner's axe poised above it. We shall present the draft poem as the poet wrote it, citing the lining, erasures, insertions, and cancellations. The asterisks are the poet's.

(1) All hungers pass away,
(2) we lose track of their dates:
(3) desires arise like births,
(4) reign for a time like potentates.
    I lie & listen   the
(5) ~~Listening~~   to the ~~morning~~ rain ~~in bed~~
(6) ~~the~~ hours before full dawn brings
(7) forward a further day & winter sun
    here
(8)   in a land where rhythm fails.
         no   springs
(9) *~~Drakensberg lies swatched in gloom~~
    Warily
(10) ~~Dreamily~~ I shake off sleep,
(11) stare in the mirror with dream-puffed eyes:
    ~~among the tables where I used~~
(12) I drag my shrunken corpulence
(13) among the tables of rich libraries.
(14) Fat hardened in the mouth,
(15) ~~the~~ famous viands tasted like ash:
(16) the mornings after of a sweet escape
    ended

(17) dreamily over bangers & mash.
(18) *starvation stalks the farms of the Transvaal.
(19) I gave those pleasures up,
(20) the sherry circuit, arms of some bland girl.
(21) Drakensberg ...
(22) What consolation comes
(23) drips away as bitterness.   (accumulates)
　　　Blithe
(24) 　　　Footfalls pass my door
(25) as I recover from the wasted years.

AKN – 11/70*

These lines were composed later:

(26) The rain abates. Face-down 　　　　$\left[\begin{array}{l}\text{bitter missery}\\\text{miserable bitterness}\end{array}\right.$
　　　 thin arms folded
(27) I lie, ~~courting oblivion,~~ half-aware
(28) of skin that tightens over pelvis.
(29) Pathetic, this, the dark posture.

AKN *

He composed the first stanza easily (lines (1), (2), (3), (4) and made no alterations to it:

> All hungers pass away,
> we lose track of their dates:
> desires arise like births,
> reign for a time like potentates.

The second stanza came easily even though he made four alterations to it. The substitution of 'I lie and listen' for 'Listening' in (5) was preferable because it is direct; whereas the participle, 'Listening' is a prosy stylization. 'I lie and listen', with its combination of related vowels and consonants, gives a sense of ease and fluency to the line which harmonizes with the tone of recumbent unease of the stanza. The poet discarded 'morning' for metrical and rhetorical reasons: for metrical reasons because the anapaest 'to the rain' in (5) emphasizes 'rain', a pivotal word in the vocabulary of the poet;[1] for rhetorical reasons because 'dawn' in (6) makes 'morning' redundant. His deletion of 'the' at the beginning of (6) fronts 'hours' for emphasis. The insertion of 'here' at the beginning of (8) is done for the same reason. The stanza is:

> I lie and listen to the rain
> hours before full dawn brings
> forward a further day and winter sun
> here in a land where rhythm fails.

The speaker, 'I', is a significant feature not only of the second stanza but of the entire poem and, we might add, of most of Nortje's poems. Though meditative and introspective, the poem also focuses on other men suffering the acerbities and absurdities of existence. The inclusive 'we' of the first stanza militates against an exclusive focus on 'I'. The poet chose 'I' to make concrete the general statement of stanza one.

The alterations to stanza two were probably made after the poet composed the germinal lines for the first four stanzas. I attest these reasons. The line (9) 'Drakensberg lies swathed in the gloom' becomes the third line of the fifth stanza. Even though the line is in its final form, he deleted it because it is not in its final place. Secondly, the speaker must elaborate the earlier condition of his existence so that the later ironic contrast starting with 'I gave those pleasures up' (19) can be established. Thirdly, below the materials for the first four stanzas and marked with an asterisk, 'Starvation stalks the farms of the Transvaal' (18) appears. This line, as well as the materials for the fifth stanza, is clearly set apart and penned in careful handwriting. The second asterisk marks a stage of the composition of the poem. Up to the asterisk, the poet composed his draft rapidly but without consideration for prosodical corrections. Satisfied that the rest of the poem will come easily, he made his revisions above the asterisk.

'Warily' appears above the deletion of 'Dreamily' (10). 'Warily' was preferred because it marks a stronger acoustical shift from the melancholy gloom of 'where rhythm fails'. Its efficacy in ringing a change arises from the medial 'r'. 'Dreamily' introduces too muffled a modulation and does not demarcate as well the next moment in the scenario: from the speaker's lying in bed to his staring into the mirror. Also, 'Dreamily' is partly repeated in 'dream-puffed' (11). The statement, deleted later, 'among the tables where I used', is a probable substitution for 'I drag my shrunken corpulence' (12). This appears to be so because 'I' is deleted at the beginning of the line, evidently to allow for the insertion of 'to' for grammatical continuity; the emphasis would have been thrown on 'corpulence' because it would have been the pivotal line of the stanza. In sum, the third stanza was composed with facility. Except for 'Warily', the poet rejected his own revisions to the stanza:

> Warily I shake off sleep,
> stare in the mirror with dream-puffed eyes,
> drag my shrunken corpulence
> among the tables of rich libraries.

The poet's alterations (15) and (17) need not concern us. What is puzzling is the line (16) which he left unaltered. In the published version the hyphenated compound, 'mornings-after', occurs.[2] No such compound exists in the poet's draft or fair copy. The line 'the mornings after of a sweet escape' is flat because 'of' makes it grammatically unsound, and 'sweet escape' is ornate. We might argue that the strategy of the poet was to establish a tone of cold bitterness (14), (15). He then wished to break up the regular and stately movement of the verse with the line (16) with its pair of weak stresses on 'of' and 'a'. This line with its exaggerated sentiment would function as a modulator of tonality between the assertive (14) and (15) and the colloquial, anticlimactic 'bangers and mash' (17):

> Fat hardened in the mouth,
> famous viands tasted like ash:
> the mornings after of a sweet escape
> ended over bangers and mash.

The juxtaposition of events and imagery in the stanza is instructive. We noted that 'Drakensberg lies swathed in gloom' (9) is in its final form but not in its final place. The line 'Starvation stalks the farms of the Transvaal' (18) and (9) evoke an experiential context different from the rest of the poem. The juxtaposition of settings is consciously executed: it is not a mere exercise in evoking a response not justified in the poem. 'Drakensberg' literally translates as mountain of the dragons. The poet's choice of 'Drakensberg lies swathed in gloom' is structurally significant in this sense: the spirit of defiance embodied by these mountains is torpid or dead, for the dragons are 'swathed' in the bandages of the maimed or the shrouds of the dead; the agents of this spirit of defiance are the victims of 'starvation' on the 'farms of the Transvaal'. The speaker has given up 'the sherry circuit' and the 'arms of a bland girl' (20) because he has found no 'consolation' in sensuous delights. The speaker is totally disillusioned because he sees his predicament but cannot act to correct it. The justification for the South African setting, then, is not mechanical, not perversely obfuscatory, but points to the poet's attempts to unify and evaluate all his experience.

> I gave those pleasures up,
> the sherry circuit arms of a bland girl.
> Drakensberg lies swathed in gloom.
> Starvation stalks the farms of the Transvaal.

Nortje composed the sixth stanza without apparent difficulty. On the right-hand side opposite (23), 'accumulates' appears in rounded brackets. He inserted 'Blithe' after composing the stanza to which 'AKN – 11/70' and his characteristic line and star are appended.

> What consolation comes
> drips away in bitterness.
> Blithe footfalls pass my door
> as I recover from the wasted years.

The last stanza was probably composed later. The stanza is written on a piece of notebook paper and is characteristically signed with a line and star below the signature; but no date is written. The present writer received a fair copy of the poem in the second week of December; it is written in a Christmas card with the salutation 'to Ray, Doreen, Inez, Lloyd/Yrs ever,/Arthur/12/70'. If we assume that the poem was written a few days before the poet's death (he died on the eighth or ninth of December) then the poem, especially the phrase 'the dark posture' (29), assumes macabre significance. Stanza seven could easily have been written below six. We could speculate interminably about an explanation. The point is the last stanza was written later, closer to the time of the poet's death when he despaired of living.

The stanza was written effortlessly. He penned 'bitter misery' and 'miserable bitterness' opposite (26), but these are not included in the poem. The only, but important, alteration is 'thin arms folded' for 'courting oblivion' in (27). The discarded phrase is a flat cliché, but it points to the dark thoughts of the speaker.

> The rain abates. Face-down
> I lie, thin arms folded, half-aware
> of skin that tightens over pelvis.
> Pathetic, this, the dark posture.

The general theme of the poem is its melancholy assertion of the transitoriness of desire. The poet enunciates this theme in his opening stanza which he wrote easily. The following five stanzas, which elaborate the theme, came to the poet without much exertion. Written as effortlessly as the first, the seventh stanza ends the poem with the notion that the speaker or poet is as transitory as the desires which cloyed his appetites.

Once Nortje had written a poem and was satisfied with a particular draft, he wrote a fair copy which he submitted to a typist to make copies. From a letter dated 3 January 1967, which he wrote to M.L.,[3] we learn that this person typed most of the fair copies of the poems that appear in *Seven South African Poets*.[4] He made the following comment about an error in the poem 'Sea-days and Summerfall':[5]

> And a rap over the knuckles for my dear typist (viz. 'things' for 'thighs' in *Sea-days*) – the malaise catches, no? Or perhaps I *did* err in the script you had, but I'm almost certain the error is a D.W. one. Anyway, I can edit it by pencil before sending it to *Black Orpheus* (Nigeria) or somewhere. The others are perfect, the super type again making me feel that the poem is somehow more deep & meaningful than it is.

Satisfied with the textual accuracy of the typed copies, he circulated them among his friends and associates for critical comment or for their inclusion in literary magazines. For example, to the present writer he sent 'Newcombe at Croydon West', 'The Times', and 'Poem for a Kitchen'. He wrote to his typist on 8 December 1966:[6]

> Incidentally, sweets, my London contact (D.B.) finds he likes *Affinity For Maggie* very much. He goes on about 'wonderful freedom of structure, etc.' If they take this thing, I hope you don't mind me keeping the title the way it is. The pun 'for' in the bracket was unintentional – usually poems are addressed 'to' people who for one reason or another one has thought much about.

There is no evidence that the poems published posthumously by Heinemann, including 'Sonnet Three' and 'All Hungers Pass Away', were regarded by the poet as being ready for circulation among his friends or for publication.

The poet should have the last word about his prosody:[7]

> For me, unlike Yeats painstakingly sketching in prose & then translating it into poetry, stripping the prose clean or filling the skeleton out with meat of meaning, as the case may be; let the emotion find its own direction, and trust that inner voice testing and hearing new sounds and phrases as they come through the brain's wind tunnel. They stand up to the poem or are rejected, but the advantage is that they clash with what already exists. The line or idea which has set the poem in motion, can throw up by turmoil a rich humus which may or may not fertilise things under two conditions: the poem must turn out to be
> (a) new
> (b) autonomous. These are vitalising criteria. Then, only then, is the *message clear*.

NOTES

1. R. J. Leitch, 'A Critical Analysis of the Poetry of Arthur Kenneth Nortje', unpublished MA thesis, University of Toronto, 1975, p. 30.
2. ibid., 'Appendix', p. 162.
3. The identity of this person is known, but it is not appropriate to disclose it.
4. Arthur Kenneth Nortje, Journal MS, unpaginated, started December 1965; pagination added to xerography by R. G. Leitch; p. 146.
5. ibid., p. 134. The poem 'Sea-days and Summerfall' is contained in *Lonely Against the Light*.
6. Journal, pp. 142–3.
7. ibid., p. 67.

Two Poems by Nortje
With a note by Dennis Brutus

T hese two poems by Arthur Nortje have not been published previously. They are an important addition to the body of his work. A portion of 'Dead Roots' appears in *Lovely Against the Light*, published at Rhodes University, Grahamstown, South Africa. It is barely intelligible and may include lines from drafts of other poems. I had hoped to use 'Dead Roots' for the collection by that name which I edited for Heinemann's African Writers Series but was unable to find the poem at the time. As can be seen from the date, Nortje was working on 'Dead Roots' shortly before his tragic death at Jesus College, Oxford, December 1970.

Apology from London

only at the particular moment how
disappointment hurts. It is another scene
that hears the lark at dawn in boughs of lush
green – we must all return and break more stone

south over the sea to where the diseased wind
rages in the dockyard of the soul.
In an English spring we litter our sorrows
following each other in a muddied file

or grouped in Highgate round a dead philosopher's
bust on a tomb, harsh-featured. Rain
washed the garlands. Your tears
eroded me. This is the short and plain

says Chaucer, Bodley. Do not sorrow wise man
goes Beowulf in an Oxford dialogue.
An apology arrives at breakfast:
your last non-appearance makes you beg

mercy. You are my blood as much as he, she,
you have as much right as any other.
There are those in that sun and rock country
who wouldn't dare call me brother.

Not over the marmalade that I'm surprised
or fierce because of trivial error.
'The longe love that in my thought doeth harbour':
it is the larger suffering symbolized

Dead Roots

What I lose will have to be lost for life
and what I endeavour be tied into a concord
on this temporary isle,
I who wear
black flower in my buttonhole
hearing the demagogues
din in my ears
from the land of my fathers.
Invisibly reversed
by boom economies, quietly mutated
through golden ages,
there still live
my several lovers

> and I do not hate
> the sun still rising
> though nostalgic
> for that alien summer's
> cornucopia.

A minute's wavering in a winter bookshop
finds me turning tomorrow's pages
instead of deciding to buy the volume
suddenly thousands of miles away
climbing Table Mountain
and hoping a snake won't slither across my finger.
I who have seen the maple and the snow
piled high in the moneyed northern streets
and came back to smell the rose among the spires
with a blessing for St George
whether the fates will choose to twist
this clothed flesh into spirals of agony
round the entrenched and articulate bones
or whether the Paraclete
will intercede for such a one as I
dispersed Hotnot ...

There were the stones wherewith
sparks were struck against the asphalt,
memory of my youth.
How they seem almost ancestral,
totems that inhabit dreams,
the carved faces now uncarvable:

> they are dead igneous, breathing rock
> on Robben Eiland,
> and I myself have lost
> sight of the long night fire.

AKN – 11/70

Poetry of the Last Five Years

Clive Wake

W ole Soyinka's recently published collection of some 250
Poems of Black Africa celebrates the remarkable fertility of
African poetry in English, French, and Portuguese since
the 1930s (and he also dips briefly into the offerings of Yoruba,
Swahili, and Zulu poetry). Readers of poetry and compilers of
anthologies have been so used to seeing this poetry as the expression of protest that they have perhaps failed to register the great
variety of its subject-matter – this is something Wole Soyinka
remedies by departing from the customary subdivisions of nation
or chronology in favour of thematic headings (nineteen in all). The
protest is there, underlying most of these poems, but Soyinka's
method reveals, too, the more predominant sensitivity to man's
relations with his fellow men and with the physical world around
him, pointing to a more positive desire to re-create the unity of the
world from the pain and suffering that men inflict upon one
another.

While Soyinka was preparing his anthology, poets continued
writing, publishers continued publishing. *African Literature
Today* has accumulated forty or so volumes sent for review which
provide perhaps an insight into some of the current trends in
African poetry. Established poets retain a certain ascendancy,
however – for various reasons. Three different editions of Senghor's work appeared in the two years 1976–7. Heinemann have
taken over the volume of *Prose and Poetry*, originally published in
1965 by Oxford University Press, and now included in their African Writers Series. This coincided with the publication by Rex
Collings of a new translation of Senghor's poems by Craig
Williamson. This translation is in some respects superior to the
earlier ones by John Reed and the author of this article –
Williamson is himself a poet, and this shows in his renderings – but
it frequently lacks precision (by this I do not mean literalness, but
the ability to find accurate equivalents in English for Senghor's

often very specific, very individual, vocabulary) and is at times simply incorrect. The translation of the poem 'Luxembourg Palace, 1939' illustrates particularly effectively both these points. Williamson's helpful introduction is essentially descriptive, presenting negritude from the point of view of negritude, and rather different from Abiola Irele's introduction to his *Selected Poems of Senghor*, which gives an excellent account of Senghor, his poetry and his theories of negritude from a constructive critical standpoint. Irele's selection is an edition of the French texts of Senghor's poetry, and he has rendered a long-awaited service to those engaged in teaching the literature of Africa.

The fact that Senghor should be re-published in this prolific way (in 1973 Seuil, his French publishers, re-issued his *Poèmes* in paperback, along with his recent new collection *Lettres d'hivernage*) suggests not that his influence as an ideologist continues – this is clearly not the case – but that his work now belongs to the classics of modern African literature. His style seems increasingly remote, his ideas have acquired the artificial air of irrelevance; it is the poet who survives for the average reader. For the rest, he belongs essentially to the study of history and the literary history of Africa. In a similar way, the poetry of David Diop and Jean-Joseph Rabearivelo appear rather late in the day in English translation. Diop's handful of poems had considerable influence in the period of protest before independence, while it has been very difficult indeed to find Rabearivelo's poetry – outside the few popularly anthologized pieces – since his suicide in the late thirties. It seems extraordinary that these two significant poets – the one a major influence, the other quite simply a very fine poet – should have had to wait so long to be translated into English. Another gap has been filled with the publication for the first time in volume form of Gabriel Okara's poetry, under the title of *The Fisherman's Invocation*; already well known, his poetry has only ever appeared before in journals and anthologies, and much of it has unfortunately been lost in the course of the poet's travels and through the mishaps of war.

Wole Soyinka began this review of the older school, and appropriately ends it. One of the youngest of the established poets, he is also probably the most outstanding. Although a major poet, Senghor nevertheless derives his importance from the ambiguous combination of poetry and politics, sensibility and ideology. Rabearivelo, more plainly a poet, through the primacy of sensibility and in his mastery of language and form, is made remote by

the romanticism of his temperament. Soyinka has a critical aggres-
siveness and realism unhindered by ideology which makes him
pre-eminently a poet of the modern world. A collection like *A
Shuttle in the Crypt*, originally published in 1972, can be re-issued
five years later, not because it is by a Nigerian poet imprisoned
through his involvement in the Biafran War, but because it is by a
modern poet imprisoned in the modern world who possesses a
mastery of language and form unrivalled in Africa at the moment.
And yet he is a supremely African poet; his latest poem, *Ogun
Abibimañ*, takes up his favourite myth of Ogun, 'God of war and
creativity ... Restorer of Rights', re-incarnated in the person of
Shaka, whose image rises symbolically out of Soweto.

> Bleak contrivances yield place
> To throats of steel. The restless dead
> Will hold a Dialogue of skulls and bones
> And set their clangour to the fortressed walls.

Soweto. Certain events have held the imagination of poets and
the people of Africa in recent years. The Biafran War was one of
them. Sharpeville was another; it forced the imagination so much
that it virtually became a symbol. Rhodesia, Angola, Mozambique
were then suddenly focused on Soweto, and Soweto emerged as the
symbol. The emphasis has shifted from the rest of Africa to southern Africa, and it seems the poets of South Africa have inherited
from those of West Africa the creative energy stimulated by aspi-
ration and protest. The bulk of the volumes I have been asked to
review – about half of them – are the work of South African poets. It
is almost as if Soyinka, with his latest poem, has turned the spot-
light firmly on to this part of the continent, and we are forced to
turn our eyes away from those writers who have held our attention
for three decades or more.

Arthur Nortje was well known before his unhappy death. In some
respects, his work reminds one of Rabearivelo's – the work of a poet
trapped within a society that held him fast, obliged to escape
deeper and deeper into himself and, ultimately, into suicide. There
is, therefore, a sadness and a seriousness about the egocentricity of
the poetry of *Dead Roots*, published posthumously, which un-
settles the reader, very conscious that he is an unwary intruder in a
private world. 'I have preyed on my emotions like a mantis,' Nortje
tells us, 'I speak this from experience, speak from me.' Nortje's
poetry suffers, as does Rabearivelo's, from the poet's introspection,
from his romanticism. One feels that, unlike Rabearivelo, he had

not yet found his real voice as a poet when he died, that he was perhaps beginning to do so in his last poems, moving towards a poetry less encumbered by the self-conscious quest for prolific, striking imagery.

Oswald Mbuyiseni Mtshali is a very different kind of poet, with a natural instinct for the impersonal that poets like Lautréamont and Eluard saw as the true basis of great poetry. Mtshali observes the world around him, transposes it into words with a simplicity of language, a tautness of style, and a vividness of imagery (using metaphor to point his moral without comment) which are almost faultless. Poems like 'The Shepherd and his Flock' and the famous 'Boy on a Swing' are excellent illustrations of his technique. The distanced approach of impersonality allows for a wit and an irony of the kind one finds in 'Sunset':

> The sun spun like
> a tossed coin.
> It whirled on the azure sky,
> it clattered into the horizon,
> it clicked in the slot,
> and neon-lights popped
> and blinked 'Time expired',
> as on a parking meter.

(Cf. Rabearivelo's 'Dawn' poems.) Similarly, in his more explicit protest poems, he bypasses the clichés and platitudes of protest to create poems rich in their human insight into the tragedy of South African life. Small wonder *Sounds of a Cowhide Drum* has been reprinted three times since it was first published in this country in 1972.

Sipho Sepamla, although inclined to be a little wordier than Mtshali, writes essentially in the same style, and writes sometimes in the popular speech which, with its various forms, offers great potential to the South African poet (a fact that Wopko Jensma, for instance, has effectively exploited). A poem like 'The Black Girl' is an interesting contrast, in its lack of rhetoric, with Senghor's famous (notorious?) 'Black Woman'. Sepamla has published three volumes in quick succession, culminating in *The Soweto I Love*, a significant celebration of this tragedy, but less impressive than the earlier volumes because of a certain prosaic quality here and there deriving from the poet's more explicit association of image and moral. Mafika Pascal Gwala (*Jol'iinkomo*) concentrates more on the abstractions of blackness and Africa, but many of his poems reveal a sense of place, an awareness of the particular as the basis of the universal, which ensure their vitality. Although it is not the most outstanding of this set of volumes, Mongane Wally Serote's *No Baby Must Weep* is in some ways the most intriguing. It is a single long poem dealing with the awareness of the black man's lot from the point of view of the child on the verge of knowledge of the world. 'Let me hold your hand/black mother' the poem begins, establishing at the outset the two symbols of the child (the African) and the mother (Africa), and through the child's sensibility it evokes the fear and pain of discovering the realities of a white-dominated world. Serote uses a stream-of-consciousness technique very effectively, the lack of punctuation emphasizing the ebb and flow of emotion, the movement outwards to the world and the retreat back to the protection of the mother, and the bewilderment of the African child. The enterprise is successful in poetic terms and one looks forward to more work by this poet. Alongside these works, Daniel P. Kunene's *Pirates Have Become Our Kings* is disappointing. It rarely displays the precision of language and image, the blending of particular and general, that one finds so successfully combined elsewhere. The poem 'The Monster' is too long, too wordy; there is a tendency throughout towards the prosaic. Perhaps he should read the poetry of Mtshali and Sepamla as guides towards the poet's mastery of language, or turn to the traditional poetry of South Africa (as illustrated, for instance, in *The Making of a Servant*, translated from the Xhosa by R. Kavanagh and Z. S. Qangule) for an awareness of the functions of simplicity and metaphor.

> Thus spake the heirs of the land
> Although it is no longer ours.
> This land will be folded like a blanket
> Till it is like the palm of a hand.
> (St J. Page Yako)

Reluctantly, one finds oneself setting white South African poets aside to be discussed separately. Yet nearly all of those gathered together for the purposes of this review are not only conscious of the South African racial situation, but respond to it in detestation of the way things are. It is not, therefore, the fact that they are white in itself that sets them apart, but rather their relationship to the situation. The black poet, like the black man generally, sees it from within in a way that none of these white poets (with the possible exception of Wopko Jensma) is able to do. One senses, for instance, that Mtshali has penetrated to the heart of the black man's burden in a poem like 'The Shepherd and his Flock', in a way Douglas Livingstone, for all his empathy, is unable to do in 'Town Tembu' (from *The Anvil's Undertone*) – we feel we know more about Livingstone's 'madam' and her family, at the end of the poem, than about the young Tembu narrator, and that we are more emotionally involved with the former than with the latter, even if it is essentially a feeling of revulsion. The one poet one senses does have a convincing emotional involvement is Mike Nicol, in *Among the Souvenirs*. The irony of the title itself points to the underlying theme of the white South African's weakening grip on a world which he thought belonged to him, but which is slowly becoming an alien land in which he is just a visitor, a collector of souvenirs. Nicol senses the unease of the white community, unsettled by the 'dire stories from the borders' – he uses this symbol of the 'borders' more than once.

> It is night again and perhaps they have come.
> Tomorrow in the rose-beds there will be
> Strange footprints. But the dogs do not bark
> And if they have come it will be weeks
> Before we know. The signs will be small.

His poem entitled 'The Refugees' is both prophetic and reminiscent of recent history, gaining its force, in fact, from this combination of the two. In another poem, he vividly evokes the situation:

> That is a violent country:
> harsh in landscape
> and government. People
> live, cold and unsmiling,
>
> with the rope's knot
> against their necks,
> waiting for the trap
> to open.

Other poets – one thinks especially of Peter Horn, Bernard Levinson, and Chris Mann – are also sensitive to the apartheid world in which they live, its injustices, its absurdities. But they, and many of the others published so richly by the Bateleur Press and the Ravan Press, are above all responsive to the South African landscape, and to the people set within that landscape, in the distinctive manner of white South African poets, sometimes purely visual and evocative (as in Chris Mann's 'Gansbaai'), at others blending the senses with a moral vision (as in David Farrell's 'The Charlie Manson False Bay

Talking Rock Blues', from the volume of the same name). There is some striking poetry about people and personal relationships – one must mention Chris Mann again, for his love poems, Sheila Roberts (*Lou's Life and Other Poems*) and above all Bernard Levinson, whose profession as a psychiatrist has inspired some remarkable insights into the private worlds of his patients (*From Breakfast to Madness*).

It is Wopko Jensma, however, who provides us with the necessary critical perspective on the achievement of current South African poetry, black or white. One is at first tempted to see him as a clever dilettante, a virtuoso who can manipulate the whole range of South African languages and express himself visually as well as verbally, in the manner of the French surrealists and their generation (and their immediate predecessors, Dada and Guillaume Apollinaire). There is a cosmopolitan touch about Jensma's work which releases it from the narrowly South African, indeed from the narrowly African, while being concerned essentially with South Africa and its tragedy. This seems to me to be the impact of the poem about Can Themba ('Till no one'), which opens *Sing for our Execution*. This derives not only, if indeed primarily, from a probably broader cultural background than most of his contemporaries, but from a mastery of language which means just that: 'mastery', as opposed to the continual struggle with it, the ephemeral control or, more often, the near control, of it that the reader is so conscious of almost everywhere else. This mastery, along with a sense of irony, gives him his freedom as a poet within the South African prison, so that one is inclined to measure the achievement of his fellow South African poets against his own.

Turning away from South Africa to East Africa, the harvest is not so rich. Mauri Yambo, with two volumes, impresses because of his vivid simplicity, as do the poems of Charles Khamwinwa and Amin Kassim in the anthology edited by Chris L. Wanjala, entitled *Singing with the Night*. Okello Oculi's *Malak* is very uneven, working most effectively when he seems to be inspired by traditional poetry. Indeed, the directness and simplicity of Swahili poetry, illustrated in Ali Jahadhmy's anthology, suggests it may be the source of the techniques of the more successful East African poets. Two collections published by the East African Literature Bureau (Joy Higiro, *Voice of Silence*, and S. N. Waititu and Y. G. Obasa, *Sleepless Nights*) are far too dependent on outmoded English models (especially the volume by Waititu and Obasa). The most interesting text from East Africa is, however, an English translation of Michel

Kayoya's *My Father's Footprints* – Kayoya was a Catholic priest executed in Burundi in 1972. Halfway between poetry and prose, it is a semi-autobiographical, meditative work in which the author turns his mind back to the Africa of his father in search of a wisdom which he has not found in European Catholicism, while at the same time honouring the white man for what he has achieved and for the simple fact that he is no less a human being than anyone else, in spite of the evils of colonialism. There is much here that is reminiscent of negritude and its oversimplifications (although Kayoya is critical of negritude – 'I have seen friends fuddled with negritude, poorly understood'), there is a tendency to moralize in the manner of clerics and once again to oversimplify, but in the context in which it was written it is a moving testimony to the need for reconciliation between Africa and Europe and for a renewal of African spirituality.

The harvest is even thinner by the time we return to West Africa: two volumes – one a pleasing collection of Joe de Graft's poems, written over the last quarter of a century and brought together for the first time; the other, a second collection by Syl Cheyney-Coker from Sierra Leone. The latter writes in tones of anger which are still rather too reminiscent of his admired Tchicaya U Tam'si, but this is not to undervalue the undoubted quality of the best poems in this volume. Joe de Graft's poems, written in various parts of Africa over an extensive period, convey impressions of Africa before and since independence, the change from one corruption to another (or the same corruption in a new guise), from white fear to black fear, the many aspects of love and of city life. This is not a major collection, there are some awkwardnesses of style, but it is a perceptive and worthwhile contribution to the corpus of West African poetry for the period out of which it grew.

De Graft's volume has brought us full circle and we are back in West Africa, where we started; but the gaze seems now to be firmly fixed on Southern Africa. Modern African poetry has been born of travail, and it looks as if it will continue to be.

> The clans are massed from hill to hill
> Where Ogun stood, behold a million brows,
> Dark bronzes from the kilns of Abibimañ
> A ring of steel against the sun, a throb
> Of feet to the ancient cry of – *Sigidi!*
>
> (W. Soyinka, *Ogun Abibimañ*)

REFERENCES

West Africa

S. Cheyney-Coker, *Concerto for an Exile*, London, Heinemann (AWS 126), 1973. New York, Humanities.

J. de Graft, *Beneath the Jazz and Brass*, London, Heinemann (AWS 166), 1975. New York, Humanities.

D. Diop, *Hammer Blows*, tr. S. Mpondo and F. Jones, London, Heinemann (AWS 174), 1975. Bloomington, Indiana University Press, 1973.

G. Okara, *The Fisherman's Invocation*, London, Heinemann (AWS 183), 1978.

J. J. Rabearivelo, *Translations from the Night*, tr. J. Reed and C. Wake, London, Heinemann (AWS 167), 1975. New York, Humanities.

L. S. Senghor, *Poèmes*, Paris, Seuil, 1973.
Prose and Poetry, tr. J. Reed and C. Wake, London, Heinemann (AWS 180), 1976.
Selected Poems/Poèmes choisis, tr. C. Williamson, London, Rex Collings, 1976.

W. Soyinka, *Selected Poems*, ed. A. Irele, Cambridge, CUP, 1977.
Poems of Black Africa, London, Secker & Warburg, 1975, and London, Heinemann (AWS 171), 1975. New York, Hill and Wang.
A Shuttle in the Crypt, London, Rex Collings, 1972; repr. 1977. New York, Hill and Wang.

South Africa

M. F. Gwala, *Jol'iinkomo*, Johannesburg, Ad. Donker, 1977.

R. Kavanagh and Z. S. Qangule (trs), *The Making of a Servant and Other Poems*, Johannesburg, Ophir/Ravan, 1974.

D. P. Kunene, *Pirates Have Become Our Kings*, Nairobi, East African Publishing House, 1978.

O. M. Mtshali, *Sounds of a Cowhide Drum*, Oxford, OUP, 1975. New York, The Third Press, 1972.

A. Nortje, *Dead Roots*, London, Heinemann (AWS 141), 1973. New York, Humanities.

S. S. Sepamla, *Hurry up to it!*, Johannesburg, Ad. Donker, 1975.

S. S. Sepamla, *The Blues Is You in Me*, Johannesburg, Ad. Donker, 1976.

S. S. Sepamla, *The Soweto I Love*, London, Rex Collings, 1977.

M. W. Serote, *No Baby Must Weep*, Johannesburg, Ad. Donker, 1975.

L. Abrahams, R. Greig, M. Kirkwood, W. Saunders, *Bateleur Poets*, Johannesburg, Bateleur Press, 1975.

D. Maclennan, S. Roberts, C. Style, P. Wilhelm, *Bateleur Poets*, Johannesburg, Bateleur Press, 1977.

D. Farrell, *The Charlie Manson False Bay Talking Rock Blues and Other Poems*, Johannesburg, Bateleur Press, 1974.

P. Horn, *Walking Through Our Sleep*, Johannesburg, Ravan Press, 1974.

W. Jensma, *Sing for our Execution*, Johannesburg, Ophir/Ravan, 1973.

W. Jensma, *I Must Show You My Clippings*, Johannesburg, Ravan Press, 1977.

B. Levinson, *From Breakfast to Madness*, Johannesburg, Ravan Press, 1974.

D. Livingstone, *The Anvil's Undertone*, Johannesburg, Ad. Donker, 1978.

M. Macnamara, *The Falls Run Back*, Johannesburg, Ophir/Ravan, 1976.

C. Mann, *First Poems*, Johannesburg, Bateleur Press, 1977.

M. Nicol, *Among the Souvenirs*, Johannesburg, Ravan Press, 1978.

P. Strauss, *Photographs of Bushmen*, Johannesburg, Bateleur Press, 1974.

East Africa

J. Higiro, *Voice of Silence*, Nairobi, East African Literature Bureau, 1975.

A. A. Jahadhmy (ed.), *Anthology of Swahili Poetry*, London, Heinemann (AWS 192), 1977. New York, Humanities.

M. Kakoya, *My Father's Footprints*, Nairobi, East African Publishing House, 1973.

O. Oculi, *Malak*, Nairobi, East African Publishing House, 1977.

S. N. Waititu and Y. G. Obasa, *Sleepless Nights*, Nairobi, East African Literature Bureau, 1975.

C. L. Wanjala (ed.), *Singing with the Night*, Nairobi, East African Literature Bureau, 1974.

M. Yambo, *Man Without Blood*, Nairobi, East African Literature Bureau, 1975.

Flame Hands, Nairobi, East African Publishing House, 1975.

Reviews

Politics and Literature

Kwabena Britwum

G.-C. M. Mutiso, *Socio-Political Thought in African Literature*, London, Macmillan, 1974, 182pp. New York, Barnes & Noble, 1974.

A 'sociological' approach to the study of African literature, it has been suggested, 'presents itself as the most apt to render a full account of modern African literature' (Abiola Irele, 'The Criticism of Modern African Literature' in *Perspectives on African Literature*, ed. C. Heywood, London, Heinemann, 1971, p. 19. New York, Africana Publishing Company, 1972.). While some of us would not like to put it so strongly, probably most people will agree that the 'social reference' of literature should be a major concern of the student of African literature.

The rather striking title of G.-C. M. Mutiso's new book appears to suggest that the author adopts a sociological perspective on literature. If the title might surprise somewhat the student of literature, the author's interest in literature is made clear at the outset: he is concerned with 'literature *per se*'. Now, since the author has chosen as the object of his investigation literature, which does not expound directly 'some specific social or political idea', he at least recognizes that one should distinguish literary texts from, say, socio-political writing whose treatment of ideas is bound to be more systematic, direct, and explicit. Moreover, by concentrating on 'literature *per se*', the author commits himself to showing in his reading of literary texts the kind of sensitive response to literature one expects from a literary critic. This would seem to be confirmed by Mutiso's aim to 'examine the social and political perceptions of

African creative writers concerning the past, the transitional present and the future of African society'.

However, the truth is that Mutiso is far less interested in literature as such. What he actually proposes to do is to 'extrapolate the major social and political concepts that will be used for the socialisation of present and future generations'. In fact, he hopes to 'construct [a] social and political theory based on literature'. The corpus on which the work is based is African literature in English from the end of World War II to 1967. The book is divided into three parts. Part One is devoted to 'Non-Literary Content in Literature'; Part Two to 'Group and Individual Identity in the African Context'; Part Three to 'African Identity in the World Context'.

The present reviewer is not primarily interested in the validity of such a theory for its own sake (in fact, such a socio-political theory could well be constructed, independently of African literature). My concern is whether or not, from reading African literature, one can plausibly 'construct' such a socio-political theory. Here the student of literature might justly be sceptical. The point is that literature is unlikely to furnish the reader with a clear-cut, unambiguous theory. When therefore the author sets out optimistically to 'extrapolate' from literature socio-political 'concepts', he forgets that establishing meaning in a literary text is a delicate and complex exercise.

A reader, preoccupied first and foremost with the referential aspect of literature, is exposed to at least two pitfalls. First, he might be tempted to introduce extraneous observations into his reading of literary texts; he might then simply look for confirmation of his views in literature. Secondly, he might be so concerned with the marshalling of his extra-literary material that he might lose sight (partially or altogether) of literature. Mutiso's book errs on both counts. For example, he writes on the role of African women in African literature: 'Women are seen as crucial factors in the modernising process, although their liberation from traditional roles often leads to alienation.' Such a statement fails to convince for at least two reasons. First, the author does not show that this observation is based on a reading of specific texts; secondly, it is a sweeping generalization which cannot be said to apply automatically to the bulk of African literary writing. One is therefore forced to conclude the author is stating his own position on the subject.

The author tends to interpret African society in his own peculiar way and this is assumed to be an interpretation derived from literature. However, since no evidence is provided to support what he claims these works are saying, it becomes difficult for the reader to ascertain the truth of an assertion such as this: 'To the extent that they [i.e. traditional outcasts in African society] were ultimately accepted into the colonial establishment as cooks, labourers, clerks, catechists ... these African converts acquired money and their status rose ...'

But even when the author is discussing particular texts, he tends to rely too much on quotations. In fact, it is no exaggeration to say that quotations are sometimes made to do the work of critical analysis (see, for example, pp. 64–71; 104–15). The question arises: how can a sentence, a long passage, taken out of its context, be used to illustrate or demonstrate a socio-political phenomenon the author happens to be discussing? (True, it is possible to 'prove' anything with such quotations.) But it is an entirely different matter as to whether a convincing socio-political theory can be constructed in this way.

More seriously, there tends to be some confusion about the type of society the author is referring to at any given time. In so far as the author discusses 'society' in literary texts, he has still got to show its correspondence with the social world outside. However, no literary text's *espace social* can be discussed as if it was automatically interchangeable with a real society. And yet the author either tends to discuss extra-textual social phenomena and simply look for evidence in texts (without showing how the general meaning of these texts relates to the world outside); or he simply discusses the social world in the texts as if he was already dealing with the real world (see, for example, pp. 76–7). It is obvious that the author's *démarche* here goes back to the nineteenth century positivistic idea of literature as a 'mirror' or a 'reflection' of society (one is thinking here of, for example, Taine and Stendhal); from this emerges the notion of literature as a 'social document'. If literature is a social document, it is perhaps only in a loose sense can this be said to be true. The point is that, even though a literary text depends on 'the real' or history for constructing its own 'sociality' or its intelligibility, nevertheless, it is only through a dialectical process of linguistic 'mediation' and imaginative enacting that social reality can be said to be embedded in a literary text. As Harry Levin rightly points out, 'literature, instead of reflecting life, we might better say, refracts it' (*The Gates of Horn: A Study of Five French Realists*, New York, OUP, 1966, p. 20).

If literature refracts life, it follows that one cannot hope to extract its social meaning by concentrating solely on the analysis of a given text's explicit content. And yet this is just what Mutiso does. For example, he quotes a character in Kachingwe's novel *No Easy Task*: 'He [the politician Dube] is a politician, and politicians are a tribe of their own. I am a journalist, not a politician.' Mutiso then infers: 'To argue that politicians are a tribe of their own is in the African context to define them as outside society – pariah to all others in their values and their interests.' The question is, how can it be said to represent the author's own views? To discuss the words of a character in a novel as if they were automatically incontrovertible or reliable is to misunderstand what meaning in literature entails. This is where thematic-formal analysis (as well as socio-political insight derived from knowledge of African society) can help one to determine the socio-political relevance of such a passage or text.

Mutiso's failure to relate 'the real' in the text to social reality leads him to misinterpret at times the political or ideological implications of a literary text. For example, the author quotes from Conton's *The African* the remark that the 'colonial politician' often gives rein to 'precisely those urges and inclinations which people of good breeding the world over try to keep in check – the incli-nation to draw the derision and scorn of others upon one's rulers for example; and the urge to acquire as much personal power and wealth as possible ... Unfortunately, as the colonies advanced toward self-government, the African politicians with whom the British officials came into contact ... have usually been much less well prepared for their careers ...' Mutiso then deduces from this: The colonial politician was primarily an agitator, and to the extent that there was scarcely a dearth of issues to agitate over, he never really learned how to develop a programme, articulate it and become accountable to the people.' However, what is interesting here is perhaps not so much what the author appears to be saying directly about the politician as what, in the process, he betrays about his own *présupposés politiques*. In other words, there emerges the ideology to which Conton implicitly subscribes. We see here a certain Westernized African intellectual (with his unmis-takably European middle-class outlook and values) viewing the 'colonial politician' as a social upstart, ill-prepared to take over the reins of government from the colonial regime. Moreover, this type of 'popular' politician is usurping the intellectual élite's natural right to rule. William Conton (himself an intellectual) lived in Ghana at the time of the country's political agitation leading to the granting of independence. What is revealing is perhaps the fact that Conton's novel brings out, implicitly, the ideological and political conflict between the radical, often far less educated, politician (appealing to the masses) and the conservative intellectual élite lacking political base at the grass-roots (see, for example, Dennis Austin, *Politics in Ghana*, London, OUP, 1964, pp. 12*ff*. New York, OUP, 1970.) It is clear therefore that what a text says cannot always, or necessarily, be taken at its face value. In the case of Conton's novel, what the author says in the text actually betrays what he does *not* say: and what he does not say becomes just as significant in the decoding of the socio-political meaning of the text. As Georges Jean aptly puts it:

> On voit de quel extraordinaire intérêt pourrait être l'observation des 'silences' dans les romans; car les romans, plus et mieux que toutes les oeuvres de la littérature, caractérisent les idéologies qui s'avouent. Le lecteur d'aujourd'hui peut donc, s'il est attentif, dépasser l'idéologie spontanée. (*Le Roman*, Paris, 1971, p. 237)

Mutiso appears to be unaware of such problems of socio-political meaning in literature. Sociological study of African literature, despite the pioneering work of scholars like Sunday Anozie (See *Sociologie du roman africain*, Paris, 1970) has still got a long way to go. E. Obiechina's recent work. *Culture, Tradition and Society in the West African Novel*, London, CUP, 1975 and New York, CUP, 1975, makes valuable contribution to the sociology of African literature. The same cannot be said, unfortunately, of Mutiso's book, which could be harmful if it falls into unwary hands.

Novels and the Colonial Experience

Eustace Palmer

M. M. Mahood, *The Colonial Encounter, A Reading of Six Novels*, London, Rex Collings, 1977, 211pp. Totawa, NJ, Rowman & Littlefield, 1977.

Professor Molly Mahood's background – her serious interest in commonweath literature and her first-hand experience of African conditions – suggests that she is eminently qualified to write an authorative work on the colonial encounter. The point must also be made that a critical work comparing in detail the responses of various writers, European and non-European, to the process of imperialism and its impact on the colonized societies, is a most exciting possibility. But given the suitability of the critic, the success of such a work would depend, to a very large extent, on the methodology and choice of novels. In order to probe the colonial experience as it is treated in fiction in depth, such a choice has to be more than merely personal. Unfortunately, Professor Mahood's selection is the first oddity that is likely to strike readers of her book.

Perhaps the choice has been dictated by the need to balance her various aims in this work, aims which are not always in consonance with each other. These could be stated simply thus:

(a) To give an affectionate scrutiny of six novels by some of those writers she admires most.
(b) To make a comparative study between novels from the developing world and those by established English authors.
(c) To bring to the scrutiny of these novels the benefit of historical and sociological information in the hope that such a treatment would result in a more balanced and accurate evaluation of the authors' attitude to the imperialist question than would otherwise be possible.

The problems immediately suggest themselves. An affectionate scrutiny might not necessarily be the most rigorous, and the choice of an 'imperialist' novel by an author one admires might not necessarily be done on the basis of quality, as Professor Mahood herself acknowledges. The need for comparative studies with 'comparative' being interpreted in a rather narrow sense, leads to some interesting consequences. Thus, in order to find a novel which pairs obviously with Achebe's *Arrow of God* in being set in colonial Africa (Professor Mahood explains the neglect of Joyce Cary's *Mister Johnson* on the grounds that she has written extensively on it in her *Joyce Cary's Africa*) she is forced to select Conrad's *Heart of Darkness* rather than his masterpiece *Nostromo* which, as the most thorough and stimulating analysis of neo-colonialism in developing countries, should surely feature in any book on the colonial encounter. This is not to suggest that *Heart of Darkness*, which is also a stimulating work on imperialism, does not merit inclusion. A satisfactory solution would have been a methodology which enables the author to evaluate the 'imperialist' attitudes of an author as a whole, and which would therefore have found space for both *Heart of Darkness* and *Nostromo*, rather than one which seeks to pair novels based on the same locality by different authors. Indeed, Professor Mahood's own constant references to other 'imperialist' novels, like *Nostromo*, by the chosen author, or by authors who are not discussed, like Joyce Cary's *Mister Johnson*, is an implicit admission of the incompleteness of her methodology.

Professor Mahood's pairs of novels are Conrad's *Heart of Darkness* with Achebe's *Arrow of God*, set in Africa; Forester's *A Passge To India* with Narayan's *The Man-Eater of Mulgudi*, set in India; and Greene's *The Comedians* with Naipaul's *The Mimic Men*, set in the Caribbean. The first two pose no problems since they are both patently significant works about imperialism. With the second pair, doubts begin to arise. One wonders what could justify the inclusion of *The Man-Eater of Malgudi* as a novel about the colonial encounter, other than the need to find a novel by an Indian, based on India, to balance Forster's *A Passage to India*. Professor Mahood is probably right in insisting that the novel has deeper meanings than is commonly supposed, but to read the relationship between Vasu and Nataraj as an analogue of that between the colonizer and the servile colonial, or to interpret Vasu's later activities as an allegory of a typical neo-colonial attitude, seems very much like forcing the novel to fit the thesis. It is difficult to see *The Man-Eater of Malgudi* as a novel about colonialism, even if one stretches the meaning of the term to include neo-colonialism. With regard to the third pair, one might possibly allow oneself to be persuaded that Naipaul's The Mimic Men is about 'the primal wrongness of Caribbean colonialism in all its phases – the creation of a slave society and economy, the prolongation through indentured labour of a form of serfdom long after black slavery ended, and the relegation of the islands for many decades to the status of slums of empire, a relegation culminating in an ill prepared "granting of independence"'. But it is also possible to suggest that the novel is about social and political (not necessarily colonial or neo-colonial) realities in Trinidad. Most important, the other half of this pair, Greene's The Comedians, surely seems to be irrelevant to the theme of this book. The mining concession, which is the only aspect of the novel that might suggest a neo-imperialist connection, features only in the final chapter of a book which has dealt very powerfully with political realities in Duvalier's Haiti. It is the work of an outsider viewing with distaste the savagery perpetrated by Haitians on Haitians in the post-independence period. It is significant that in her actual discussions of some of these works Professor Mahood gives lengthy and at times very stimulating analyses of them as individual texts, barely glancing at the theme of imperialism. But discussion, brilliant though it is, of works which do not seem to be relevant to the theme, seriously impairs the coherence of The Colonial Encounter.

Professor Mahood's chosen methodology is both critical and historical/sociological. This can have its advantages. The careful documentation of a work's historical and sociological references could be invaluable in clarifying ambiguities and confusions, and could lead to lasting insights. Not surprisingly, Professor Mahood is at her best with Conrad's Heart of Darkness where her thorough and painstaking research into events, attitudes and currents of thought at the time leads her to a very powerful presentation of Conrad's shifting feelings and gives a plausible and valuable explanation of the ambiguities that lie at the heart of his treatment of imperialism. With Achebe's Arrow of God the weaknesses of the method begin to appear. The historical/sociological approach is only valuable where it leads to elucidation of genuine difficulties or enhances our understanding of the work's meaning. It should not be regarded as an automatic 'open sesame' which is valuable per se. And quite often, whatever sociological or historical information is needed, it will probably be provided by the author himself in the text, as Achebe does copiously in Arrow of God. Professor Mahood's detailed documentation of the socio-anthropological background, backed by an impressive list of authorities, does no more, therefore, than confirm Achebe's fidelity to anthropological fact. But is it really necessary that it should have been confirmed? Would it have mattered, in fact, if it were not confirmed? Professor Mahood also comes dangerously near equating fidelity to sociological fact with literary excellence: '... so clear a pointer by the novelist cannot be ignored, and first and foremost *Arrow of God* – his richest book to date – presents itself as the documentation of a way of life which is confirmed in all its details by historians and anthropologists'. The element of 'affectionate scrutiny' is very evident in the discussion of *Arrow of God*. Where a number of readers object to the preponderance of anthropological material in that novel, Professor Mahood is prepared, rather unconvincingly, to make a case for the relevance of the sociological material, including all the songs. Significant though that work is, it will be difficult to demonstrate that Achebe has been as adroit in the handling of the sociological as he was in *Things Fall Apart*.

With *A Passage to India* Professor Mahood shows that Forster was close to the historical facts, demonstrating that the novel grew out of the incidents consequent on the Amritsar massacre. But although Professor Godbole's character is strikingly illuminated in the course of the discussion, this delving into history does not offer much elucidation. It does not help us very much to be told that Forster has got Mr Das right or that the latter behaves correctly as a typical Indian magistrate, since this is enacted in the text itself. The real problem with Forster, as with Conrad, is the ambiguity of his attitude towards imperialism. Why is it that in spite of his contempt for the Anglo-Indians Forster prevents himself from making a final denunciation of imperialism, withdrawing instead into the arena of personal relationships for a solution to the world's racial problems? This is the kind of difficulty one would have liked to see illuminated by Professor Mahood's method in the discussion of *A Passage to India*.

With *The Man-Eater of Malgudi* the method breaks down or becomes quite unnecessary. Professor Mahood quite rightly refrains from presenting background in order to illuminate difficulties because the mythological explanations we need – such as that Vasu represents the Man-eating god – are given in the novel by people like Sastri. Of course, in the discussion of the last two novels, Professor Mahood seems to have lost all interest in the historical/sociological approach.

A discussion of six such novels by six different novelists, purporting to be about imperialism, obviously invites comparative evaluation, but Professor Mahood, in her own words, avoids making cross-references in the body of the work, leaving 'the initiative in comparison and contrast to the reader' instead. In a concluding chapter, however, she attempts to pull the strands together, making use of the 'pairings already suggested by the arrangement I have given these essays'. She quite rightly concludes that *Heart of Darkness* and *Arrow of God* have a strong affinity of theme and attitude. 'Both are virtually [to make use of Conrad's phrase] "about a man who went mad in the centre of Africa" ... Both explore the ultimate cause of their hero's alienation in the imperial intrusion into Africa and develop the theme that a man who cuts himself off from his natural community ends by serving dark gods.' But Professor Mahood is not as happy in some of her other judgements. For instance she declares that the expatriate novelists – Forster, Conrad and Greene – see the colonial encounter as a painful disruption, just like the African Chinua Achebe. This is certainly true of Conrad, but is it true of Forster? In spite of the oppression of the imperialists, the Indian cultural tradition presented by Forster shows no signs of disruption. It still remains durable, proud, and dignified. To an extent it is even an implacable and unfathomable mystery to the imperialists who prefer to leave it untouched. It is difficult to agree with Professor Mahood that this disruption comes through Adela, since the latter is not, in fact, an imperialist agent. The point is surely made again and again in the novel, that while the events at Chandrapore imposed a strain on relationships, they were far from disrupting a continent.

The Colonial Encounter confirms one's impression of Professor Mahood as an eminent critic of the old school who is at her best with literary evaluation and is rather uncomfortable with the historical/sociological approach, although she feels called upon, now and then, to use it. This work will be valuable for providing stimulating insights into her chosen texts as individual novels; but it does not quite come off either as an analysis of the colonial encounter or as a demonstration of the value of the historical/sociological method.

West Indian Literature

Rosamund Metcalf

Kenneth Ramchand, *An Introduction to the Study of West Indian Literature*, Caribbean, Nelson, 1976, 183pp.

Kenneth Ramchand's *Introduction to the Study of West Indian Literature* is ill-served by a title which promises at once more and less than is delivered. The term 'introduction' inevitably gives rise to expectations of broad critical survey, and this is exactly what Dr Ramchand does not intend. As he explains in his preface, his lecturing experience at the University of the West Indies since 1969 has led him to the conclusion that the time for introductory surveys of Caribbean literature has now passed, and that the present function of criticism should be to provide students with stimulating material which will enable them to arrive at their own generalizations. Accordingly, he has not here attempted any comprehensive account of his field, but instead has put together eleven separate pieces on individual works, by means of which he hopes to provoke exploration of wider critical issues. Though his immediate range seems restricted – nine novels and two poets – the ultimate reference is intended to be broad.

In his opening remarks Dr Ramchand declares a policy: the avoidance of the well-trodden paths of historical, sociological, and thematic criticism. Students of Caribbean literature, weary of repeated explications of the socio-cultural context, may be cheered by the prospect of this new approach, and they will not be disappointed – at least in cases where major works are concerned. In discussing Jean Rhys's *Wide Sargasso Sea* (1966), for instance, he refuses to engage in the usual debate about social relevance and accuracy, and instead reads on the personal level, concentrating on the psychological and emotional reactions of the two main characters, Antoinette Mason and her husband. Though this approach may seem naïve at first, he achieves through it not only a fresh and sympathetic response to the couple's predicament but also a breadth of insight which is often, paradoxically, lost in the socio-cultural analysis. Where the relationship is usually examined in terms of a conflict between West Indian and European values, Dr Ramchand looks at it from the individual point of view. By so doing

he arrives at an understanding of the husband at once more complex and compassionate than the norm – he sees him as the victim
not only of his national, racial, and cultural limitations, but also of
the dehumanizing processes of modern society in general –
materialism, social ambition, and the dominance of the mechanical
intellect. Similarly, in the case of V. S. Naipaul's *A House for Mr
Biswas* (1961), he turns aside from the established critical analysis
of the problems of the Indian community in Trinidad and their
relation to the total West Indian experience. He chooses instead to
concentrate again on personal aspects – specifically, the relationship of Mr Biswas to his son Anand, and its significance in the
total scheme of the novel. Here, once more, he succeeds in deepen-
ing our emotional understanding, and, incidentally, in refuting
George Lamming's notorious dismissal of Naipaul as merely a
heartless and 'castrated' satirist.

It would not, however, be possible or even desirable for a critic of
Caribbean literature at the present time to steer entirely clear of the
socio-cultural debate. In discussing H. G. de Lisser's *Jane's Career*
(1914), and even Roger Mais's *The Hills Were Joyful Together*
(1953), Dr Ramchand finds himself constrained to adopt a more
sociological approach – though in the case of *The Hills Were Joyful*
he protests that such an approach is unfair to Mais, to whom 'man's
relation to the cosmos was at least as important ... as a knowledge
of the workings of a given society'. Sometimes the need to strike a
balance between essential historical background and immediate
critical insight produces a certain awkwardness in presentation –
in his chapter on V. S. Reid's *New Day* (1949), Dr Ramchand only
arrives at his main topic after a three-page excursion around the
novels of George Lamming and Michael Anthony. The same is true
of the piece on *A Brighter Sun* (1952), in which discussion of
Samuel Selvon is preceded by a fairly detailed account of Edgar
Mittelholzer's *Corentyne Thunder* (1941). The comparison is
clearly relevant, since Mittelholzer, like Selvon, was concerned to
present a peasant protagonist, but it functions here as an irritating
diversion in a book which has promised to avoid the historical
survey technique. Much more satisfying are the chapters in which
Dr Ramchand engages the reader's attention by an immediate
plunge into his main topic – as he does in his chapter on *A House
for Mr Biswas*, which begins: 'Late one afternoon, bored and all
alone in Mr Biswas's newly-built house on the Shorthills estate,
Anand goes through Shama's bottom drawer, finding in turn his
parents' marriage certificate, the birth certificates of his sisters and

himself, photographs of Pundit Tulsi and the Tulsi family ...'

All through *An Introduction to the Study of West Indian Literature* the reader is conscious of conflicting impulses in Dr Ramchand – the teacher's desire to use his lectures (from which this book has evolved) to stimulate independent thought, and the critic's desire to make all plain. The teacher usually wins, and sometimes this can result in frustration for the reader – critical hares are started but not chased; appetites are whetted but not satisfied. In his introduction, for instance, Dr Ramchand refers to the possibility of illuminating comparison between the differing reactions to landscape of writers from different territories, but it remains only a possibility. Again, in the chapter on *Jane's Career*, the reader is tantalized by a passing mention of the importance of feminist themes in West Indian literature. Moreover, the form of Dr Ramchand's book itself is a limiting factor, in that certain complex critical issues can only be mentioned, not dealt with. Thus the vexed question of what exactly constitutes a 'West Indian' novel crops up from time to time, but is always left dangling. Similarly, the difficult problem of the relationship of sound to sense in poetry is touched on in the chapter on Edward Brathwaite, but it seems darkened rather than clarified by too hasty explanation.

In general this book must convince us of the excellence of Dr Ramchand's teaching methods – particularly his power to encourage students to think for themselves – rather than of his skill in putting together a critical work capable of standing alone. As he implicitly admits in his preface, *An Introduction to the Study of West Indian Literature* requires the support of classroom and tutorial work to fulfil its potential. This is true, but should not be taken as a reflection on the author's critical ability. When he chooses to write conventional accounts of themes, characters, and techniques, as he does in the chapters on *A Brighter Sun* and Michael Anthony's *The Games Were Coming* (1963), or when he chooses to provide straightforward summaries of literary careers, as he does in the first half of the chapter on the work of Derek Walcott, he is admirably clear, full, and illuminating. Students who do not enjoy the benefit of his tutorial presence may find these the most satisfying, though they are also the least ambitious, sections of his book.

Vernie February

Sipho Sepamla, *The Soweto I Love*, London, Rex Collings, 1977, 53pp.

Soweto, acronym for South Western Township, is an oft-found word in the Western press ever since the 'slaying of the innocents' in June 1976 in South Africa. Although a non-African word, it seems to have acquired an African connotation even linguistically, one suspects. Few people outside the political and sociological context of South Africa would know the true meaning of Soweto. Through the years, it has come to mean several things. To the black inhabitants of Soweto, it stands for ghetto township, dehumanization and oppression, institutionalized violence and, since June 1976, the wanton shooting-down of children. But there is also a heroic tinge to the word. Like all places, even of poverty, it is home to the dispossessed of the world.

Several South African poets in exile and at home found inspiration in the holocaust at Soweto. Daniel Kunene exploits the word in its total socio-linguistic and political sense in his poem called 'Soweto' and the effect is traumatic. James Matthews, who lives inside South Africa, sees Soweto as the beacon which lights the way to freedom. Lewis Nkosi's 'Children of Soweto' is an angry indictment and a cry of anguish. Some of the breakaway members of the African musical group Ipi Tombi have now decided to call themselves Soweto Sounds. Thus even black South African artists have pounced on the 'cult value' of Soweto in Western countries.

Sipho Sepamla's collection, *The Soweto I Love*, is particularly interesting because his is an inside, one would almost hope 'god-eye', view of the black struggle, suffering and hopes for the future. It is no accident that a simple tabulation of the words used in his poems and their meanings would invariably have to do with fear, anger, stench, and humiliation. Thus I counted the following words and phrases which all link up, one way or the other with the concept of fear: terror, fleeing, cowed, scared, alarm, frantic, scare, cowardly, hounded, panic, scurry and scuttle, tremble.

These words and phrases find their complements in each other such as: scavenger, rodents, stench and smell of death, pain of humiliation, storm raging, choking dust. This imagery defines Sepamla's landscape and society which is consumed with fear, hatred, and predators. Upon first reading his poetry, one tends to think of it as simple and naïve. A critic at Wisconsin made a similar observation about Daniel Kunene's poem 'Soweto'. A second and more thorough scrutiny teaches that the simplicity is singularly deceptive and hides a deeper, more profound meaning. The terror of his South African landscape is poignantly portrayed precisely through this simplicity of language; the, at times, inverted sentence structure further creates the impression of an awkwardness with the English language. Only when he abandons his special style, however, does he really sound awkward, as for example in the poem 'I Saw This Morning' where the very direct 'he was crippled by' and 'he was wheeling round his teacher' jar. This simplicity, coupled with a staccato English and fairyesque quality – the Big Bad Wolf image – is hauntingly portrayed in 'A Child Dies'. His poem 'Like a Hippo' must at first glance appear to the Western reader like the work of a child, which impression quickly gives way to an understanding of the greater symbolism in the poem – again deceptively simple, like some of the oral stories with a tremendous sting in the tail. The Hippo becomes the state = Afrikanerdom = apartheid.

Sepamla has hitherto successfully avoided writing 'poetry conscripted for the victims'. Like the Afro-American artist, the poet in South Africa can to a large extent function as a 'guerrilla fighter who can talk Black English and ignore accepted aesthetics'. There is after all the fundamental realization that while the language of the black artist in South Africa is Western, his idiom is definitely non-Western (black if one wishes).

The poet's anger is contained with poise and does not spill over into a bitterness, a vituperation. He seldom allows himself a comic ironic stance, yet when he does exploit humour as a device, the effect is clear, as for example in 'Shop Assistant' which evokes images of another South African poet, Adam Small who writes in Afrikaans and his lampooning of white women in the poem 'Oppie parara' (On the parade). Sepamla's 'Civilization Aha' falls short of the reference to 'Western Syphilization' by the Afro-American poet Jon Eckels. Although oral in tone at times, his poetry draws its strength from the urban proletariat environment which spawned him, the poet. Despite the fact that Soweto has, in the words of the poet, 'made of mourning a way of life', he can still say 'I love you

Soweto', thus recalling Can Themba's affection for that other black cheap reservoir of labour which defined the landscape of the generation of black writers two decades ago – namely, Sophia Town. Of the gulf between white and black, Sepamla can write:

> go measure the distance from cape town to pretoria ...
> you'll never know how far i stand from you ...

Yet, he can still find the strength and the moral courage to conclude in all humility, a quality in which white South Africa is totally deficient:

> but a wish of mine remains
> peace at all times with all men.

This moving collection is another affirmation of the Afro-American Nikki Giovanni's belief that 'There is no difference between the warrior, the poet and the people.'

Antoine-Roger Bolamba
Esanzo: Songs for my Country

Lulu Wright

Antoine-Roger Bolamba, *Esanzo: Songs for my Country*, Preface by Léopold Sédar Senghor, translated by Jan Pallister, Sherbrooke, Québec, Canada, Editions Naaman, 1977, 73pp.

This edition of Bolamba's poems leaves a strong impression of unfairness to the author. Senghor's somewhat grudging praise and the mediocrity of the translation contribute equally to this impression.

While being apparently struck by the directness and immediacy of Bolamba's poetry and recognizing his expression of the great themes of negritude, Senghor is obviously irritated by the poet's lack of sophistication. He affirms that Bolamba thinks Negro in French; that he carries his native ideas and rhythms into French; he wants to charm his people but not with the methods of those who have mastered the art; his poetry does not express ideas; he is not well read; it is a gamble for him to be writing in French which is the language of culture and polite expression. Senghor hints at the little awkwardnesses that purists might find in his style. Finally, he asserts that Bolamba pulverizes syntax. This is indeed a formidable list of indictments.

A note on page 11 already questions the validity of Senghor's assertions, chiefly in the ground that Bolamba is a surrealist poet. If we agree that his kind of poetry with its sometimes elliptical, suggestive mode of expression merits the description 'surrealist', which seems a reasonable proposition, then Senghor's statements do appear unjustifiable. That the poet is not well read and that he uses a syntax of juxtaposition which pulverizes syntax seem to be irrelevant within the context of the genre that Bolamba has selected. The poems are intended to probe moods, appeal to the emotions, almost mesmerize the reader, rather than delineate and describe. In this respect they show affinities with Césaire's poems rather than with Senghor's more expository poems. The criticism about syntax is hardly fair for, with one or two exceptions such as 'Chant du soir', the poems are syntactically normal in spite of the deceptive absence of punctuation marks. In fact, Senghor's own poems take no liberties with syntax but they can drag the reader sinuously through as many as six long lines, which include some curious inversions, before a main verb is even indicated. Further-more, Senghor's poetry smacks heavily of French influence which is sometimes an enrichment but at others a troublesome intrusion. In his poem 'L'Ouragan', for example, the echo of romantic diction is unmistakable;

> Servante, suspends ton geste de statue et vous, enfants, vos rires d'ivoire.

This line could almost be a parody of Lamartine's

> O temps, suspends ton vol! et vous, heures propices,
> Suspendez votre cours!

Romantic verbal excesses, particularly grandiloquent repetition, find many a parallel in Senghor's poetry. In his 'Nuit de sine', the

three consecutive lines beginning with the formula 'Voici que ...'
are reminiscent of some of Victor Hugo's measured repetitions.

It would seem, therefore, that Senghor's frigid reaction to the
simplicity and incisiveness of Bolamba's short poems stems from
his own literary and stylistic preferences. The mixture of tones
Senghor achieves in his poetry is a result of his complex experience
whereas Bolamba's poems spring from a modest, more subdued,
but perhaps more authentically African background. However,
Senghor's preface poses the problem faced by Bolamba and all
second-language creative writers who try to be thoroughly themselves while at the same time using a foreign vehicle of expression.
Perhaps, too, Senghor's reaction is tinged with envy at the complete lack of affectation in Bolamba's poetry.

Jan Pallister's translation produces a very uneven result. Sometimes a really felicitous choice of expression brings an image alive,
e.g. in 'Dans ube tempête':

> Let us plough the waterfield with our oar.

This is a close and sensitive rendering of:

> Labourons de la pagaie le champs de l'eau.

However, far too often, Ms Pallister's versions tend to be stilted and
unimaginative, sometimes literal to the point of absurdity. This is
inexcusable in conditions where no concessions need to be made to
rhyme or regular rhythm. Lines such as:

> which instil in our minds
> a burst of madness

from the poem quoted above, for:

> qui font éclore la folie
> dans les esprits,

apart from consisting of a string of ill-assorted words, do little with
the metaphor 'éclore', the phrase 'instil in our minds' being wholly
discordant. In 'Songe grave', translated 'Grave dream', Bolamba's
phrase 'des baillements sonores' produces the ugly combination
'sonorous yawns' while in 'Lokolé', 'les pagnes solennels' are
'solemn loincloths'. In West Africa we might have called these
vestments 'ceremonial lappas' (wrappers): In the same poem,
the delightful image of the breeze caressing the poet's brow and
retiring like a shy maiden, is rendered thus:

Ah! the breeze
it deposits a kiss on my forehead
and
like a reticent virgin
steals away.

The incidence of such ill-reflected versions is uncomfortably high. Worse still, a few of the translations are quite inaccurate. While the difficulty of handling poetry, especially this kind of evocative poetry with its symbolic use of vocabulary is recognized, one cannot help being conscious in the present translation of a tendency bordering on caricature, which springs from a desire to interpret rather than translate. Sometimes the reader wonders whether Ms Pallister's inaccuracies are a result of unfamiliarity with African life. The translation of 'nourrices' in the first poem 'Bonguemba' as 'wet nurses' is ludicrous. Surely these dancers are nursing mothers. Similarly we are left wondering what is wrong with a phrase such as 'women in labour' or 'women in child-bed' for 'les femmes en gésine', whom the translator describes ambiguously as 'delivering women'. In the same poem, the light, brisk rattle of the drum, evoked by Bolamba in the sound 'touptoup, touptoup', becomes a heavy 'bam bam bam bam' in the English version, showing that the translator is not in tune with the mood and quality of sound involved. In fact Ms Pallister hardly reacts to noise words and sound effects which are important in these poems. Her pestles 'singing in the mortars' for 'Les pilons chantent bas dans les mortiers' in the poem 'Les voix sonores' are unrealistic, as is the tongue in 'Portrait' which 'wags like a flag', when Bolamba's 'ma langue claquer comme un étendard' definitely suggests sound and movement combined. It is true that in the translation of poetry absolute accuracy is impossible; on the other hand, even though some degree of interpretation is indispensable and personal reaction inevitable, it must be admitted that honesty to the poet is paramount.

These are poems about African life. They conjure up its scenes, suggest its ways and its atmosphere. It is refreshing to be in the world of the sighing pawpaw tree, to hear sunny April singing a hearty song in the mango trees, to see the canoe skimming the waves, the cupped leaves laden with rainwater; to watch the vigorous dancers in their gaudy scarves. There are also evocations of Africa's mystery and magic. The gong in 'Lokolé' is a messenger of peace to men who have lost their way in the darkness of error. This image is repeated in another poem, 'Bonguemba', and its apocalyptic tone brings its message and strengthens the poet's intense optimism, expressed repeatedly in the poems, about the black existence and purpose. Of course we have heard this before, as Senghor points out, but Bolamba offers us his vision in an interesting way. He does treat universal themes such as beauty which for him is mirrored in the mind; the power of memory in the perception and satisfaction of beauty; the transience, precariousness, and fragility of happiness; the value of human warmth and tenderness. Such themes are banal enough and there is no lofty development given to them but rather the light touch of unexpected insights. The 'milk' of human yearning in 'Esanzo' surprisingly casts, on a common experience normally associated with frustration and despair, a glow of worth. There is a wealth of thought here. Even though the poems are couched in relatively simple language, apparently artless, they are rich in undertones.

One reservation the reader could have concerns the translations of Mongo poems. These may be a worthy tribute to the language in the original but after two bouts of translation they do appear embarrassingly insubstantial. They could well have been omitted. For the rest, Bolamba's poems, though slight in dimension, can stand up to a repeated reading which should prove that the author deserves a place among Senghor's 'poètes de l'Anthologie'.

Index

Laye, Camara, 10, 95, 109, 110, 114
'Legend of the Saifs, The', 133
Letters to Martha, 49
Lettres d'hivernage, 234
Leusse, Hubert de, 124
Levin, Harry, 245
Levinson, Bernard, 238, 239
'Like a Hippo', 257
Lindfors, Bernth, 4, 205
Lion and the Jewel, The, 99
Lisser, H. G. de, 254
'Lokolé', 260, 261
Longfellow, H. W., 39
Lorca, Jose Garcia, 35
Lord of the Flies, 17
Lorgoligi Logarithms and Other Poems, 50
Lou's Life and Other Poems, 239
Lovely Against the Light, 231
Lowenthal, Leo, 184
'Luxembourg Palace, 1939', 234

Machiavelli, Nicolo, 3
Madubuike, Ihechukwu, 40, 100
Mahood, M. M., 248–52
Maillu, D. G., 52, 178, 179, 180, 182, 183, 184, 185, 187, 188
Mais, Roger, 254
Making of a Servant, The, 237
Malak, 239
Mallarmé, Stephane, 35
Malraux, André, 28
Man Died, The, 15
Man-Eater of Mulgudi, The, 249, 251
Man of the People. A, 25, 26, 99, 223
Mangua, Charles, 177, 178, 183, 188
Mann, Chris, 238, 239
Mann, Thomas, 106
Maran, René, 17–18, 97
Marriage of Anansewa, The, 78
Masiye, Andreya, 65
Mason, 202
Matthews, James, 256
Maugham, W. Somerset, 202
Mazrui, Ali A., 44, 108, 109, 117
Mbari, 28, 34
Measures Taken, The, 69
Melville, Herman, 35
'Mercedes Funeral, A', 26
'Messiahs, The', 51
Mhudi, 28
Mightier Sword, The, 65
Milton, John, 91, 222
Mimic Men, The, 249, 250
Mirili Ngahiika Ndenda, 2–3
Mister Johnson, 249
Mittelholzer, Edgar, 254
Mofolo, 19, 28
'Monster, The', 237
Moore, Gerald, 44, 92, 93, 125
Moremi, 62

Mother Is Gold, 93
Mphahlele, Ezekiel, 7, 11, 12, 13, 14, 49, 191–201, 202
Mqayisa, Khayalethu, 77
Mrs Dalloway, 16
Mtshali, Oswald Mbuyiseni, 49, 50, 236, 237
'Mubenzi Tribesmen, The', 27
Mugo, Micere Githae, 2, 65, 66, 68–70
Mulcaster, Richard, 90
Munonye, 86
Muntu, 61, 62
Murasaki, Shikibu, 116
Murder in Majengo, 186
Muse, The, 47
Mutiso, G.-C. M., 243–7
Mwaura, 182
My Dear Bottle, 182, 187
My Father's Footprints, 240
My Mercedes Is Bigger Than Yours, 27

Naipaul, V. S., 249, 250, 254
Naked Gods, The, 22
Nandwa, E., 177
Nanjala, Elizabeth, 181
Narayan, 249
Narrow Path, The, 95
Nazareth, Peter, 168, 173
Ndeti, Kivuto, 177, 186
Ndu, Pol, 39, 51
Neuburg, Victor E., 177, 179, 188
'New Brooms, The', 51
New Day, 254
'Newcombe at Croydon West', 229
Ngugi wa Thiong'o 2, 3, 14, 22, 23, 26, 27, 66, 68–70, 108, 111, 135, 153–66, 167–76, 179, 181
Nicol, Mike, 238
'Nigerian Death Ride, A', 34
'Night Rain', 98
Nkosi, Lewis, 34, 196, 256
Nnolim, 107
No, 183, 184
No Baby Must Weep, 237
No Easy Task, 246
No Time to Die, 48
Nortje, Arthur Kenneth, 224–30, 231–2
Nostromo, 249
'Novelist as Teacher, The', 95
'Nuit de sine', 259
Nwankwo, Nkem, 20, 22
Nwanodi, Okogbule Glory, 35
Nwapa, 86, 94
Nwoga, Donatus I., 29, 107
Nwoga, Pat, 46
Nwoko, Demas, 70
Nzekwu, Onuora, 86, 94

'O Roots', 51
Oba Ko So, 61
Obaluaye, 62
Obasa, Y. G., 239
Obeng, 28
Obiechina, Prof. E. N., 126–7, 184, 188, 247

Oculi, Okello, 20, 46–7, 239
Odili, 26
Oduor-Otieno, Barry, 50
Ofeimun, Odia, 50, 51
'Offal Kind', 20
Ogieriaixi, Evinma, 65
Ogun Abibiman, 235, 240
Ogunde, Hubert, 70
Ogungbesan, 42
Ogunniyi, 'Laolu, 75
Ogunyemi, Wale, 61, 62, 65
Okai, Atukwei, 50
Okara, Gabriel, 33, 34, 44, 86, 97, 98, 234
Oke, 108
Okigbo, Christopher, 2, 4, 35, 38, 39, 41, 42, 47, 48, 86–7, 89, 93, 97, 107
Okike, 40, 47, 50, 51
Okoampa VI, Nana, 71
Old Masters, The, 66
Oludhe-Macgoye, Marjorie, 180, 185, 187
Omabe, 45, 47
Omotosho, Kole, 20, 23, 39, 44
One by One, 178, 182, 183, 184
Onwechekwa, 100
Onyango-Ogutu, 177
'Oppie Parara', 257
Orphan, 47
Osadebey, Dennis, 33, 35, 89
Oti, Sonny, 66
Ouluoguem, Yambo, 29, 86, 99, 107, 109, 110, 111, 124–33, 160, 165
'L'Ouragan', 259
Ousmane, 20, 156, 162, 165
Ovonramwen Nogbaisi, 65, 66
Owen, Wilfred, 36
Owusu, Martin, 65
Oyadiran, Sola, 183
Oyono, Ferdinand, 25, 97, 108, 132, 181
Ozidi, 61

Pallaster, Jan, 260, 261
Palm-wine Drinkard, The, 8
Palmer, 114–17
Passage to India, A, 249, 251
'Path of Thunder', 41, 42, 47, 48, 51
p'Bitek, Okot, 4, 10, 38, 39, 40, 43, 46, 47, 178, 179, 188
Patchen, 36
Pater, Walter, 207
Peau noir, masques blancs, 91
People of the City, 202
Perspectives on African Literature, 243
Petals of Blood, 2, 14, 16, 21, 23, 24, 25, 26, 27, 153–66
Peters, Lenrie, 35
Petrarch, 36, 90
Pilgrim's Progress, The, 210
Pirates Have Become Our Kings, 237
Plaatje, Sol T., 28
Plato, 88
Pléiade, 90
'Poem for a Kitchen', 229
Poèmes, 234

266   Index